James Corbet Burcher is a planning barrister at No5 Chambers.

He has acted in many Green Belt cases since 2012, including residential and commercial development of all kinds.

In March 2025, he secured permission for one of the first Grey Belt residential schemes at appeal.

He regularly advises development industry clients on Grey Belt applications and acts for them at appeal inquiries/hearings and plan examination hearings.

A Practical Guide to Securing Planning Permission on Grey Belt Land in the Green Belt

A Practical Guide to Securing Planning Permission on Grey Belt Land in the Green Belt

James Corbet Burcher, BA (Hons) LLM
Barrister, Lincoln's Inn

Law Brief Publishing

Published 2025 by Law Brief Publishing, an imprint of Law Brief Publishing Ltd
30 The Parks
Minehead
Somerset
TA24 8BT

www.lawbriefpublishing.com

Paperback: 978-1-914608-84-1

PREFACE

The current Government is committed to major reform of Green Belt policy. In the Deputy Prime Minister's words: "*A Green Belt designed for England in the middle of the twentieth century now must be updated for an England in the middle of the twenty first.*"[1]

Grey Belt policy is at the vanguard of these reforms. Since the first publication of the National Planning Policy Framework on 12 December 2024, there has been a marked increase in the grant of planning permission on Green Belt sites, both by local planning authorities at "first instance" and by Inspectors and the Secretary of State on appeal. Ultimately, Grey Belt policy should have a notable effect on the delivery of new homes and jobs across England. The policy's introduction is one of the most significant changes in planning policy in the past 70 years.[2]

This book provides a short, practical introduction to the relevant sections of the National Planning Policy Framework and the Planning Practice Guidance, as well as some of the key legislative provisions and case law. It focusses on some of the main points that are currently arising in practice (both at application and on appeal), in an easily accessible format. The text will be of interest to all those who are involved in promoting and determining Grey Belt applications.

The book is structured in two main parts. Part I introduces the general legislative and policy framework, and provides general practical advice for applications, appeals and court challenges. Part II then considers each of the policy tests within NPPF 155-159, structured around the four Criteria in NPPF 155a to 155d. Additional sections are also provided on (a) the Very Special Circumstances test under NPPF 153, as a reserve

---

1 Rt Hon Angela Rayner MP, the Deputy Prime Minister and Secretary of State for Housing, Communities and Local Government, Written Ministerial Statement: "Building the homes we need" (30 July 2024)

2 Taking the Circular 42/55 (3 August 1955) as the starting point for modern Green Belt policy

position and (b) the Presumption in Favour of Sustainable Development under NPPF 11d(ii).

The law is up to date as at 1 May 2025.

James Corbet Burcher
May 2025

CONTENTS

PART I

THE GENERAL FRAMEWORK

CHAPTER ONE

WHAT IS GREY BELT POLICY?

(1) The National Planning Policy Framework

1.1. Under NPPF 153, all development in the Green Belt is subject to the Very Special Circumstances ("VSC") test, unless subject to a specified exception:

> "*Inappropriate development is, by definition, harmful to the Green Belt and should not be approved except in very special circumstances.*"

1.2. Grey Belt development is the most important such exception in force today.

1.3. By the operation of NPPF 155, all forms of development are to be considered an exception to inappropriate development where <u>all</u> of the tests in NPPF 155a, 155b, 155c and (as applicable) 155d (incorporating NPPF 156) are met. Throughout this book, these sub-paragraphs shall be labelled Criteria A, B, C and D (for shorthand and in line with two early planning appeal decisions in this field):[1]

---

1 3347424 – Great Barr, Walsall (14 February 2025) and 3346228 – Hadlow (21 February 2025). For brevity, all appeal decisions shall be referred to by their 7-digit reference number, a settlement name within the address and their date.

[NPPF 155]

155. The development of homes, commercial and other development in the Green Belt should also not be regarded as inappropriate where all the following apply:

[Criterion A]

a. The development would utilise grey belt land and would not fundamentally undermine the purposes (taken together) of the remaining Green Belt across the area of the plan;

[Glossary Definition]

Grey belt

For the purposes of plan-making and decision-making, 'grey belt' is defined as land in the Green Belt comprising previously developed land and/or any other land that, in either case, does not strongly contribute to any of purposes (a), (b), or (d) in paragraph 143. 'Grey belt' excludes land where the application of the policies relating to the areas or assets in footnote 7 (other than Green Belt) would provide a strong reason for refusing or restricting development.

[Criterion B]

b. There is a demonstrable unmet need for the type of development proposed;

[Criterion C]

c. The development would be in a sustainable location, with particular reference to paragraphs 110 and 115 of this Framework; and

[Criterion D: The Golden Rules]

d. Where applicable the development proposed meets the 'Golden Rules' requirements set out in paragraphs 156-157 below.

[NPPF 156]

156. Where major development involving the provision of housing is proposed on land released from the Green Belt through plan preparation or review, or on sites in the Green Belt subject to a planning application, the following contributions ('Golden Rules') should be made:

a. affordable housing which reflects either: (i) development plan policies produced in accordance with paragraphs 67-68 of this Framework; or (ii) until such policies are in place, the policy set out in paragraph 157 below;

b. necessary improvements to local or national infrastructure; and

c. the provision of new, or improvements to existing, green spaces that are accessible to the public. New residents should be able to access good quality green spaces within a short walk of their home, whether through onsite provision or through access to offsite spaces.

1.4. Each of the Criteria target a range of different policy objectives.

1.5. Criterion A (NPPF 155a) controls for the principal Green Belt harms,[2] by focussing Grey Belt development on sites that make a less than "strong" contribution to the Green Belt purposes (listed in NPPF 143(a), (b) and (d)). It also acts as a filter to ensure that the development is not subject to any major environmental /

2 NPPF (December 2024), Glossary: "Grey belt"

technical constraint providing a strong reason for refusing or restricting development (as listed in NPPF 11's footnote 7).[3]

1.6. Criterion B (NPPF 155b) ensures that Grey Belt policy only applies where there is a "demonstrable" unmet need. In the housing context, this will automatically be triggered by a housing land supply of less than 5 years or where the Housing Delivery Test score was below 75% of the housing requirement over the previous 3 years. The concept of "unmet need" is broad, but in simple terms, it acts (alongside the presumption in favour of sustainable development) to support the grant of permission where the existing development plan or historic approaches to development management have not released sufficient land to meet up-to-date needs. It is also a clear incentive to adopt an up-to-date plan in line with contemporary national planning policy.

1.7. Criterion C ensures that the site/development is sustainably located,[4] by cross-reference to NPPF 110 and 115. This ensures that the distribution of Grey Belt development is in the right locations, whilst still mindful of the broader imperative of meeting needs across a variety of different types of site.

1.8. Criterion D finally applies the Golden Rules to applications for major housing development, i.e. a significant portion of all Green Belt applications today. The Golden Rules seek to secure additional investment to meet Government's ambitions for the housing sector.[5] NPPF 156(a) requires that all Grey Belt applications for housing must provide a specific percentage of affordable housing (as defined by NPPF 157 or in due course the new development plan). NPPF 156(b) ensures that applications also make necessary infrastructure contributions (i.e. not under-

---

3 NPPF Footnote 7

4 NPPF 155

5 NPPF 156 and 159

provide on this component to meet the affordable housing target). Finally, NPPF 156 (c) requires applications to provide or make contributions to new/improved accessible Green Space on or off-site (as defined by NPPF 159). If all of these requirements are met, then a decision-taker must accord the development's compliance with the Golden Rules significant weight, as a new, free-standing benefit within the planning balance.[6]

1.9. The Grey Belt decision-taking policy is therefore revolutionary in two senses. First, it expressly encourages the release of specific areas of Green Belt early <u>ahead</u> of the Local Plan adoption. Second, the policy's wording, intricate structure and use of parallel PPG guidance is advanced in its specificity and clarity. It provides a very clear route-map to permission, if all the tests are met. Grey Belt policy is therefore both a radical break with past Green Belt policy, and in important ways, a "pathfinder" for the future of the English planning system.

<u>(2) Grey Belt Policy's Formal Status as a Material Consideration</u>

1.10. Grey Belt policy's formal status is that of a "material consideration", for the purposes of Section 70(2) of the Town and Country Planning Act 1990 ("TCPA") and Section 38(6) of the Planning and Compulsory Purchase Act 2004 ("PCPA"). All underlining is added both here and throughout the book:

Section 70(2) TCPA: "*(2) In dealing with an application for planning permission…the authority shall have regard to—*

(a) the provisions of the <u>development plan</u>, so far as material to the application,

…

---

6 NPPF 158

(c) any other material considerations."

Section 38(6) PCPA: "*(6) If regard is to be had to the development plan for the purpose of any determination to be made under the planning Acts the determination must be made in accordance with the plan unless material considerations indicate otherwise.*

1.11. Grey Belt policy formally extends beyond NPPF 155-159 and the NPPF's Glossary Definition of "Grey Belt land" to the Planning Practice Guidance ("PPG") Green Belt Chapter (published on 27 February 2025) and Written Ministerial Statements on the topic.

1.12. Each of the different forms of policy enjoy equivalent weight (as confirmed by the Court of Appeal in *Mead Realisations v Secretary of State for Housing, Communities and Local Government* [2025] EWCA Civ 32). That is subject to an important practical proviso that greater weight would ordinarily be accorded to the most recent expression of national policy. For example, the NPPF text of 12 December 2024 plainly post-dates the initial descriptions of the intentions of the policy in the 30 July 2024 Written Ministerial Statement.

(3) National Development Management Policies

1.13. At present, national policy does not have express legislative status in decision-taking beyond that within s70(2) TCPA and s38(6) PCPA. However, the English plan-making system is presently undergoing an important (albeit protracted) legislative change to the decision-making provisions in Section 38 PCPA.

1.14. Under the Levelling-up and Regeneration Act 2023 ("LURA"), Section 38(6) PCPA is due to be repealed in England and replaced by Section 38(5A)-(5C) PCPA. The new Section 38 will preserve the emphasis upon "the development plan" at sub-sections 38(5A) and (5B) but will also introduce a new parallel consideration: "national development management policies" ("NDMPs"). Subsection 38(5C) crucially makes clear that in any case of conflict between NDMPs and the development plan, the NDMPs will override/prevail:

"*38(5A) For the purposes of any area in England, subsections (5B) and (5C) apply if, for the purposes of any determination to be made under the planning Acts, regard is to be had to—*

(a) the development plan, and

(b) any national development management policies.

(5B) Subject to subsections (5) and (5C), the determination must be made in accordance with the development plan and any national development management policies, taken together, unless material considerations strongly indicate otherwise.

(5C) If to any extent the development plan conflicts with a national development management policy, the conflict must be resolved in favour of the national development management policy."

1.15. New Section 38ZA PCPA describes NDMPs as follows:

"*A "national development management policy" is a policy (however expressed) of the Secretary of State in relation to the development or use of land in England, or any part of England, which the Secretary of State by direction designates as a national development management policy.*"

1.16. Section 38ZA also controls the procedure for making and revoking NDMPs, including initial consultation, consideration of climate change mitigation/adaptation matters and later consultation on material changes to the NDMPs.

1.17. It is therefore open to Government to transport the entirety of Green Belt policy presently in NPPF Chapter 13 into a single comprehensive NDMP, or separate NDMP documents.

1.18. The new provisions would not necessarily prevent Government from publishing other forms of policy (notably through further Written Ministerial Statements and Planning Practice Guidance). However, such policy would not have the specific Section 38(5C) status, and it can be envisaged that arguments would be made that separate policy published under these routes would not carry the same weight in decision-taking. In summary, the direction of travel is towards a national policy that enjoys a very strong status indeed, especially in cases where the development plan is out-of-date.

1.19. In the next Chapter, we shall consider how Grey Belt policy emerged as a response to early 21st century Green Belt policy, (as developed throughout the second half of the 20th century) to discern key principles for how the policy should be applied in applications and appeals today.

CHAPTER TWO

THE HISTORY AND DEVELOPMENT OF GREY BELT POLICY

(1) Introduction

2.1. To understand the purpose of Grey Belt policy, it is important to begin by reflecting on the scale of the existing Green Belt in 2024 when the policy was first proposed. In the Written Ministerial Statement (30 July 2024), the Deputy Prime Minister expressly noted:

"*The Green Belt today accounts for more land in England than land that is developed – around 13 per cent compared to 10 per cent.*"

2.2. At the end of 2024, Green Belt land covered 12.5% of England's total area (1.6m out of a total 13m hectares).[7] Importantly, the Green Belt was concentrated around almost all major urban areas. The 16 separate Green Belts measured as follows (in descending order of size):[8]

(1) London (508kha)

---

7 Local Authority Green Belt 2023-24 Statistical Release (12 December 2024) – all figures rounded down. For comparison, at the same time developed land amounted to just 8.7% of all land, National Parks for 9.3%, and National Landscapes (formerly AONB) for 15%.

8 The only major urban areas without a Green Belt are Leicester, Kingston Upon Hull, Plymouth, Southampton and Reading.

(2) South & West Yorkshire (Leeds, Bradfield, Sheffield) (245 ha)

(3) Merseyside and Greater Manchester (245k ha)

(4) Birmingham (Coventry and Wolverhampton) (226k ha)

(5) Tyne and Wear (98k ha)

(6) Bath and Bristol (71k)

(7) Derby and Nottingham (59k ha)

(8) Stoke-on-Trent (44k ha)

(9) South-West Hampshire and SE Dorset (35k ha)

(10) Oxford (34k ha)

(11) York (27k ha)

(12) Cambridge (26k ha)

(13) Cheltenham and Gloucester (6k ha)

(14) Blackpool (2.5k ha)

(15) Carnforth, Lancaster and Morecombe (1.5ha)

(16) Burton upon Trent and Swadlincote (0.7k ha)[9]

2.3. At the core of the new Grey Belt concept was an acceptance by the incoming Government that the Green Belt had grown far too large

---

The full spatial extent of the Green Belt can be observed on the MHCLG's Planning Data Map: https://www.planning.data.gov.uk/map/?dataset=green-belt

and that it was acting as an unacceptable constraint in the very locations that most needed to grow.

2.4. Grey Belt policy is therefore best understood as a decisive response to systemic problems that had developed over a long period of time: notably (a) the inflexibility and opacity of the Very Special Circumstances test (as introduced by Circular 42/55 (1955)) and (b) the gridlock in plan-led Green Belt release in the 2010s and early 2020s, especially just prior to the 2024 General Election.

2.5. This Chapter examines the origins of these issues, tracing the development of today's Grey Belt policy in eight key phases:

(1) Pre-1955 History

(2) The 1955 Circular

(3) 20th Century Green Belt Policy (1955-2012)

(4) The NPPF Era (2012-2024)

(5) The 2024 General Election: The Emergence of "Grey Belt"

(6) The 2024 First Written Ministerial Statement and the NPPF Consultation

(7) The 2024 NPPF Publication

(8) Post-NPPF 2024 Developments

(2) Pre-1955 History

2.6. Today's Green Belt policy has its origins in the demographic, industrial and physical expansion of urban areas in England commencing in the 1500s and surging through the first half of the 1900s. Throughout this period, there was a recognition that urban growth needed to be checked, but limited legislative mechanisms to do so, and little consensus as to (a) the form of constraint that should be used and (b) the purpose to which the land kept free from development should be put.

2.7. The first main legislative steps to promote urban containment at scale began in London in the 16th and 17th centuries.[10] In 1580, Elizabeth I issued a Royal Proclamation forbidding any new building on any site within three miles of the city gates of London. In 1657, the Commonwealth passed an "Act for preventing the multiplicity of buildings in and about the Suburbs of London and within ten miles of the same."[11] This required new houses within ten miles of London each to have four acres of land. This legislation was undermined by the purchase of dispensations, and plainly, was of very limited long-term effect without a modern system of urban planning controls.

2.8. As London and other major cities grew significantly through the 19th century, there were increasing calls for the imposition of constraints on development. A range of objectives were cited, including the preservation of agricultural land, the protection of health and public amenity and the creation of recreational opportunities. The most famous example, at the turn of the 20th century, was Ebenezer Howard's work *Garden Cities of To-Morrow* (1898) which proposed a polycentric "garden city" (or "city of gardens"), surrounded and integrated by green space. As the modern town and country planning system established itself in the early 1900s, the concept of constraints around the whole city gathered ever-increasing interest.

---

10 For a full historical survey, see notably *Green Belts: Past; present; future?* by John Sturzaker and Ian Mell (2017) and *The Green Belt, Housing Crises and Planning Systems* by Charles Goode (2025)

11 C.J., vii., 566, 577; Scobell, ii., 484, Cap. XXIV

2.9. A principal catalyst for new legislative controls came after the First World War, when London experienced significant economic growth and internal migration from across the UK. In 1927, the Greater London Regional Planning Committee was tasked to consider whether London could be provided with "*something which might be called an agricultural belt, as has often been suggested, so that it would form a dividing line between Greater London as it is and the satellites or fresh developments that might take place at a great distance.*" In 1933, the Committee's technical adviser, Raymond Unwin proposed a "green girdle" of smaller open space areas just beyond the city's urban limits.

2.10. This resulted in the first and only Green Belt legislation to date: (1) the Restriction of Ribbon Development Act 1935 and (2) the Green Belt (London and Home Counties Act) 1938. The 1935 and 1938 Acts were focussed on land acquisition. The Acts promoted the preservation of land for public amenity purposes, through the use of council purchase and the imposition of restrictive covenants. The 1938 Act was, however, critical in instituting for the first time the terminology of "Green Belt", as both a physical entity and a concept.

2.11. By the early 1940s, Green Belt designation was recognised as the primary vehicle for urban containment in each of the four main reports which formed the basis for the post-war planning system (Barlow, Scott, Uthwatt and Reith). Patrick Abercrombie's County of London Plan 1943 and Greater London Plan 1944 illustrated London with an Inner Urban Ring, a Suburban Ring, a Green Belt Ring and finally an Outer Country Ring. Abercrombie's Report described the Green Belt Ring as "*a zone with sufficient openness to have enabled attempts to be made to create a Green Belt, a zone in which the communities still maintain some semblance of distinct individuality*".

2.12. The Town and Country Planning Act 1947 then provided the legislative basis for more widespread adoption of Green Belt post-war, through the mandatory requirement for local authorities to prepare and adopt development plans. Importantly, the 1947 Act did not use the term "Green Belt" or any equivalent wording. This has remained the position in all modern legislation to date.

(3) The 1955 Circular

2.13. Circular 42/55 ("the 1955 Circular") is regarded as the starting point for modern Green Belt national policy. The 1955 Circular was short, but remains an important reference point even today, outlining both the vision of the policy and displaying its inherent limitations.

2.14. The Circular was produced in a very specific context. By early 1955, there had been marked progress towards a Green Belt for London but relatively limited progress towards the adoption of Green Belts elsewhere. The Minister for Housing and Local Government, Duncan Sandys MP, was concerned about the slow rate of adoption nationally. This reflected a common view in the immediate post-war period that all major cities should explore constraints on their growth: to limit interwar-style sprawl, to encourage regeneration of their bomb-damaged cores and to preserve the rural character of the surrounding countryside.

2.15. On 25 April 1955, the Minister issued a statement in Parliament, which was later attached to the Circular and therefore forms an important part of its interpretive context today. He noted the establishment of Green Belt around London and recommended the adoption of a Green Belt around other cities:

"I am convinced that, for the well-being of our people and for the preservation of the countryside we have a clear duty to do all we can to prevent the further unrestricted sprawl of the great cities.

The Development Plans submitted by the local planning authorities for the Home Counties provide for a Green Belt, some 7 to 10 miles deep, all around the built-up area of Greater London. Apart from some limited rounding off of existing small towns and villages, no further expansion is to be allowed within this belt.

These proposals, if strictly adhered to, should prove most effective. For this the authorities in the Home Counties deserve much credit.

In other parts of the country certain planning authorities are endeavouring by administrative action to restrict further building development around the large areas but I regret that nowhere has any formal Green Belt as yet been proposed. I am accordingly asking all planning authorities concerned to give this matter further consideration with a view to submitting to me proposals for the creation of clearly defined green belts wherever this is appropriate. …"

2.16. Three months later, on 3 August 1955, the Ministry of Housing and Local Government issued Circular 42/55. The full text is worth considering today (notably the three chosen Green Belt purposes in paragraph 3 and the exceptions in paragraph 5):

"*1. Following upon his statement in the House of Commons on April 26th last (copy attached), I am directed by the Minister of Housing and Local Government to draw your attention to the importance of checking the unrestricted sprawl of the built-up areas, and of safeguarding the surrounding countryside against further encroachment.*

2. He is satisfied that the only really effective way to achieve this object is by the formal designation of clearly defined Green Belts around the areas concerned.

3. The Minister accordingly recommends Planning Authorities to consider establishing a Green Belt wherever this is desirable in order:

(a) *<u>to check the further growth of a large built-up area</u>*

(b) *to prevent neighbouring towns from merging into one another; or*

(c) *to preserve the special character of a town.*

4. Wherever practicable, a Green Belt should be several miles wide, so as to ensure an appreciable rural zone all round the built-up area concerned.

5. Inside a Green Belt, approval should not be given, except in very special circumstances, for the construction of new buildings, or for the change of use of existing buildings for purposes other than agriculture, sport, cemeteries, institutions standing in extensive grounds, or other uses appropriate to a rural area.

6. Apart from a strictly limited amount of "infilling" or "rounding off" (within boundaries to be defined in Town Maps) existing towns and villages inside a Green Belt should not be allowed to expand further. Even within the urban areas thus defined, every effort should be made to prevent any further building for industrial or commercial purposes: since this, if allowed, would lead to a demand for more labour, which in turn would create a need for the development of additional land for housing.

7. A Planning Authority which wishes to establish a Green Belt in its area should, after consulting any neighbouring Planning Authority affected, submit to the Minister, as soon as possible, a Sketch Plan, indicating the approximate boundaries of the proposed Belt. Before officially submitting plans, authorities may find it helpful to discuss them informally with this Ministry either through its regional representative or in Whitehall.

8. In due course, a detailed survey will be needed to define precisely the inner and outer boundaries of the Green Belt, as well as the boundaries of the towns and villages within it. Thereafter these particulars will have to be incorporated as amendments in the Development Plan.

9. This procedure may take some time to complete. Meanwhile it is desirable to prevent any further deterioration of the position. The Minister, therefore, asks that where a Planning Authority has submitted a Sketch Plan for a Green Belt, it should forthwith apply provisionally, in the area proposed, the arrangements outlined in paragraph 5 and 6 above."

2.17. The brevity of this Ministerial instruction for such a significant national-scale initiative seems remarkable today. However, perhaps not as remarkable as the continuity with the 21st century national policy text. Current policy retains much of the key terminology: "sprawl", "encroachment", "(in)appropriate" and "infilling" as well as the "very special circumstances" test itself. In particular, the Circular's three "purposes" for the Green Belt remain almost unchanged. Indeed, they are those which are expressly referred to in the Grey Belt Glossary definition: ("*(a) to check the further growth of a large built-up area; (b) to prevent neighbouring towns from merging into one another; or (c) preserve the special character of a town*"), each expressed in the alternative, noting different settlement patterns and objectives.

2.18. The 1955 Circular contained brief reference to a Green Belt potentially serving a purpose beyond mere containment. Paragraph 4 notably referred to the need for the Green Belt to form an "*appreciable <u>rural</u> zone*". However, the 1955 Circular contained no analysis of "need" – whether for housing, industrial or any form of development. Beyond paragraph 8's "detailed survey", there was little reference to Green Belt assessment, i.e. exactly how the exercise of designation should be carried out. Whilst the strong controls on development within the Green Belt were to be strictly subject to a plan-led approach, the text was less than clear as to how the designation should later be reviewed, and if necessary, adjusted.

2.19. Since 1955, the population of England has increased by over 25%.[12] There have been countless technological, geographical and societal changes, affecting how people work, move about, acquire goods and live their lives. When one further considers the elapse of seven decades, multiple legislative reforms and emergence of entirely new doctrines of growth (e.g. sustainable development), it is clear that the Circular's approach could not sensibly be continued into the middle of the 21st century – as the Government's First Written Ministerial Statement in 2024 would later expressly observe.

(4) 1955-2012: 20th Century Green Belt Policy

1955-79: Establishment of Green Belts and Subsequent Circulars

2.20. The majority of today's Green Belt land was designated during the quarter-century from 1955 up to the early years of the Thatcher-led Government in the 1980s. In parallel, public enthusiasm for the Green Belt grew rapidly. This was in turn matched by political support (both locally and at Westminster).

2.21. The practicality and suitability of the policy was however the subject of great debate from professional and academic quarters from the outset. Within the Ministry, it was acknowledged early on that the designation of Green Belt land and prohibition on major development in this manner could create significant tensions with meeting emerging residential and economic needs in the post-war era. In 1957, the Ministry reflected in an annual report: "*the establishment of a green belt is, however, a step which calls for most careful deliberation. The strict control of development that needs to be exercised in green belt areas in order to resist the pressure of urban sprawl cannot be justified, except where the position urgently demands*

12 1955 Population Estimates: 44m; 2024 Population Estimates: 58m

it."[13] In the same year, the Ministry issued Circular 50/57 which provided for detailed guidance on boundary definition, including designation of "white land" which would not fall within the Green Belt but might be suitable for development in the future. By 1960, the Government had become particularly concerned at a growing shortage of housing and employment land and issued Circular 37/60 recommending the balancing of Green Belt with identification of other land for development elsewhere. Concerns continued to be expressed at the official and academic level throughout the 1960s.

2.22. Wider professional/academic studies such as: '*The Containment of Urban England*' (1973) by Peter Hall and others, also began to critically review the policy. It was increasingly observed that the introduction of Green Belt policy, without an underlying strategic vision would give rise to significant issues for long-term delivery of development needs in the right locations.

2.23. Successive Governments were, however, unable or unwilling to make fundamental reforms. The Department for the Environment (as successor to the Ministry for Housing and Local Government) issued Circular 122/73 "Land Availability for Housing" which largely preserved the status of Green Belt policy.

<u>1979-1997: Circular 14/84 (1984), Planning Practice Guidance Note 2 (1988) and the Planning Practice Guide 2 (1995)</u>

2.24. In the early 1980s, the Thatcher Government explored the relaxation of Green Belt controls to promote economic growth. This proved politically unpopular and the Government opted instead to reiterate its commitment to Green Belt.

---

13 MHLG, Report of the Ministry of Housing and Local Government for the Year 1956 (1957)

2.25. In 1984, the Department for the Environment issued Circular 14/84 emphasising (paragraph 1) that "*it reaffirms the objectives of Green Belt policy and the related development control policies set out in the Ministry of Housing and Local Government Circular 42/55*", thereby again upholding the 1955 Circular's central VSC test, and a limited approach to exceptions. It also added a key reference to "permanence" that remains today: "*The essential characteristic of Green Belts is their permanence and their protection must be maintained as far as can be seen ahead*" (paragraph 3).

2.26. In 1988, the Department further published Planning Policy Guidance 2 on Green Belts ("PPG2"). PPG2 emphasised continuity. Paragraph 1 stated:

> "*1 The Government attaches great importance to Green Belts, which have been an essential element of planning policy for more than three decades. The purposes of Green Belt policy and the related development control policies set out in 1955 remain valid today.*"

2.27. PPG2 further re-emphasised the very special circumstances test:

> "*12. The general policies controlling development in the countryside apply with equal force in Green Belts but there is, in addition, a general presumption against inappropriate development within them.*
>
> *13. Inside a Green Belt, approval should not be given except in very special circumstances, for the construction of new buildings, or for the change of use of existing buildings for purposes other than agriculture, sport, cemeteries, institutions standing in extensive grounds, or other uses appropriate to a rural area.*"

2.28. The 1955 "very special circumstances" wording was therefore re-confirmed without change.

2.29. In 1988, the Department for the Environment also re-issued the short 1962 pamphlet, "Green Belts" for a public readership expressly "*to demonstrate the continuity of the policy and <u>our strong commitment</u> to Green Belts.*" In 1993, the Department published a major report entitled "The Effectiveness of Green Belts" which recommended the retention of the policy with some targeted amendments, none of them on a scale comparable to Grey Belt.

2.30. In 1995, the Government published Planning Policy Guidance 2 replacing PPG2 (1988) and the earlier Circulars. Whilst the PPG2 (1995) echoed the earlier PPG2 (1988) wording, it re-numbered and expanded certain key paragraphs. This structure would later be preserved extensively in the NPPF:

> "*3.1 The general policies controlling development in the countryside apply with equal force in Green Belts but there is, in addition, a general presumption against inappropriate development within them. <u>Such development should not be approved, except in very special circumstances</u>. See paragraphs 3.4, 3.8, 3.11 and 3.12 below as to development which is inappropriate.*
>
> *3.2 Inappropriate development is, by definition, harmful to the Green Belt. It is for the applicant to show why permission should be granted. <u>Very special circumstances to justify inappropriate development will not exist unless the harm by reason of inappropriateness, and any other harm, is clearly outweighed by other considerations.</u> In view of the presumption against inappropriate development, the Secretary of State will attach substantial weight to the harm to the Green Belt when considering any planning application or appeal concerning such development.*"

<u>1997-2010: The Labour Government</u>

2.31. Following the 1997 General Election, the Labour Government chose to retain the existing PPG2 in full, save for one minor update in 2001 in respect of park and ride schemes. This aligned with a programme of promoting city regeneration. The Conservative

Government's PPG2 (1995) text was therefore to remain in force for over 17 years.

2.32. The era did however see key legislative changes in plan-making, which temporarily promised reform and the potential for Green Belt release. The Planning and Compulsory Purchase Act 2004 introduced a revised system of strategic and local plans, notably the Regional Spatial Strategies (later Regional Strategies), which were intended to explore how to meet development needs at a strategic level, including through Green Belt release.

2.33. The era was also characterised by political structural change, as planning assumed a more distinctive role within Government's functions. The Department of the Environment's responsibilities were initially conducted by the Office for the Deputy Prime Minister (OPDM) (from 2001) and then latterly the Department for Communities and Local Government (DCLG) (from 2006), whose name survives substantially today in the Ministry's current title (MHCLG).

(5) 2012-2024: The Coalition/Conservative Governments and the National Planning Policy Framework

Localism and the NPPF

2.34. Between 2010-2015, the Coalition Government made two significant legislative and policy changes which had a significant bearing on decision-taking and plan-making within Green Belt in the subsequent years up to July 2024.

2.35. First, through the Localism Act 2011, the new Government abolished the Regional Strategies, requiring authorities to address their own individual needs, subject to a new Duty to Cooperate,[14] which was widely considered to be far more light-touch in terms of

[14] Section 33A of the Planning and Compulsory Purchase Act 2004

addressing cross-boundary matters. This largely removed the opportunity for coordinated Green Belt release at the strategic scale, save through certain joint plans. The only major example outside London has been the Places for Everyone plan (adopted March 2024), promoted by the Greater Manchester Combined Authority and nine constituent LPAs.

2.36. Second, DCLG sought to streamline the text of national planning policy, bringing together the collected PPG and PPS documents into a single, much shorter document. The core of PPG2 remained, but with much of the text considerably reduced. There was then considerable continuity in the text of Green Belt policy for the 12 year period from 2012 to 2024, save for focussed changes to the exceptional circumstances test in 2018 and then again in 2023. The 2018 version added express criteria to guide the circumstances in which exceptional circumstances could be demonstrated for Green Belt release. The December 2023 change confirmed that there was no obligation to release Green Belt land. The decision-making text therefore remained in a format largely unchanged from PPG2 (1995) paragraph 3.2's wording.

2.37. Outside the NPPF changes, the Coalition Government (2010-2015) and the successor Conservative Government (2015-2024) also pursued more ad hoc ways to emphasise their opposition to Green Belt release. This was exemplified by the Written Ministerial Statement of 17 January 2014, when the Minister for Planning set out an approach to both gypsy and traveller and conventional housing, which heavily emphasised the strictness with which the very special circumstances test would be applied:

"*The government's planning policy is clear that both temporary and permanent traveller sites are inappropriate development in the green belt and that planning decisions should protect green belt land from such inappropriate development. I also noted the Secretary of State's policy position that* <u>*unmet need, whether for traveller sites or for conventional housing, is unlikely to outweigh harm to the green belt*</u>

and other harm to constitute the "very special circumstances" justifying inappropriate development in the green belt.

The Secretary of State wishes to re-emphasise this policy point to both local planning authorities and planning inspectors as a material consideration in their planning decisions."

2.38. The WMS had a chilling effect upon Green Belt site promotion for several years. It was never expressly withdrawn prior to 2024, although its terms were not incorporated in subsequent versions of the NPPF in 2018, 2019, 2023. Collectively, the WMS wording presented a significant obstacle to the promotion of housing schemes on Green Belt sites, until a small, but notable wave of appeal decisions at Inspector level around 2021 and 2022.[15]

2.39. By the latter years of the Conservative Government, popular support for the Green Belt as a major constraint was no longer as assured as in earlier decades. Significant public concern was expressed, especially amongst those in their 20s and 30s, with the lack of availability of housing and its general unaffordability. This was coupled with repeated business/commercial sector statements on the need to release land around major cities to boost industrial and economic activity (notably in the life sciences, advanced manufacturing and logistics sectors).

2.40. At a time when the need for development had never been greater, existing national policy seemed less and less effective. The final 18 months of the Conservative Government (December 2022 through to July 2024) saw many local plans suspended prior to submission, and others at examination even withdrawn after Inspectors had completed their examination reports and recommended adoption. There was a sense of a perpetual crisis in plan-making and a need for radical reform.

15 For example, 3265925 and 3265926 – Colney Heath (14 June 2021)

(6) The 2024 Labour Manifesto and the General Election (4 July 2024)

2.41. The Labour Party entered the 2024 General Election with a commitment to targeted Green Belt release through a new approach, based around two key concepts: "the Grey Belt" and "the Golden Rules". This was, in effect, an attempt to re-brand Green Belt release, through the simple but subtle re-labelling of the target areas, and the type of benefits that could be delivered.

2.42. On 19 April 2024, the Labour Party issued a press release proposing five "golden rules" which would apply to all Green Belt release:

(1) Within the Green Belt, any brownfield land would have to be "prioritised for development" ahead of a new category: "grey belt" land;

(2) Grey Belt land should then be preferred ahead of "nature-rich, environmentally valuable land in the green belt";

(3) Where "grey belt" was to be released, the plans should include the provision of at least 50 per cent affordable housing;

(4) Proposals must also boost public services and local infrastructure;

(5) There should be no building on "genuine nature spots" and plans for the development of grey belt land should also include "improvements to existing green spaces" and meet "high environmental standards".

2.43. By 13 June 2024, the Labour Party Manifesto adopted a broader, less specific position reiterating the emphasis on "grey belt" and "golden rules". The text was vaguer in respect of all other matters: specific affordable housing targets, improvements to accessibility and the exact approach to prioritisation:

> "*The dream of homeownership is now out of reach for too many young people. The Conservatives have failed to act even though the housing crisis is well known to be one of the country's biggest barriers to growth. Labour will get Britain building again, creating jobs across England, with 1.5 million new homes over the next parliament.*
>
> *We will immediately update the National Policy Planning Framework to undo damaging Conservative changes, including restoring mandatory housing targets. We will take tough action to ensure that planning authorities have up-to-date Local Plans and reform and strengthen the presumption in favour of sustainable development….*
>
> *Labour is committed to preserving the green belt which has served England's towns and cities well over many decades. Under the Conservatives, greenbelt land is regularly released for development but haphazardly and often for speculative housebuilding. Without changing its purpose or general extent, Labour will take a more strategic approach to greenbelt land designation and release to build more homes in the right places. The release of lower quality 'grey belt' land will be prioritised and we will introduce 'golden rules' to ensure development benefits communities and nature...*"

2.44. The Manifesto's suggestion that Green Belt release had been "regular" under the Conservative Government was, of course, highly questionable after years of Secretary of State refusals and strict application of the VSC test. However, the remaining text drew an accurate picture: an ever-growing crisis of housing unaffordability, slow Local Plan adoption and a need for a system with greater certainty.

2.45. The landslide General Election result of 4 July 2024 provided the Government with a clear mandate for both legislative and policy change and the early months were characterised by a distinct reforming momentum.

(7) The First Written Ministerial Statement (30 July 2024) and the NPPF 2024 Consultation

The First Written Ministerial Statement (30 July 2024)

2.46. On 30 July 2024, Angela Rayner MP, the Deputy Prime Minister and Secretary of State for Housing, Communities and Local Government, issued a Written Ministerial Statement "Building the homes we need" which heralded a new approach to Green Belt policy, in particular through decision-making on Grey Belt land:

"*BUILDING IN THE RIGHT PLACES*

...

It is however also clear that brownfield land can only be part of the answer, and will not be enough to meet our housing needs – which is why a Green Belt designed for England in the middle of the twentieth century now must be updated for an England in the middle of the twenty first. The Green Belt today accounts for more land in England than land that is developed – around 13 per cent compared to 10 per cent. Yet as many assessments show, large areas of the Green Belt have little ecological value and are inaccessible to the public. Much of this area is better described as 'grey belt': land on the edge of existing settlements or roads, and with little aesthetic or environmental value. It is also true that development already happens on the Green Belt, but in a haphazard and non-strategic way, leading to unaffordable houses being built without the amenities that local people need.

This Government is therefore committed to ensuring the Green Belt serves its purpose, and that means taking a more strategic approach to Green Belt release. We will start by requiring local authorities to review their Green Belt boundaries where they cannot meet their identified housing, commercial or other development needs. There will be a sequential approach, with authorities asked to give consideration first to brownfield land, before moving onto grey belt sites and then to higher performing Green Belt land – recognising that this sequence may not make sense in all instances, depending on the specific opportunities available to individual local authorities. We are defining grey belt land through reference to the specific reasons for which the Green Belt exists, so that it captures sites that are making a limited contribution to the Green Belt's purposes, with additional guidance set out in the consultation. Existing protections for land covered by environmental designations, for example National Parks and Sites of Special Scientific Interest, will be maintained – and there will be a safety valve to ensure Green Belt is not released where it would fundamentally undermine the function of the Green Belt across the area of a local plan as a whole.

But we cannot wait for all release to come through plan making. Where authorities are under performing – be that lacking a sufficient land supply or failing to deliver enough homes as measured by the Housing Delivery Test – we will therefore also make it clear that applications for sites not allocated in a plan must be considered where they relate to brownfield and grey belt land. This route will maintain restrictions on the release of wider Green Belt land, meaning it would remain possible for other Green Belt land to be released outside the plan-making process where 'very special circumstances' exist, but such cases would remain exceptional. We are also strengthening the general presumption in favour of sustainable development, by clarifying the circumstances in which it applies and introducing new safeguards to make clear that its application cannot justify poor quality development.

Whenever Green Belt land is released, it must benefit both communities and nature. That is why we have today translated our 'golden rules' into policy, meaning that development on Green Belt will need to: target at least 50 per cent of the homes onsite being affordable for housing developments; be supported by the necessary infrastructure, like schools, GP surgeries and transport links; and provide accessible green space."

2.47. On the same date, the Government initiated a consultation on the new NPPF text, to take place over a three-month period up to 24 September 2024. It also issued letters to Local Planning Authorities, the development sector and separately to the Planning Inspectorate in respect of local plan examination.[16] The NPPF Consultation text amplified the WMS, setting out the nature of the objective (with bolded text in the original):

> *2. But brownfield development alone will not be enough to meet our housing need. To deliver the homes and commercial development this country needs, we are proposing the targeted release of grey belt land.* ***This government recognises the important role the Green Belt plays in preventing urban sprawl and remains committed to its continued protection – but we must review the post-war Green Belt policy to make sure it better meets the needs of present and future generations.*** *Without altering the general extent or purpose of the Green Belt, our proposed changes will support local planning authorities facing acute housing and development pressures to meet their needs, while securing environmental improvements, affordable housing and other infrastructure upgrades communities care about.*
>
> *3. Instead of the haphazard release we see under the status quo, release will be strategic and underpinned by clear safeguards. We propose to make changes to the NPPF to make clear that, where a local planning authority is unable to meet housing, commercial or other needs after fully considering all opportunities to make effective and efficient use of brownfield and wider opportunities, it should undertake a Green Belt review. <u>This review should look to release poor quality grey belt land from the Green Belt through both plan-making and decision-making to meet local needs. This release will be subject to the sustainable</u>*

16 https://www.gov.uk/government/consultations/proposed-reforms-to-the-national-planning-policy-framework-and-other-changes-to-the-planning-system/proposed-reforms-to-the-national-planning-policy-framework-and-other-changes-to-the-planning-system#chapter-5--brownfield-grey-belt-and-the-green-belt

development principles that underpin national planning policy, and to clear 'golden rules' as set out later in this chapter.

4. The Green Belt serves a specific planning purpose, in terms of preserving openness and preventing sprawl, but is not an environmental designation or a marker of any environmental importance. Much of it is inaccessible to the public and of poor ecological status. We want our proposal to not simply offset the loss of Green Belt land, but to bring about positive improvements for the quality and enjoyment of the environment. We propose a two-stage process for doing this. First, land that is safeguarded by existing environmental designations, for example National Parks, National Landscapes and Sites of Special Scientific Interest, will maintain its current protections. Second, any development on land released from the Green Belt must bring benefits, via not only mandatory Biodiversity Net Gain, but also through new rules that will secure improved access to good quality greenspace.

...

Defining the grey belt

8. As set out above, we must look to a wider set of low-performing sites where this is necessary. We propose defining grey belt land as Green Belt land which makes a limited contribution to the Green Belt's purposes, as set out in paragraph 143 of the current NPPF. To maintain existing environmental protections, we propose excluding land of environmental value from the definition, or assets of particular importance, as set out in footnote 7 of the NPPF. We are interested in whether additional exclusions are necessary, such as areas identified in draft or published Local Nature Recovery Strategies, that could become of particular importance for biodiversity.

9. To support a consistent and transparent approach to identifying land, we propose inserting a new definition of grey belt land into the glossary of the NPPF. This will provide criteria for assessing whether land makes a limited contribution to the Green Belt purposes. This definition will read as follows:

Grey belt: For the purposes of Plan-making and decision-making, grey belt is defined as land in the Green Belt comprising Previously Developed Land and any other parcels and/or areas of Green Belt land that make a limited contribution to the five Green Belt purposes (as defined in para 140 of this Framework) but excluding those areas or assets of particular importance listed in footnote 7 of this Framework (other than land designated as Green Belt).

10. We are interested in whether further support is needed to assist authorities in judging whether land makes a limited contribution to the Green Belt purposes. We propose incorporating the following into the glossary appended to the NPPF but welcome views on the most effective way of providing this guidance: Land which makes a limited contribution to the Green Belt purposes will:

a) Not strongly perform against any Green Belt purpose; and

b) Have at least one of the following features:

i. Land containing substantial built development or which is fully enclosed by built form

ii. Land which makes no or very little contribution to preventing neighbouring towns from merging into one another

iii. Land which is dominated by urban land uses, including physical developments

iv. Land which contributes little to preserving the setting and special character of historic towns

11. We have chosen to avoid prescribing specific and quantifiable measures of terms such as "substantial built development" at this point.

However, we are interested in whether respondents believe more specific criteria or further guidance are needed.

12. We want this approach to protect land which makes a strong contribution to any Green Belt purposes, while allowing authorities to consider a range of Green Belt land based on its merits for potential development.

13. We want to ensure that our definition of grey belt land acts to accurately identify land with a high sustainable development potential, while also avoiding providing incentives to allow the degradation of existing Green Belt Land. We believe that defining the grey belt in terms of its contribution to the purposes should help to prevent this, but we are interested in whether additional protections or requirements are necessary.

14. We do not want our proposals to undermine existing protections for best and most versatile agricultural land. Our proposals do not remove the requirement for planning policies and decisions to recognise the benefits of the best and most versatile agricultural land, and, where significant development of agricultural land is demonstrated to be necessary, areas of poorer quality should be preferred.

15. We are clear that sustainability remains an overarching objective and that development in the grey belt should meet the expectations set out in the NPPF, around effective use of land and access to transport.

2.48. The consultation text was very much a first draft. It included the two key definitional constraints for Grey Belt: land could only qualify if it made a "limited" contribution to all five purposes and all areas within Footnote 7 areas were excluded. There was however a key recognition that this definition might prove too narrow in the parallel draft PPG definition offered. The consultation text also referred to all sites providing at least 50% affordable housing. A draft NPPF Annex 4 was produced setting out a national approach to viability. All of these proposals were the subject of detailed consultation responses and over the next five months, the policy was developed further, with significant, but focussed, textual changes.

(8) The Second Written Ministerial Statement (12 December 2024) and the 2024 NPPF Publication

2.49. On 12 December 2024, the Minister of State, Matthew Pennycook MP, presented the final version of the NPPF to Parliament, also issuing a new WMS again entitled "Building the homes we need". The Minister confirmed the intention to progress the Grey Belt initiative, albeit with some important targeted adjustments to the consulted policy wording to reflect consultees' concerns:

"But we know that there are simply not enough sites on brownfield land registers to deliver the volume of homes that the country needs each year, let alone enough that are viable and in the right location. And that is why we have grasped the nettle and proposed a modernised, strategic approach to Green Belt land designation and release, fit for the 21st century.

In the first instance, it requires local authorities to use the local plan process to adopt a 'sequential approach', considering brownfield, then grey belt, and only then higher performing land – all while ensuring that sustainability is a central consideration throughout. We expect authorities to conduct Green Belt reviews, to identify the right land to bring forward in their areas. Where authorities fail to meet development needs, developers may bring forward proposals on low-performing grey belt land outside of the plan process, but with higher performing land protected from this form of release.

Through our consultation we found broad support for this strategic approach to Green Belt release, and for the concept of grey belt, which recognises that there are significant parts of the Green Belt that contribute little by way of aesthetic, public access, or ecological value. However, we did see evidence that our proposed definition of grey belt was likely to leave too much room for subjectivity and debate. In response, we have set out a clearer description of how to assess whether land meets the definition, and we will be providing further guidance in the new year. We remain clear that existing protections for land covered by environmental and national landscape designations – for example National Parks, Areas of Outstanding Natural Beauty and Sites of Special Scientific Interest – will remain.

At the centre of our reformed Green Belt policy lie our golden rules, which mean that housing can only be built on Green Belt land if developers deliver high levels of affordable housing, appropriate local infrastructure, and accessible public green space. Our consultation proposed rules requiring that residential schemes across the country would deliver 50 percent affordable housing, while recognising that because land values vary, the limited use of viability assessments should be permitted within certain constraints. The objective of these rules was to make sure that the public would receive the fair share of the 'planning uplift' driven by the new rules, and that returns to landowners would be fair but not excessive.

We received significant feedback from a wide range of stakeholders who welcomed the ambition of these rules and the commitment to maximising affordable housing delivery, but who shared strong evidence that fixing the affordable housing requirement at 50 percent nationally would not reflect regional variations in viability and would hinder delivery. This risked leaving authorities with a choice: allow flexibility and turn the amount of affordable housing into a negotiation; or hold firm and make sites unviable, delivering no homes, affordable or otherwise. Responding to this, our final policy introduces a 15 percentage point premium on top of existing affordable housing requirements, up to a maximum of 50 percent, and rules out any negotiation until we have strengthened national planning practice guidance on viability – in which we will consider the case for permitting viability negotiations on previously developed land and larger strategic sites, likely to carry greater infrastructure costs.

In a majority of authorities, this will result in an affordable housing requirement of 50 percent. Local authorities will be required to adopt their own ambitious golden rules through the local plan process, which will supersede these national requirements as new plans come into force. This revised approach delivers on our commitment to sharing the proceeds of land value uplift fairly, securing clear public benefits, while delivering more homes and more affordable homes than a flat 50 percent rate. It will increase the speed of housing provision by giving all actors greater certainty about what is required and what will achieve planning permission."

<u>The Consultation Response Document (12 December 2024)</u>

2.50. The Government's consultation response was published in parallel, and confirmed the importance placed on clarity and certainty, and the clear wish to ensure that the policy did not apply to an overly narrow category of land:

"<u>After carefully considering the consultation responses, the government has provided a new definition of grey belt, that seeks to clarify the relationship between Previously Developed Land and other grey belt land to ensure that both routes to development provide clear and separate tests.</u>

<u>We have also clarified that grey belt land is Green Belt land which does not strongly contribute to Green Belt Purposes (a), (b), and (d).</u>

We have included a clear statement that development brought forward on Green Belt land, or on land released from the Green Belt, should be sustainable, and in line with the requirements to promote sustainable transport as set out in Chapter 9 of the National Planning Policy Framework.

We have made changes to ensure that the protections given to other protected areas, as listed in footnote 7 of the National Planning Policy Framework, are not weakened by our changes to Green Belt policy, by being clear that development or release of Green Belt land should not proceed where these policies give a strong reason for refusal.

We also recognise the need for further guidance to ensure a more consistent approach to assessing Green Belt land. We will be providing further guidance in January 2025. To ensure that local authorities are supported to implement the changes in the National Planning Policy Framework, we will also provide a funding contribution to local authorities that will need to undertake Green Belt reviews as a result of our policy changes. Local authorities that meet our eligibility criteria will be able to submit an Expression of Interest (EoI) to receive a share of this funding.

Our revised grey belt definition will allow for development on land that is not already previously developed as we believe it is important that we also consider the development potential of land which, though it may be formally designated as Green Belt, no longer adequately serves the Green Belt purposes. However, our definition of grey belt will still make it clear that high performing Green Belt land should be protected, and that Previously Developed Land should be prioritised for development.

We do not consider that additional protections are needed to protect agricultural land, or that a formal exclusion is needed from the grey belt to protect agricultural land. The National Planning Policy Framework is already clear that the value of the best and most versatile agricultural land should be recognised in both plan-making and decisions. However, we have concluded that the Local Nature Recovery Strategies will benefit from new guidance and updates to the existing planning practice guidance to clarify the role of Local Nature Recovery Strategies when it comes to enhancing the Green Belt.

…

The government recognises that greater clarity is needed to assist authorities in identifying grey belt land so as to ensure development does not come forward in inappropriate locations. We have revised and streamlined our proposed definition of grey belt to focus on the role that land plays in protecting against sprawl, preventing the merging of settlements, and preserving the setting of historic towns. These purposes focus on the spatial role played by Green Belt land, and so will prevent intentional degradation of Green Belt parcels in order to meets grey belt criteria.

We will also be publishing further guidance on Green Belt reviews in January 2025, to ensure a more consistent approach to the identification of grey belt land. This will assist in ensuring inappropriate or high performing land is not identified for release or development and will set out how the performance of Green Belt should be assessed. This guidance will also provide guidance on how to ensure that parcels of land identified for development do not fundamentally undermine the purpose of the wider Green Belt."

(9) Post-NPPF Developments

2.51. From 5 September 2024 through to early 2025, the House of Lords Select Committee conducted an inquiry in respect of Grey Belt, culminating in a letter from its Chair to the Deputy Prime Minister/Secretary of State (dated 5 February 2025) and a response from the Minister of State (dated 19 March 2025). The Committee's conclusions expressed doubts about the efficacy of the policy. However, of greater interest are the remarks of Minister of State himself at the session on 18 December 2024, very shortly after the NPPF publication. The Minister was pressed on the question of scale of release, with his response emphasising that taking account for necessary local specificity, the extent of Green Belt release would be "modest but would make a difference":[17]

17 https://committees.parliament.uk/work/8503/the-grey-belt/publications/

"*Lord Mair: Minister, our Chair has already referred to the significance of the grey belt in terms of how much difference it will make, and I want to pursue that point. What is your estimate of the scale of housing development that will be enabled through the release of grey-belt land? Are you able to give any indication, numerically or as a proportion of your overall housing target? What is your feel for the likely significance of the grey belt? Are we talking about 10% of the overall housing target, or is it higher or much smaller than that?*

Matthew Pennycook MP: In general terms, I am happy to say that we do not think it will be a significant quantity of land; it will be a modest amount of land that will make a difference.

Without being evasive in any way, I cannot give you a specific figure, because it is very difficult for us sitting here in Westminster to quantify the precise amount. I say both of those things—this is a prelude to what I will come on to say—for the following reasons.

Regarding the amount of grey belt, we are talking specifically about parcels of land, which is what the definition speaks to, rather than the green belt as a whole across the local authority area. Parcels of land will be identified locally through locally led assessments undertaken by local planning authorities. How they assess grey belt for a green-belt review will obviously depend on the particular geography and development needs of their local areas, although the department intends to bring forward guidance in the new year to assist local authorities with greenbelt reviews. Some, as I mentioned earlier, have undertaken green-belt reviews, but lots have not, and we think they need some support. Principally, identifying those sites would be a locally led activity.

Then—this is where we could perhaps stray into some of the assessments that have been made by others, such as Lichfields and LandTech, which have made an estimate of the total proportion of grey-belt sites across the country—the locally led assessment also needs to be overlaid with the question of whether these sites meet the other national planning policy requirements. For example, are they in sustainable locations? Do they meet the other requirements in the NPPF? Do they meet our golden rules on what is required to bring them forward?

The precise amount will differ in every local area where land needs to be released. Just to take a step back, we are talking about release only where local authorities are unable to meet assessed housing need through brownfield development alone. Where it does need to be released, it will be based on a local figure, and that will differ in lots of different areas, so I am afraid it is not as easy as plucking a single-digit figure out of the air for the national total as a whole.

<u>Lord Mair</u>: I was not expecting you to be able to pluck a single-digit figure out of the air, but I and my colleagues on the committee want to get a feel from you as to the likely scale of this. Will it make a real difference, or is it just a small adjustment to existing green belt?

<u>The Chair</u>: This is the difficulty. The Minister wants to say that it is not significant, but it will make a difference. He has used both those terms. I understand why you might want to tread that line, but we would like to probe a little bit.

<u>Matthew Pennycook MP</u>: Let me therefore expand on my answer in a way that might be helpful. Several studies have been produced. I referenced Lichfields, which I think gave a total quantum of 15% of the green belt released, and LandTech, which gave a figure of 9%. They are independent assessments that make a number of assumptions, as any assessment does. We would take issue with them replicating exactly the policy approach that we have ultimately taken forward. The figures in those ranges are not overlaid with the policy requirements I have talked about.

Let us take the Lichfields figure of 15%. You have to overlay on top of that the question of whether that 15%, in terms of individual parcels of land, meets the other requirements of the NPPF in terms of sustainability, et cetera. Also, does it meet our golden rules? <u>Taking</u>

that in the round, I am confident that the total proportion of the green belt that will be released through grey belt will be in single digits. That is what I mean by "not significant". We are not talking about 40%, 50% or 60% of the green belt being released. In many parts of the country, that simply would not be possible without undermining, across the plan area, the fundamental purposes of the green belt. That is the backstop that exists.

However, I would slightly challenge the Chair's assertion that even a single-digit release quantum of the total green belt is not meaningful in terms of land coming forward that is appropriate for development.

The Chair: I do not think I said that, to be fair.

Matthew Pennycook MP: Modest will still be impactful, even if we are not talking about a significant quantum of the green belt as a whole being released through this method.

The Chair: I did not quite say that. I was quoting you; you used both those terms. That is a much fuller and more helpful answer."

The Planning Practice Guidance (27 February 2025)

2.52. On 27 February 2025, the Government published the Planning Practice Guidance update. The brief delay beyond the promised January 2025 publication date no doubt reflected (i) the technical complexity of setting national guidance and (ii) the helpful clarificatory judgment in *Mead Realisations v Secretary of State for Housing, Communities and Local Government* [2025] EWCA Civ 32, confirming that there was no legal constraint on PPG clarifying and indeed expanding upon the NPPF.

2.53. The following month, the Minister of State issued a response to the House of Lords Select Committee (19 March 2024) which was positive and robust, identifying the reforms as part of a wider programme:[18]

"I am grateful for the Committee's focus on this important topic, which forms a key part of our recent reforms to the planning system. As you know, the government is committed to preserving Green Belts which have served England's towns and cities well over many decades, not least in terms of checking the unrestricted sprawl of large built-up areas and preventing neighbouring towns merging into one another.

However, we are taking more strategic approach to greenbelt land designation and release to build more homes in the right places. These changes, along with our wider programme of planning reform, support the delivery of our Plan for Change milestone of building 1.5 million safe and decent homes in this Parliament.

I am pleased that the Committee welcomes the positive contribution that grey belt land can make to meeting housing targets in a sustainable way, and that the Committee sees potential for our reforms to enable more pragmatic decision-making and ensure the right development comes forward in the right places.

I note the Committee's concerns as to the evidence underpinning these planning reforms, how they will work alongside other changes to national policy, and whether the planning system is capable of delivering these ambitions."

(10) Summary

2.54. Grey Belt policy represents a clear break with the past. Government is plainly committed to the Green Belt, but only where it serves a contemporary purpose. There has been a clear recognition that it is not sufficient to apply Green Belt as an absolute constraint, both to decision-making in an era of an "acute and entrenched housing

18 https://committees.parliament.uk/work/8503/the-grey-belt/publications/

crisis" and in respect of plan-making for Local Plans that look to the 2040s and beyond. The concept of Green Belt "permanence" (dating from as far back as Circular 14/84) is plainly now a much more conditional concept.

2.55. Taking the longer historical view back as far as 1955 reveals some intriguing continuities between Grey Belt and the original vision for the Green Belt, as revealed in the text of the 1955 Circular. For example, the 2025 Planning Practice Guidance emphasises that Green Belt purpose B relates solely to "towns", and not "villages", directly reflecting the initial 1955 wording. The original vision of a Green Belt "several miles wide" might be said to be far closer to Grey Belt policy than the 12.5% total coverage across England of today. That said, it is clear that Government wishes to look ahead.

2.56. Historic Green Belt policy text has often been considered to have some interpretive significance in cases of textual ambiguity. In several modern NPPF-era cases, the courts have considered historic policy from as far back as the 1980s to interpret terms that were ambiguous and unclear (see notably the discussion in *Redhill Aerodrome Ltd v Secretary of State for Communities and Local Government* [2014] EWCA Civ 1386 [15]-[17] and *Sefton MBC v Secretary of State for Housing, Communities and Local Government* [2021] EWHC 1082 (Admin), [10]-[13] and [30]-[59], both excerpted in Chapter 20). However, the historic cases were concerned with express statements by Government that Green Belt policy had <u>not</u> changed. The same cannot necessarily be said for Grey Belt given its introduction of entirely new concepts. Grey Belt policy now requires interpretation and application afresh, considering the precise text used, its immediate and wider NPPF context, the accompanying Planning Practice Guidance, and wider Government statements as to the intention of the policy.

2.57. In Chapter 3, we shall examine the structure of NPPF Chapter 13's decision-making provisions, followed (in Chapter 4), by those in respect of plan-making. Collectively, this provides vital context to how the Grey Belt provisions are to operate.

CHAPTER THREE

THE DECISION-TAKING CONTEXT

(1) Introduction

3.1 The NPPF Chapter on Green Belt comprises 19 paragraphs (NPPF 142-160). Grey Belt decision-taking policy occupies 5 paragraphs (NPPF 155-159), plus a Glossary definition for "Grey Belt land" incorporating NPPF 143. The text of the whole Green Belt Chapter merits close scrutiny as part of any planning application.

3.2 The Grey Belt innovations should be read alongside other policy innovations in the 2024 NPPF, notably the revised presumption in favour of sustainable development (NPPF 11d) and various changes to housing policy (NPPF Chapter 5) and economic policy (NPPF Chapter 6).

3.3 This Chapter considers the following five key topics/paragraphs. These collectively provide the strong presumption against development in the Green Belt, to which Grey Belt policy is an express exception (but critically a broad exception):

(1) "Great Importance" (NPPF 142)

(2) The "Fundamental Aim" and "Openness" (NPPF 142)

(3) The Green Belt Purposes (NPPF 143)

(4) Inappropriate Development and Very Special Circumstances (NPPF 153)

(5) Specified Exceptions (NPPF 154)

3.4 In the next Chapter, we shall examine the plan-making legislation and the NPPF policy provisions, including the plan-led approach and transitional arrangements (NPPF 144-150 and Annex 1, NPPF 234-235) and the Exceptional Circumstances and the new sequential approach to Green Belt release (NPPF 148).

(2) "Great Importance" (NPPF 142)

3.5 NPPF 142 emphasises the "great importance" of Green Belts:

"*142. The government attaches great importance to Green Belts...*"

3.6 There is symbolic continuity here with historic national policy. The use of the term "importance" began with the 1955 Circular.[19] The adjective "great" was first introduced in Circular 14/84. The express term "great importance" is not used elsewhere in the NPPF. "Great weight" is to be accorded in the protection of nationally designated landscapes,[20] and heritage,[21] both of which reflect express statutory protections. The same term is used for the promotion of mineral extraction.[22] There are other isolated

---

19 Circular 42/55, Paragraph 1: "*I am directed by* [the Minister] *to draw your attention to the importance of checking the unrestricted sprawl of the built-up areas, and of safeguarding the surrounding countryside against further encroachment*"

20 NPPF 189: "*Great weight should be given to conserving and enhancing landscape and scenic beauty in National Parks, the Broads and Areas of Outstanding Natural Beauty which have the highest status of protection in relation to these issues*"

21 NPPF 212: "*When considering the impact of a proposed development on the significance of a designated heritage asset, great weight should be given to the asset's conservation*"

22 NPPF 224: "*When determining planning applications, great weight should be given to the benefits of mineral extraction, including to the economy*"

references in respect of sites within existing settlements[23] and educational development.[24]

(3) The "Fundamental Aim" and "Openness" (NPPF 142)

3.7 National Policy continues to describe a single fundamental aim for Green Belt policy, expressed in two parts:

> *"142.... The fundamental aim of Green Belt policy is to prevent urban sprawl by keeping land permanently open; the essential characteristics of Green Belts are their openness and their permanence."*

3.8 Two key points arise: (a) the spatial nature of Green Belt policy and (b) the methodological and legal complexity of the "openness" test.

Green Belt as a Spatial Policy

3.9 Green Belt is fundamentally a "spatial" policy. It is purely concerned with keeping designated Green Belt land "permanently open" (subject to Grey Belt and other exceptions).

3.10 It is not an "environmental" policy in the sense that its primary aim is to protect substantive environmental goals (e.g. landscape or ecology), or even to reduce emissions from travel through more sustainable patterns of growth. The protection of the Green Belt *may* achieve those other aims as a secondary effect, but these are primarily to be protected through their own separate, respective policy protections.

3.11 This formal separation is important and reflects a long-standing governmental concern to focus the policy's purpose, to simplify its application. The 1955 Circular simply referred to "*checking*

---

23 NPPF 73d

24 NPPF 100a

unrestricted sprawl" and "*safeguarding the surrounding countryside against further encroachment*". PPG2 (1995) narrowed the description, but also noted additional agricultural and sustainability objectives.[25] These references were lost in the NPPF consolidation exercise in 2012.

3.12 It is particularly important that certain phrases in the current Government's pre-December 2024 NPPF publications are not misconstrued, when applying the current text. The first WMS (30 July 2024) stated prominently that "*This Government is therefore committed to ensuring the Green Belt serves its purpose*" without precisely explaining what the dominant purpose was. This was followed by a reference that: "*large areas of the Green Belt have little ecological value and are inaccessible to the public*". The Second Written Ministerial Statement (12 December 2024) confirms expressly that the Grey Belt limitation to purposes (a), (b) and (d) was based on the clear spatial focus: "*These purposes focus on the spatial role played by Green Belt land*". All of this emphasises that Grey Belt development, aside from bespoke provisions such as the third Golden Rule (NPPF 156(c): publicly accessible green space) is not required to promote any specific ecological or landscape improvement role in its own right.

3.13 In planning applications/appeals, it may become important to emphasise this spatial character when assessing any Green Belt case (including Grey Belt), and not to become diverted by considerations of landscape quality and the secondary effects of

---

25 PPG 2, paragraph 1.4: "*The fundamental aim of Green Belt policy is to prevent urban sprawl by keeping land permanently open; the most important attribute of Green Belts is their openness. Green Belts can shape patterns of urban development at sub-regional and regional scale, and help to ensure that development occurs in locations allocated in development plans. They help to protect the countryside, be it in agricultural, forestry or other use. They can assist in moving towards more sustainable patterns of urban development (see paragraph 2.10).*"

Green Belt protection. Third party objections that merge landscape, biodiversity, agricultural and climate change considerations within the Green Belt are quite common, and they can occasionally appear within Officer's Reports as well.

Openness

3.14 The phrase "permanently open" and the term "openness" have been the subject of considerable dispute and litigation over the years. Grey Belt policy should be understood as an express response to the stricture and complexity of the test, effectively removing it from consideration altogether.

3.15 The PPG explains the term "openness", as having both "spatial" and "visual" aspects, but being fundamentally a question of planning judgement:

What factors can be taken into account when considering the potential impact of development on the openness of the Green Belt? [26]

Assessing the impact of a proposal on the openness of the Green Belt, where it is relevant to do so, requires a judgement based on the circumstances of the case. By way of example, the courts have identified a number of matters which may need to be taken into account in making this assessment. These include, but are not limited to:

- *openness is capable of having both spatial and visual aspects – in other words, the visual impact of the proposal may be relevant, as could its volume*

[26] Paragraph: 013 Reference ID: 64-013-20250225

- *the duration of the development, and its remediability – taking into account any provisions to return land to its original state or to an equivalent (or improved) state of openness*

- *the degree of activity likely to be generated, such as traffic generation*

How should harm to the Green Belt including harm to its openness be considered if a development is not inappropriate development?[27]

Footnote 55 to the NPPF sets out that if development is considered to be not inappropriate development on previously developed land or grey belt, then this is excluded from the policy requirement to give substantial weight to any harm to the Green Belt, including to its openness.

This is consistent with rulings from the courts on these matters that, where development (of any kind, now including development on grey belt or previously developed land) is not considered to be inappropriate in the Green Belt, it follows that the test of impacts to openness or to Green Belt purposes are addressed and that therefore a proposal does not have to be justified by "very special circumstances".

3.16 Throughout the 2010s, the term "openness" was the subject of much litigation including the following (non-exhaustive) list of cases:

- *Europa Oil and Gas Limited v SSCLG* [2013] EWHC 2643 (Admin) (minerals development);

- *Fordent Holdings Limited v SSCLG & Cheshire West and Chester Council* [2013] EWHC 2844 (Admin) (caravan and campsite development);

[27] Paragraph: 014 Reference ID: 64-014-20250225

- *Timmins v Gedling Borough Council* [2014] EWHC 654 (Admin) (cemetery/crematorium development);

- *R (Lee Valley Regional Park Authority) v Epping Forest District* Council [2016] EWCA Civ 404 (agricultural development);

- *Euro Garages Ltd v SSCLG & Anor* [2018] EWHC 1753 (Admin) (petrol filling station development);

- *Turner v SSCLG & East Dorset Council* [2016] EWCA Civ 466 (residential development);

- *R (Amanda Boot) v Elmbridge BC* [2017] EWHC 12 (Admin) (sports facility development)

3.17 Finally, in *R (Samuel Smith Old Brewery (Tadcaster) and others) v North Yorkshire County Council* [2020] UKSC 3, the Supreme Court endorsed the Court of Appeal's judgment in *Turner v SSCLG & East Dorset Council* [2016] EWCA Civ 466 and effectively confirmed the dual spatial/visual nature of "openness" (now expressed in the PPG). This judgment will be explored in Chapter 20 as part of the Very Special Circumstances test.

3.18 As the revised PPG now confirms, the focus of Grey Belt assessment is purely on the Green Belt purposes, and not openness as a free-standing test. An assessment of openness will only be required if the planning case retains a Very Special Circumstances argument.

(4) Green Belt Purposes (NPPF 143)

3.19 NPPF 143 retains the five purposes unamended:

143. Green Belt serves 5 purposes:

(a) to check the unrestricted sprawl of large built-up areas;

(b) to prevent neighbouring towns merging into one another;

(c) to assist in safeguarding the countryside from encroachment;

(d) to preserve the setting and special character of historic towns; and

(e) to assist in urban regeneration, by encouraging the recycling of derelict and other urban land.

3.20 The precise wording and interpretation of these five purposes shall be explored in Part II, Chapters 9-11 and 14.

3.21 As noted in the previous Chapter, purposes (a), (b) and (d) closely echo the three purposes identified in the 1955 Circular's paragraph 3: "*(a) to check the further growth of a large built-up area; (b) to prevent neighbouring towns from merging into one another; or (c) to preserve the special character of a town.*"

3.22 The decision to exclude purpose (c) "*safeguarding the countryside from encroachment*" in the Grey Belt land Glossary Definition is particularly notable. On many greenfield/agricultural sites, it has often been difficult to identify no harm to this purpose, and indeed, far higher gradings of harm have been identified than for the other purposes.

(5) Inappropriate Development and Very Special Circumstances (NPPF 153)

3.23 NPPF 153 retains the core concept of "inappropriate development", and the Very Special Circumstances ("VSC") test:

153. When considering any planning application, local planning authorities should ensure that substantial weight is given to any harm to the Green Belt, including harm to its openness. Inappropriate development is, by definition, harmful to the Green Belt and should not be approved except in very special circumstances. 'Very special circumstances' will not exist unless the potential harm to the Green Belt by reason of inappropriateness, and any other harm resulting from the proposal, is clearly outweighed by other considerations.

3.24 Prior to the introduction of Grey Belt and the Golden Rules, the Very Special Circumstances provisions (e.g. NPPF (2023) 152-153) presented a formidable challenge, both because of the height of the threshold, and the lack of clarity as to what might amount to VSC.

3.25 Whilst the VSC test remains in place, the immediate and wider context is now considerably altered, such that the effect can no longer be said to be the same. In particular, all major residential development must now satisfy the Golden Rules via NPPF 156 (explored further in Part II, Chapters 17-19). The position has therefore moved from one of significant uncertainty/risk far closer towards (if not completely) a brightline pass/fail test.

3.26 The precise structure and interpretation of the VSC test shall be explored in Part II, Chapter 20.

(6) Exceptions (NPPF 154)

3.27 NPPF 154 provides a consolidated list of 14 exceptions, comprised of eight types of development which are definitionally "not inappropriate" and a further list of six types which are not inappropriate, provided that they "*preserve its openness and do not conflict with the purposes of including land within it*":

154. Development in the Green Belt is inappropriate unless one of the following exceptions applies:

a) buildings for agriculture and forestry;

b) the provision of appropriate facilities (in connection with the existing use of land or a change of use), including buildings, for outdoor sport, outdoor recreation, cemeteries and burial grounds and allotments; as long as the facilities preserve the openness of the Green Belt and do not conflict with the purposes of including land within it;

c) the extension or alteration of a building provided that it does not result in disproportionate additions over and above the size of the original building;

d) the replacement of a building, provided the new building is in the same use and not materially larger than the one it replaces;

e) limited infilling in villages;

f) limited affordable housing for local community needs under policies set out in the development plan (including policies for rural exception sites); and

g) limited infilling or the partial or complete redevelopment of previously developed land (including a material change of use to residential or mixed use including residential), whether redundant or in continuing use (excluding temporary buildings), which would not cause substantial harm to the openness of the Green Belt.

h) Other forms of development provided they preserve its openness and do not conflict with the purposes of including land within it. These are:

i. mineral extraction;

ii. engineering operations;

iii. local transport infrastructure which can demonstrate a requirement for a Green Belt location;

iv. the re-use of buildings provided that the buildings are of permanent and substantial construction;

v. material changes in the use of land (such as changes of use for outdoor sport or recreation, or for cemeteries and burial grounds); and vi. development, including buildings, brought forward under a Community Right to Build Order or Neighbourhood Development Order.

3.28 The list remains disparate, prioritising a range of different economic and social objectives, but without a coherent overall structure. The list is a mixture of simple, singular terms ("buildings for agriculture") and more relative terms going to scale/number (e.g. "disproportionate additions" and "limited infilling"). The exceptions list can therefore be seen as the vestige or accretion of exceptions from 1955 onwards.

3.29 The exceptions have generated a significant amount of case law over the years, especially in respect of the term "openness" (as listed above). There are a number of reasons for the extent of historic litigation over the exceptions, but fundamentally, the policy wording was simply not clear enough. Grey Belt policy can therefore be understood as an attempt both (a) to remove debates about openness altogether and (b) as an effort to reach a greater level of definitional precision across all of the policy tests to avoid litigation.

(7) Summary

3.30 This Chapter has considered the context in which Grey Belt policy sits. Unlike the Very Special Circumstances test and the other Exceptions, Grey Belt policy is intended to set a pathway that provides a considerably higher level of certainty, for a much wider category of development than the existing exceptions.

3.31 In the next Chapter, we shall examine the interaction with the plan-making process, before considering key points to consider for the various stages/pathways through which a Grey Belt application may pass.

CHAPTER FOUR

THE PLAN-MAKING CONTEXT

(1) Introduction

4.1. The focus of this book is on how to secure permission outside the plan-making process. Definitionally, the majority of Grey Belt permissions will be granted in local planning authorities where the development plan is out-of-date and in the process of review and preparation of a new plan. In many cases, the date of adoption of that new document may be some years away. The plan-making process will however be relevant to most Grey Belt applications in one of several ways.

4.2. First, and most importantly, Government has tasked all local planning authorities with Green Belt land to conduct a review of Green Belt boundaries as part of the plan-making process (see notably NPPF 147-149 and the PPG Green Belt Chapter). As part of this exercise, reports will be produced which will situate all LPA decision-making as to whether the land falls within the Glossary definition. On 27 February 2025, Government announced the grant funding of a total of £9.38 million to 134 local planning authorities, comprised mostly of individual grants of £70,000 per authority to support the cost of undertaking Green Belt reviews. The exact timetable for delivery and publication is unclear, but most will report as part of the plan-making process.

4.3. Second, ahead of the completion of this exercise, LPAs may seek to refer to the historic Local Plan evidence base which may have explored the nature of a site's contribution to the Green Belt purposes as part of the Glossary Definition for the purposes of

Criterion A (NPPF 155a). The PPG provides a somewhat cautionary note over the use of such documents, but does not prohibit their use.[28]

4.4. Third, the local plan preparation process (both historic and current) may become relevant to identifying whether a given site meets Criterion B (NPPF 155b) (i.e. the extent of unmet need) and also Criterion C (NPPF 155c) (i.e. locational sustainability).

4.5. Finally, the extent of progress of the local plan process may be relevant as a broader material consideration, i.e. the weight to be accorded the benefits of delivering the development (over and above NPPF 158 and the requirement to accord "significant weight" to major housing development which meets the Golden Rules). Any local plan delay will also be a material consideration for a very special circumstances case, if this is argued as a reserve position.

4.6. Almost all applications and appeals will therefore need to consider the plan-making process under the current Part 2 of the Planning and Compulsory Purchase Act 2004 ("PCPA") and the different phases of plan-making that have either taken place historically or are ongoing.

4.7. It will also become increasingly important to look to the new Local Plan system under the Levelling-up and Regeneration Act 2023, Schedule 7.

4.8. This Chapter therefore begins with a summary of the legislative framework within Part 2 of the Planning and Compulsory Purchase Act 2004 and then examines the NPPF provisions in respect of Green Belt release, culminating in a list of some of the

28 Paragraph: 002 Reference ID: 64-002-20250225 "*When updating or preparing plans, authorities will need to consider whether any existing Green Belt assessment remains up to date.*"

key documents/processes that any Grey Belt application will need to track.

(2) The Legislative Framework

4.9. Whilst the LURA 2023 puts in place arrangements for new-style Local Plans (considered further below), the majority of authorities are encouraged to prepare and submit for examination development plan documents prior to December 2026. The NPPF Consultation Response (12 December 2024) stated:

> "*[W]here plans at reg 19 need to be revised to account for the revised National Planning Policy Framework and local housing need, the expectation for plans to be submitted in 18 months will be extended to December 2026 where LPAs have to do significant additional work (defined as returning to the regulation 18 consultation). All earlier stage plans progressing under this version of the National Planning Policy Framework will be expected to be submitted for examination under the existing 2004 Act system no later than December 2026.*"[29]

4.10. The PCPA Part 2 sets out a series of 12 separate (but overlapping) steps/activities that an LPA must take to prepare and adopt a Local Plan:

(a) The duty to survey (Section 13 PCPA)

(b) The preparation of a Local Development Scheme, comprising development plan documents (Section 15 PCPA)

---

[29] NPPF Consultation Response (12 December 2024), Section 12: 12. The future of planning policy and plan making Response to Questions 103-104 https://www.gov.uk/government/consultations/proposed-reforms-to-the-national-planning-policy-framework-and-other-changes-to-the-planning-system/outcome/government-response-to-the-proposed-reforms-to-the-national-planning-policy-framework-and-other-changes-to-the-planning-system-consultation

(c) Parallel preparation of a Policies Map alongside the DPD

(d) Plan preparation (Section 19 PCPA)

(e) Sustainability appraisal (Section 19 PCPA)

(f) The Duty to Cooperate (Section 33A PCPA)

(g) Statutory consultation (Regulations 18 and 19)

(h) Plan submission (Section 20 PCPA)

(i) Plan examination (Section 20 PCPA)

(j) Modification and Reporting (Section 20 PCPA)

(k) Plan adoption (Section 23 PCPA)

(l) Plan review (Regulation 5)

4.11. This is an iterative process. The extensive evidence that is gathered (and consulted upon), informs the drafting of policies (notably allocations and designations) and supporting text, all of which is again consulted upon. The final draft text is ultimately scrutinised through formal examination by an Inspector (or Inspectors) appointed by the Secretary of State.

4.12. The NPPF text under NPPF Chapter 13 (and allied paragraphs) which governs Green Belt release through plan-making is a critical consideration throughout these stages.

4.13. For the sake of brevity, this summary will not include reference to the detailed guidance on plan-making in the various PPG Chapters or the Planning Inspectorate's Guidance, now collected in a single webpage.[30]

(a) The Duty to Survey

4.14. Under Section 13 PCPA, all local planning authorities are required to undertake a survey of their area and "*keep under review the matters which may be expected to affect the development of their area or the planning of its development.*"

4.15. Section 13(2) and (3) PCPA specifies the following mandatory considerations:

(2) These matters include–

(a) the principal physical, economic, social and environmental characteristics of the area of the authority;

(b) the principal purposes for which land is used in the area;

(c) the size, composition and distribution of the population of the area;

(d) the communications, transport system and traffic of the area;

(e) any other considerations which may be expected to affect those matters;

(f) such other matters as may be prescribed or as the Secretary of State (in a particular case) may direct.

(3) The matters also include–

(a) any changes which the authority think may occur in relation to any other matter;

30 https://www.gov.uk/government/collections/create-or-update-a-local-plan

(b) the effect such changes are likely to have on the development of the authority's area or on the planning of such development.

4.16. The duty to survey is not regularly discussed at examination or in the decision-taking context. Nevertheless it situates LPAs' subsequent plan-making activity and is the statutory basis for the substantial introductory content at the start of most development plans, including their description of the extent of existing Green Belt designations. and where applicable, the process that has been undergone to identify Grey Belt land for release.

<u>(b) The Local Development Scheme: The Duty to Prepare and Maintain</u>

4.17. Section 15 PCPA requires the authority to "*prepare and maintain…a local development scheme*". This is formally a list of the relevant documents which comprise the development plan, and allied documents, e.g. Supplementary Planning Documents (SPDs). The development scheme is to specify the "development plan documents", as part of a wider subset of "local development documents".

4.18. Development Plan Documents are often colloquially termed "Local Plans", The initials "DPD" shall be used to disambiguate from the <u>future</u> "Local Plans" under the LURA reforms (covered below).

4.19. The content of Development Plan Documents is defined by Regulation 5 of Town and Country Planning (Local Planning) (England) Regulations 2012 ("the Local Plan Regulations"):

5(1) For the purposes of section 17(7)(za) of the Act the documents which are to be prepared as local development documents are—

(a) any document prepared by a local planning authority individually or in cooperation with one or more other local planning authorities, which contains <u>statements regarding one or more of the following</u>—

(i) the development and use of land which the local planning authority wish to encourage during any specified period;

(ii) the allocation of sites for a particular type of development or use;

(iii) any environmental, social, design and economic objectives which are relevant to the attainment of the development and use of land mentioned in paragraph (i); and

(iv) development management and site allocation policies, which are intended to guide the determination of applications for planning permission;

(b) where a document mentioned in sub-paragraph (a) contains policies applying to sites or areas by reference to an Ordnance Survey map, any map which accompanies that document and which shows how the adopted policies map would be amended by the document, if it were adopted.

4.20. Green Belt policy can be considered to fall within the category of development management policies under Regulation 5(1)(a)(iv), and any allocations on Grey Belt land sites would also fall within this category and potentially Regulation 5(1)(a)(i).

4.21. All DPDs in Green Belt areas (adopted prior to December 2024) will contain at least one development management policy which confirms the existence of the Green Belt and sets out how applications on Green Belt land are to be determined. The wording will often either closely match national policy at the time that the document was adopted, or incorporate future policy by reference.

4.22. Where an LPA wishes to release land from the Green Belt for a specific allocation, then it will ordinarily state this change and make a corresponding allocation policy.

(c) The Policies Map

4.23. A DPD will be accompanied by a policies map (based on an OS Map) which is formally separate from the plan but which "*illustrate geographically the application of the policies in the adopted development plan.*" (Regulation 9(1)(c)).

4.24. The DPD formally designates certain land as Green Belt and the Policies Map records the boundary and designation. In many cases, this will simply have involved carrying over designations made in historic development plans, including those adopted under previous legislation.

4.25. In guidance issued on 27 February 2025, the Government emphasised the importance of a standard format for the Policies Map across all LPAs. [31] This includes the use of OS basemap (as required by Regulations 2 and 9(1)(a) of the Town and Country Planning (Local Planning) (England) Regulations 2012/767) in OS Open Greyscale with Labels or OS MasterMap Topography Layer. However, the guidance goes further in seeking standardised colour schemes and hatching, including denoting broader area-based, environmental policies such as Green Belt. The intention would appear to be an approach that is not merely universal and easier to understand for the human viewer, but also increasingly capable of computer-based measurement at scale and across LPA boundaries.

(d) Plan Preparation

4.26. The preparation, examination and adoption of DPDs is currently governed by Sections 19, 20 and 23 PCPA. This is the key phase which will generate the local plan evidence that may guide Grey Belt assessment at the application phase. This could take place a

31 https://www.gov.uk/guidance/how-to-present-your-policies-map

number of months or even years prior to plan submission, and thus presents a critical event in the application/appeal process.

4.27. The key characteristics of the DPD preparation process are set out under Section 19(1)-(1C) PCPA:

19(1) Development plan documents must be prepared in accordance with the local development scheme.

(1A) Development plan documents must (taken as a whole) include policies designed to secure that the development and use of land in the local planning authority's area contribute to the mitigation of, and adaptation to, climate change.

(1B) Each local planning authority must identify the strategic priorities for the development and use of land in the authority's area.

(1C) Policies to address those priorities must be set out in the local planning authority's development plan documents (taken as a whole)

4.28. Local Planning Authorities are therefore instructed to prepare DPDs in a specific way, having regard to strategic priorities. There is no formal cut-off date by which to do so in the legislation, nor in current national policy. The legislation is also largely silent in respect of meeting any specific development needs (e.g. housing needs) and the balance to be struck with other protective designations, including Green Belt. Instead, that is left to NPPF or other national policy.

4.29. Section 19(2) PCPA sets out a series of requirements in respect of preparation, most notably:

19(2) In preparing a development plan document or any other local development document the local planning authority must have regard to–

(a) national policies and advice contained in guidance issued by the Secretary of State;

4.30. The primary example of a "national policy" is the NPPF, e.g. the current NPPF Chapter 13. The PPG can be considered "advice contain in guidance", but is also in effect "national policy".

(e) Sustainability Appraisal

4.31. LPAs are also required by Section 19(5)(a) to undertake a sustainability appraisal ("SA"):

19(5) The local planning authority must also–

(a) carry out an appraisal of the sustainability of the proposals in each development plan document

(b) prepare a report of the findings of the appraisal.

4.32. This process incorporates the retained EU obligation to carry out Strategic Environmental Assessment, in accordance with the Environmental Plans and Programmes Regulations 2004 ("the SEA Regulations"), and the SA will therefore formally be an "environmental report" for the purposes of Regulations 2, 5 and 12. Schedule 1, paragraph 1 of the SEA Regulations requires an environmental report to record: "*An outline of the contents and main objectives of the plan or programme, and of its relationship with other relevant plans and programmes.*" Most SAs will therefore explore current and prospective Green Belt status as part of the wider environmental assessment process. The SA is not a free-standing Green Belt Assessment. The analysis of existing settlement sustainability (or different "reasonable alternatives" e.g. sustainable urban extensions) may however be of greater significance to the assessment of Criterion C (NPPF 155(c)) when assessing locational sustainability.

(f) The Duty to Cooperate

4.33. The Duty to Cooperate under Section 33A(1) PCPA 2024 requires authorities to cooperate in "*maximising the effectiveness with which [plan preparation] is undertaken*" further defined as "*(2)(a) to engage constructively, actively and on an ongoing basis*". The duty was to be repealed under the LURA 2023 provisions, but remains in force for all current DPDs. It is unlikely to be of direct impact for most Grey Belt applications save that in certain cases, applicants may wish to argue that the Criterion B test of "demonstrable unmet need" includes cross-boundary under-provision, stemming from failures to meet the duty. Allegations that the Duty to Cooperate is not being met in current plan-making exercises may also feature in arguments about likely delay to that process.

(g) Statutory Consultation

4.34. The development plan document must be subject to statutory consultation both prior to the submission of the Development Plan Document (Regulation 18 of the Town and Country Planning (Local Planning) (England) Regulations 2012) and post-submission (Regulations 19 and 20). Crucially, in the latter phases, the LPA should have published the bulk of its evidence base, including the Green Belt Assessment, identifying Grey Belt land. This sets a clear time marker for when this information should be in the public domain and thus a material consideration for all Grey Belt applications and appeals.

(h) Plan Submission

4.35. A development plan document will then be submitted to the Secretary of State for examination under Section 20 PCPA.

4.36. From this point, it may be argued that the weight to be accorded the emerging plan will increase, but much will depend on the steady progress of the examination, in accordance with NPPF 49:

49. Local planning authorities may give weight to relevant policies in emerging plans according to:

(a) the stage of preparation of the emerging plan (the more advanced its preparation, the greater the weight that may be given);

(b) the extent to which there are unresolved objections to relevant policies (the less significant the unresolved objections, the greater the weight that may be given); and

(c) the degree of consistency of the relevant policies in the emerging plan to this Framework (the closer the policies in the emerging plan to the policies in the Framework, the greater the weight that may be given).

<u>(i) Plan Examination</u>

4.37. Under Section 20 PCPA, the development plan document is then subject to independent examination by an Inspector (or Panel of Inspectors), who will conduct a part-written and part-hearing process to consider submissions on the content of the submitted development plan.

4.38. The purpose of the examination is to determine whether the Development Plan Document has complied with various substantive / procedural requirements, notably the following:

20(5) The purpose of an independent examination is to determine in respect of the development plan document–

(a) whether it satisfies the requirements of sections 19 and 24(1), regulations under section 17(7) and any regulations under section 36 relating to the preparation of development plan documents;

(b) whether it is <u>sound</u>

(c) whether the local planning authority complied with any duty imposed on the authority by section 33A in relation to its preparation.

4.39. The soundness test is defined within national planning policy, not within legislation. An LPA must therefore have regard to the Secretary of State's national policy (presently within NPPF Chapter 13 for the Green Belt) for the purposes of preparing the plan. In certain transitional cases (set out in NPPF Annex 1), the Secretary of State may direct the authority to have regard to an earlier version of the NPPF.

(j) Modification and Reporting

4.40. Under Section 20 PCPA, once they have completed the examination hearings, the LPA will consult upon modifications to the plan to make the plan sound. The Inspector(s) will then issue a Final Report.

4.41. The publication of the Final Report will be a critical phase for Grey Belt application cases, in addressing the question of "demonstrable unmet need". LPAs may seek to argue that there is no longer such a "need" once the Report has been published, as this will be met by the emerging allocations and policies. The countervailing argument will be that the need has not been fully addressed or met until the date of publication itself, or indeed until the relevant permissions have been granted.

(k) Plan Adoption

4.42. Under Section 23 PCPA, the local planning authority must make all the modifications recommended. They can then formally adopt the plan, by resolution. It is only at this point that the new Development Plan Document is fully in force.

(l) Plan Review

4.43. Under Regulation 10A of the 2012 Regulations, there is a general requirement to complete a plan review every five years:

(1) A local planning authority must review a local development document within the following time periods—

(a) in respect of a local plan, the review must be completed every five years, starting from the date of adoption of the local plan, in accordance with section 23 of the Act (adoption of local development documents);...

4.44. This is not accompanied by any specific statutory provisions, and is not explained further in national planning policy guidance, thereby creating a significant and problematic lacuna in the system.

(3) New Local Plans under Schedule 7 of the Levelling-up and Regeneration Act 2023

4.45. Sections 93 and 94 and Schedule 7 of the Levelling-up and Regeneration Act 2023 introduce a new Local Plans structure/framework which represents the direction of travel for all plans submitted in 2027 and beyond. At the time of writing, Schedule 7 is not yet in force.

4.46. The objective is for Local Plans to be:

(i) singular;

(ii) mandatory; and

(iii) with specific content specified in statute.

4.47. The core provisions of Schedule 7 relevant to Green Belt can be summarised as follows:

Mandatory Adoption

4.48. Every local planning authority must prepare a Local Plan (Sections 15C(1) and (2) PCPA 2004).

4.49. The Local Plan is to be distinguished from Spatial Development Strategies ("SDSs") (at the strategic tier) that are non-mandatory, and from supplementary plans ("SPs") which provide for more localised policy on specific sites.

Local Plan Timetable

4.50. The Local Plan must be prepared in accordance with the published Local Plan Timetable (Section 15CA(1) PCPA). Once adopted, an LPA must comply with the Local Plan Timetable.

Policy Content

4.51. The Local Plan must set out policies in relation to amount, type and location of, and timetable for development in the LPA's area (Section 15C(3) PCPA).

4.52. The local plan may include *"(a) other policies (however expressed) in relation to the use or development of land in the local planning authority's area which are designed to achieve objectives that relate to the particular characteristics or circumstances of their area, any part of their area or one or more specific sites in their area*" (Section 15C(4) PCPA).

Assessment

4.53. The Local Plan "*must take account of an assessment of the amount, and type, of housing that is needed in the local planning authority's area*": (Section 15C(8) PCPA).

Non-Duplication of National Development Management Policies

4.54. The Local Plan cannot "*be inconsistent with or (in substance) repeat any national development management policy*" (Section 15C(9)(b) PCPA 2004).

Timescale and Transition

4.55. The exact timetable for the transition to the new Local Plans system has not been specified at the time of writing, although various deadlines have been suggested in the consultation documents. At present LPAs are expected to follow the current Part 2 PCPA system for an extended period up to the December 2026 deadline, save where they are subject to the transitional provisions in Annex 1 of the NPPF. All plans submitted after December 2026 will need to follow the new Local Plans system.

Summary

4.56. The new-style Local Plans are likely to be different to those prepared under the existing PCPA 2004 regime.

4.57. The Local Plans will be increasingly spatial in their focus, with a primary concentration on (a) housing and commercial allocations (including on Grey Belt land) and (b) protective designations, including the remaining Green Belt boundaries. The bulk of decision-taking policy will be covered by the NDMPs, including the Very Special Circumstances test and also Grey Belt policy itself.

(4) The Plan-Led Approach to Green Belt Release

4.58. The NPPF encourages a plan-led approach to Green Belt release. However, this is now strictly conditional upon rapid/timely plan preparation.

4.59. The Government's vision is that all LPAs should achieve universal plan adoption within 5 years (i.e. before the end of the current Parliament in mid-2029), on the basis of plans that have met their identified needs in full, including under the exceptional circumstances approach detailed below.

4.60. The NPPF (2024) provisions apply to all DPD preparation, save for the limited category of plans seeking to apply transitional arrangements under Annex 1: Implementation. These permit certain LPAs to continue plan-making under the previous NPPF where (i) their plan-making is advanced but also (ii) where the housing requirement within the draft plan is sufficiently close to the new local housing need figures:

234. For the purpose of preparing local plans, the policies in this version of the Framework will apply from 12 March 2025 other than where one or more of the following apply:

a. the plan has reached Regulation 19 (pre-submission stage) on or before 12 March 2025, and its draft housing requirement meets at least 80% of local housing need;

b. the plan has been submitted for examination under Regulation 22 on or before 12 March 2025;…

235. Where paragraph 234 a, b, c, d or e apply, the plan will be examined under the relevant previous version of the Framework.

4.61. In the months between 12 December 2024 and 12 March 2025, only a relatively small number of authorities sought to take advantage of the transitional provisions in NPPF 234(b) by submitting their plans prior to the deadline.

4.62. Technically, the operation of Annex 1 would retain the older provisions of the NPPF (2023), which provided:

145. Once established, there is <u>no requirement</u> for Green Belt boundaries to be reviewed or changed when plans are being prepared or updated. Authorities may <u>choose</u> to review and alter Green Belt boundaries where exceptional circumstances are fully evidenced and justified, in which case proposals for changes should be made only through the plan-making process.

4.63. However, throughout the latter half of 2024 and early 2025, Inspectors appointed to examine a number of plans rejected the proposition that Green Belt release was "optional", in the face of significant shortfalls against even the older Local Housing Need figures. The precise nature of the former NPPF policy is therefore still being worked out in practice, and Inspectors will scrutinise when and how Green Belt should be released through draft plans at examination and/or future plans.

4.64. Moreover, NPPF 78(c) creates an uplift in housing requirements in just 18 months by 1 July 2026, for any plan adopted in the past, applying a 20% increase to the housing requirement of any authority reliant on a plan figure adopted in the past 5 years (i.e. on the basis of the pre-NPPF 2024 local housing need figures):

c) From 1 July 2026, for the purposes of decision-making only, [the buffer is]

- 20% where a local planning authority has a housing requirement adopted in the last five years examined against a previous version of this Framework [41], *and whose annual average housing requirement is 80% or less of the most up to date local housing need figure calculated using the standard method set out in national planning practice guidance.*

[Footnote 15] Or the housing requirement is more than five years old and the relevant strategic policies have been reviewed and found not to require updating.

4.65. There is therefore a major incentive for all local planning authorities not only to prepare development plan documents which make provision for Green Belt release but also to use their general development management powers to grant applications on Grey Belt land under NPPF 155.

4.66. It is also necessary to recognise the significant prominence given to housing delivery and economic growth by Government.

4.67. The NPPF Consultation emphasised the importance of two twin objectives: (i) a boost in housing delivery up to 1.5 million homes over the Parliament and (ii) economic growth, and these are best understood as intertwined aims:

1. The Government has made clear that sustained economic growth is the only route to improving the prosperity of our country and the living standards of working people. Our approach to delivering this growth will focus on three pillars: stability, investment and reform.

...

3. Today, we set out specific changes we propose to make immediately to the NPPF following this consultation. These changes – amending the planning framework, and universal, ambitious local plan coverage – are vital to deliver the Government's commitments to achieve economic growth and build 1.5 million new homes.

4.68. These twin "growth" imperatives sit at the heart of current Green Belt policy, in a manner unprecedented within previous versions of the NPPF. They are writ large through NPPF Chapters 5 and 6, the various Written Ministerial Statements, HM Treasury announcements, and a whole range of other publications. These set the crucial context to the reforms to the exceptional circumstances test, especially the emphasis on the release of Grey Belt land under NPPF 146, which requires needs to be met "in full".

(5) The Exceptional Circumstances Test and the New Sequential Approach

4.69. The NPPF continues to retain the "exceptional circumstances" approach as a single test, but accompanied by an extensive set of procedural/substantive requirements. NPPF Chapter 13's plan-making components are broken down and analysed in outline below. The precise manner in which these will be fully evidenced, presented by LPAs and subject to testing at Local Plan examination falls outside the scope of this book. This book is instead focussed on the opportunities that may be created from the evidence base, once published, for Grey Belt applications / appeals.

4.70. The evidence base for the exceptional circumstances test will provide substantial guidance on the preparation of the evidence base on almost all four Criteria, including (a) Grey Belt eligibility (through LPA-wide Green Belt Assessments); (b) the extent of unmet need (through Strategic Housing Market Assessments; locational sustainability (e.g. through Local Plan Transport Assessments and Sustainability Appraisal); (d) questions of affordable housing viability (albeit without reducing the percentage requirement) and green space availability (e.g. through Open Space Assessments).

4.71. For ease of reference, the sentences are sub-divided by square brackets to assist in description of the component sentences:

<u>NPPF 144: New Green Belts</u>

4.72. NPPF 144 allows for the creation of new green belts. However, it emphasises that "*The general extent of Green Belts across the country is already established.*" Given the emphasis on meeting housing and employment needs, it is highly debatable whether new Green Belts will be created or indeed existing Green Belts expanded.

<u>NPPF 145: Exceptional Circumstances</u>

4.73. NPPF 145 then sets out the introductory or core principles which are to govern the exceptional circumstances exercise:

145. [1] *Once established, Green Belt boundaries should only be altered where exceptional circumstances are fully evidenced and justified through the preparation or updating of plans.* [2] *Strategic policies should establish the need for any changes to Green Belt boundaries, having regard to their intended permanence in the long term, so they can endure beyond the plan period.* [3] *Where a need for changes to Green Belt boundaries has been established through strategic policies, detailed amendments to those boundaries may be made through non-strategic policies, including neighbourhood plans.*

4.74. The width of the exceptional circumstances test is now also placed effectively beyond doubt by the provisions, notably NPPF 146 on the importance of meeting housing needs in full. There had previously been a considerable amount of litigation in respect of the term "exceptional circumstances". The High Court notably held in *Compton Parish Council v Guildford Borough Council* [2019] EWHC 3242 (Admin), [70]-[72] that the exceptional circumstances test is a <u>lower</u> threshold than very special circumstances:

70. <u>"Exceptional circumstances" is a less demanding test than the development control test for permitting inappropriate development in the Green Belt, which requires "very special circumstances." That difference is clear enough from the language itself and the different contexts in which they appear</u>, but if authority were necessary, it can be found in R(Luton BC) v Central Bedfordshire Council [2015] EWCA Civ 537 at [56], Sales LJ. As Patterson J pointed out in IM Properties Development Ltd v Lichfield DC [2014] EWHC 2240 at [90-91 and 95-96], there is no requirement that Green Belt land be released as a last resort, nor was it necessary to show that assumptions upon which the Green Belt boundary had been drawn, had been falsified by subsequent events.

4.75. The Court continued by emphasising the width of the planning judgement to be applied in the application of the test, disagreeing with submissions made on the basis of earlier case law that there was any particular framework to be applied, beyond the text itself:

> *71. There is however a danger of the simple question of whether there are "exceptional circumstances" being judicially over-analysed. This phrase does not require at least more than one individual "exceptional circumstance". The "exceptional circumstances" can be found in the accumulation or combination of circumstances, of varying natures, which entitle the decision-maker, in the rational exercise of a planning judgment, to say that the circumstances are sufficiently exceptional to warrant altering the Green Belt boundary.*
>
> *72. General planning needs, such as ordinary housing, are not precluded from its scope; indeed, meeting such needs is often part of the judgment that "exceptional circumstances" exist; the phrase is not limited to some unusual form of housing, nor to a particular intensity of need. I accept that it is clearly implicit in the stage 2 process that restraint may mean that the OAN is not met. But that is not the same as saying that the unmet need is irrelevant to the existence of "exceptional circumstances", or that it cannot weigh heavily or decisively; it is simply not necessarily sufficient of itself. These factors do not exist in a vacuum or by themselves: there will almost inevitably be an analysis of the nature and degree of the need, allied to consideration of why the need cannot be met in locations which are sequentially preferable for such developments, an analysis of the impact on the functioning of the Green Belt and its purpose, and what other advantages the proposed locations, released from the Green Belt, might bring, for example, in terms of a sound spatial distribution strategy. The analysis in Calverton PC of how the issue should be approached was described by Jay J as perhaps a counsel of perfection; but it is not exhaustive or a checklist. The points may not all matter in any particular case, and others may be important especially the overall distribution of development, and the scope for other uses to be provided for along with sustainable infrastructure.*

4.76. The *Compton* judgment is one of many in recent years to confirm that decisions on Green Belt release through the development plan are to be approached rigorously. Fundamentally it entails a series of planning judgements by the promoting local planning authority and ultimately the Inspector examining the plan, and the court cannot intervene in such judgements absent clear legal error.

4.77. Litigation is inevitable in the plan-making process, especially given the scale of the controversy that attaches to all Green Belt release. However, the collected provisions under NPPF 145-149 now present an even more formidable challenge than before, given that Green Belt release is now expressly required by NPPF 146.

NPPF 146: Meeting Needs in Full

4.78. NPPF 146 requires Green Belt to be released to meet development needs "in full". This represents perhaps the single most important change in Green Belt plan-making policy in several decades:

> *146.* [1] *Exceptional circumstances in this context include, but are not limited to, instances where an authority cannot meet its identified need for homes, commercial or other development through other means.* [2] *If that is the case, authorities should review Green Belt boundaries in accordance with the policies in this Framework and propose alterations to meet these needs in full, unless the review provides clear evidence that doing so would fundamentally undermine the purposes (taken together) of the remaining Green Belt, when considered across the area of the plan.*

4.79. NPPF 146[2]'s reserve provision: "*unless such alterations would fundamentally undermine the function of the Green Belt across the area of the plan as a whole*" is a relatively high threshold, as confirmed by the PPG:

How can the impact of releasing or development on the remaining Green Belt in the plan area be assessed? [32]

A Green Belt assessment should also consider the extent to which release or development of Green Belt land (including but not limited to grey belt land) would fundamentally undermine the purposes (taken together) of the remaining Green Belt across the plan area as whole.

In reaching this judgement, authorities should consider whether, or the extent to which, the release or development of Green Belt Land would affect the ability of all the remaining Green Belt across the area of the plan from serving all five of the Green Belt purposes in a meaningful way.

4.80. This is self-evidently a high threshold and it is difficult to think of scenarios where it would readily arise. It is arguable that the total Green Belt release would need to be of an extremely large character. We shall return to this question in Part II, Chapter 14 below when considering Criterion A (NPPF 155(a)).

4.81. The primary significance of this stage to Grey Belt applications is that an LPA must establish early on what the targets will be for the purposes of NPPF 155(b), thereby demonstrating the extent of the current "demonstrable unmet need". This applies as much to commercial/employment development, as to housing.

NPPF 147: Assessment of All Reasonable Options

4.82. Under NPPF 147, it is necessary next to examine "all reasonable options for meeting [the LPA's] identified need for development":

"*147.* [1]*Before concluding that exceptional circumstances exist to justify changes to Green Belt boundaries, the strategic policy-making authority should be able to demonstrate that it has examined fully all*

32 Paragraph: 008 Reference ID: 64-008-20250225

other reasonable options for meeting its identified need for development. [2] *This will be assessed through the examination of its strategic policies, which will take into account the preceding paragraph, and whether the strategy:*

a) makes as much use as possible of suitable brownfield sites and underutilised land;

b) optimises the density of development in line with the policies in chapter 11 of this Framework, including whether policies promote a significant uplift in minimum density standards in town and city centres and other locations well served by public transport; and

c) has been informed by discussions with neighbouring authorities about whether they could accommodate some of the identified need for development, as demonstrated through the statement of common ground."

4.83. NPPF 147 carries forward the old NPPF (2023) 143, which was originally brought in by NPPF (2018). The "alternatives" exercise has however been considerably simplified/clarified by the confirmation under NPPF 146 that the needs are to be met "in full". An LPA therefore has a clear starting figure for housing need (subject only to arguments concerning other restrictive designations, such as National Park and National Landscape (AONB) protected landscape designations and others under NPPF 11d(i) and footnote 7).

4.84. NPPF 147(a), (b) and (c) each require a detailed assessment of existing land under the respective categories. Ordinarily, NPPF 147(a) would be met through a specific Brownfield Land Assessment document, although this may be incorporated in another document, identifying the particular status and deliverability of identified brownfield sites. NPPF 147(b) is a more complex requirement, requiring both an assessment of the impact of densification generally and also in relevant areas (towns, city centres and other locations well served by local transport). Finally, NPPF 147(c) relates closely to the wider soundness requirements under NPPF 36(a), (c) and NPPF 24-28 in respect of discussions with adjacent and proximate authorities.

4.85. All of these exercises are likely to feed into the assessment against Grey Belt Criterion B (NPPF 155(b)) in the same way as explored above – specifically the extent to which the LPA can realistically meet its needs through other routes.

NPPF 148: The Sequential Approach

4.86. NPPF 148 builds on NPPF 146 and 147. It requires a sequential search for sites progressing through three different geographical stages:

> *148.*[1] *Where it is necessary to release Green Belt Land for development, plans should give priority to previously developed land, then consider grey belt which is not previously developed, and then other Green Belt locations.* [2] *However, when drawing up or reviewing Green Belt boundaries, the need to promote sustainable patterns of development should determine whether a site's location is appropriate with particular reference to paragraphs 110 and 115 of this Framework.* [3] *Strategic policy-making authorities should consider the consequences for sustainable development of channelling development towards urban areas inside the Green Belt boundary, towards towns and villages inset within the Green Belt or towards locations beyond the outer Green Belt boundary.*

4.87. NPPF 148[1]'s emphasis on previously developed land (PDL) is a repeat of the earlier NPPF (2023) 143(a) and, save in certain authorities, likely to yield only relatively small amounts of Green Belt land for development. It is therefore likely that the bulk of release will therefore have to come through both Grey Belt release and "other Green Belt locations".

4.88. It is important to note that the NPPF does not distinguish or set apart the "site search" exercise in NPPF 148 and the specific provisions in NPPF 155-159. It is therefore perfectly open to a developer whose site is confirmed as Grey Belt eligible (i.e. meeting the Glossary definition) to promote their site at any stage, including ahead of Local Plan adoption.

The PPG and Green Belt Review

4.89. At this point it is necessary to break off from the NPPF text, to consider how the PPG informs the structure of the Green Belt review process.

4.90. The introductory section observes:

> ***Assessing Green Belt to identify grey belt land***
>
> *This guidance is relevant to those authorities performing a review of Green Belt boundaries to meet housing or other development needs (either prior to or as part of the plan making process), those authorities otherwise required to determine whether land constitutes grey belt in decision making, and others seeking to identify grey belt land.*
>
> *Where grey belt is identified, it does not automatically follow that it should be allocated for development, released from the Green Belt or for development proposals to be approved in all circumstances. The contribution Green Belt land makes to Green Belt purposes is one consideration in making decisions about Green Belt land. Such decisions should also be informed by an overall application of the relevant policies in the National Planning Policy Framework (NPPF).*

4.91. There is therefore a cautionary note that Grey Belt Assessments should not automatically lead to grants of permission. However, in practice, a positive finding that the Site is Grey Belt land will be highly influential for a prospective application on Criterion A (NPPF 155a) compliance.

4.92. The PPG continues:

Why should authorities assess their Green Belt to identify grey belt land?[33]

As set out in national policy, the review and alteration of Green Belt boundaries should take place, where necessary, as part of the plan making process. In doing so, we expect authorities to identify grey belt land to inform this review and the prioritisation detailed in paragraphs 147 and 148 of the NPPF.

National policy also requires authorities to identify, where necessary, whether land is grey belt for the purpose of considering applications on Green Belt land. Where land is identified as grey belt land, any proposed development of that land should be considered against paragraph 155 of the NPPF, which sets out the conditions in which development would not be inappropriate on grey belt land.

How should authorities assess their Green Belt to identify grey belt land?[34]

In order to identify grey belt land, authorities should produce a Green Belt assessment, either as part of the review of Green Belt boundaries during the preparation or updating of a local plan, or at another relevant point. This assessment should be informed by the guidance below.

We expect most Green Belt assessments to be undertaken by local authorities or appropriate groups of local authorities. Green Belt assessments should also inform the preparation of Spatial Development Strategies where these will be setting the strategic context for land release.

---

33 Paragraph: 001 Reference ID: 64-001-20250225

34 Paragraph: 002 Reference ID: 64-002-20250225

When updating or preparing plans, authorities will need to consider whether any existing Green Belt assessment remains up to date.

4.93. The message is clear that Green Belt Assessments will almost invariably need to be undertaken afresh, taking on board the new criteria and guidance within the PPG.[35]

4.94. The key steps are summarised as follows (with square brackets added):

<u>What are the key steps in a Green Belt assessment?</u>[36]

In order to assess the Green Belt in the relevant local or strategic development area effectively, authorities will need to:

[1] *identify the location and appropriate scale of area/s to be assessed*

[2] *evaluate the contribution each assessment area makes to Green Belt purposes (a), (b), and (d), using the criteria identified below*

[3] *Consider whether applying the policies relating to the areas or assets of particular importance in footnote 7 to the NPPF (other than Green Belt) would potentially provide a strong reason for refusing or restricting development of the assessment area*

[4] *identify grey belt land*

[5] *identify if the release or development of the assessment area/s would fundamentally undermine the five Green Belt purposes (taken together) of the remaining Green Belt when considered across the area of the plan*

---

35 Paragraph: 005 Reference ID: 64-005-20250225

36 Paragraph: 003 Reference ID: 64-003-20250225

4.95. The PPG continues (again with square brackets added):[37]

<u>How should authorities define the land to be assessed?</u>

In assessing their Green Belt, it will in most cases be necessary for authorities to divide their Green Belt into separate assessment areas for the purpose of identifying grey belt. <u>The number and size of assessment areas can be defined at a local level and respond to local circumstances</u>. However, the following principles will need to be considered:

[1] *when identifying assessment areas, authorities should consider all Green Belt within their Plan areas in the first instance*

[2] *to ensure any assessment of how land performs against the Green Belt purposes is robust, assessment areas should be sufficiently granular to enable the assessment of their variable contribution to Green Belt purposes*

[3] *a small number of large assessment areas will not be appropriate in most circumstances – authorities should consider whether there are opportunities to better identify areas of grey belt by subdividing areas into smaller assessment areas where this is necessary*

[4]*authorities should consider where it may be appropriate to vary the size of assessment areas based on local circumstances. For example, the assessment of smaller areas may be appropriate in certain places, such as around existing settlements or public transport hubs or corridors*

4.96. A number of important points therefore arise for applications and appeals.

4.97. First, the Green Belt Review should ordinarily be LPA-wide. All prospective development sites will be the subject of a review within the survey period, within a period of circa 12 to 24 months from

37 Paragraph: 004 Reference ID: 64-004-20250225

the PPG's publication on 27 February 2025. It will be important for those promoting the sites to know when the review will commence and when the document will be published.

4.98. Second, the Review must be sufficiently "granular", to identify smaller areas and not rest on more strategic-scale parcels. This may follow logical boundaries on the ground, but it could also potentially reflect individual ownerships, if there is a clear physical demarcation on the ground. Whilst there is no formal requirement to consult on the Green Belt Review exercises, it is likely that there will be some measure of information-gathering by the assessors, both on practical matters (e.g. site access) but potentially plot configuration. This may allow landowners and developers the opportunity indirectly to input into the assessment process, and to track likely publication dates.

4.99. Third, whilst there is no specification as to format, it would appear likely that a significant amount of the work will be carried out by larger consultancies, adopting a common methodological format. It will therefore become progressively easier to predict how these exercises will be carried out and accordingly how the individual criteria will be applied. In cases of disputes and challenges, it may be necessary to identify inconsistency in the application of the methodology between different parcels and in certain narrow cases, between different Reviews conducted in separate LPAs.

NPPF 148 (continued)

4.100. Returning to the NPPF text, NPPF 148[2] emphasises the importance of locational sustainability, by express reference to NPPF 110 and 115. We shall return to these themes in Chapter 16 when examining Criterion C: NPPF 155(c): "*The development would be in a sustainable location, with particular reference to paragraphs 110 and 115 of this Framework*". It is critical to note that NPPF 148 does not necessarily mandate development in locations that are *already* sustainable, but may encompass those that can be made so, with new transport infrastructure.

NPPF 149

4.101. NPPF 149 then continues the list of final requirements of a more general character, carrying forward the old NPPF (2023) 148:

149. When defining Green Belt boundaries, plans should:

(a) ensure consistency with the development plan's strategy for meeting identified requirements for sustainable development;

(b) not include land which it is unnecessary to keep permanently open;

(c) where necessary, identify areas of safeguarded land between the urban area and the Green Belt, in order to meet longer-term development needs stretching well beyond the plan period;

(d) make clear that the safeguarded land is not allocated for development at the present time. Planning permission for the permanent development of safeguarded land should only be granted following an update to a plan which proposes the development;

(e) be able to demonstrate that Green Belt boundaries will not need to be altered at the end of the plan period; and

(f) define boundaries clearly, using physical features that are readily recognisable and likely to be permanent.

4.102. NPPF 149(a) is a further instruction to consider the importance of "sustainable patterns of development", notably the benefit in locational terms of releasing Green Belt land which is already close to existing urban areas, including services and facilities. This paragraph is essentially an echo of NPPF 146[1]'s "identified needs" and 148[2]'s "sustainable patterns of development". Its addition is largely a legacy of earlier drafting and its retention might therefore be said to be vestigial.[38]

4.103. NPPF 149(b) is, in essence, a fine detail provision whose primary purpose is to address residual anomalies in a Green Belt boundary – especially those which follow grants of permission for small-scale development, or the extension of garden land as a material change of use.

4.104. NPPF 149(c) and (d) refer to safeguarded land: a much larger concept, originating in earlier national policy documents. Importantly, the designation can only cover land that will be needed to cover long-term development needs "well beyond" the plan period. Again, the utility of this provision may be questionable in a context of much greater focus upon Green Belt release to meet existing needs, i.e. where existing safeguarded land is released and where there is limited scope to identify additional land for those needs arising beyond the plan period.

4.105. NPPF 149(e) is essentially another echo of NPPF 145[2] as described above, emphasising the importance of permanence in boundaries.

4.106. Finally, NPPF 149(f) sits alongside NPPF 149(b) and (e) as a key guide to where a specific boundary should be placed, at a "readily recognisable" and "permanent" physical feature. This may include

---

[38] The provision also echoes s39 of the Planning and Compulsory Purchase Act 2004, which requires any person/body preparing a development plan document to "*exercise the function with the objective of contributing to the achievement of sustainable development.*" The High Court held in *IM Properties v Lichfield DC* [2014] EWHC 2440 (Admin), [98] that Section 39 and the predecessor provision (NPPF (2012) 84)) "*That is clear advice to decision makers to take into account the consequences for sustainable development of any review of green belt boundaries. As part of that patterns of development and additional travel are clearly relevant.*"

a building, a road, a river or a canal, and may extend even wider to topographical features.

NPPF 151: Additional/Compensatory Uses

4.107. NPPF 151 finally provides:

151. Once Green Belts have been defined, local planning authorities should plan positively to enhance their beneficial use, such as looking for opportunities to provide access; to provide opportunities for outdoor sport and recreation; to retain and enhance landscapes, visual amenity and biodiversity; or to improve damaged and derelict land. Where Green Belt land is released for development through plan preparation or review, the 'Golden Rules' in paragraph 156 below should apply.

4.108. We shall consider NPPF 156-157 and 159 in respect of infrastructure and the Golden Rules contributions in Part II, Chapters 17-19.

(6) Summary

4.109. In conclusion to this chapter, the various NPPF provisions will require a significant evidence base to be gathered, much of which will be of direct relevance to the various Grey Belt Criteria. It will therefore be of importance to understand how this evidence will be gathered and presented, when and with opportunity for consultation, challenge, discussion and amendment/revision:

(1) Green Belt Assessment (Criterion A (NPPF 155(a))

- NPPF 145[1]: "fully evidenced and justified"

- NPPF 146[2]: "purposes of the remaining Green Belt…across the area of a plan"

- NPPF 148[1]: "first consider [PDL]…then grey belt…then other sustainable Green Belt locations"

<u>(2) Housing and Commercial/Employment Needs Assessment (Criterion B (NPPF 155(b))</u>

- NPPF 146[1]: "identified need for homes, commercial and other development"

- NPPF 146[2]: "to meet these needs in full"

<u>(3) Brownfield Land Assessment and Housing Density Assessment (Criterion A (NPPF 155(a) and Criterion B (NPPF 155(b))</u>

- NPPF 147[1]: "all other reasonable options for meeting its identified need"

- NPPF 147[2] and (a)-(c): brownfield, density optimisation, cooperation

<u>(4) Transport Assessment / Sustainability Appraisal (Criterion C (NPPF 155(c))</u>

- NPPF 148[2]: "sustainable patterns of development"

- NPPF 148[3]: "channelling development towards urban areas"

<u>(5) Affordable Housing Assessment and Viability Assessment (Criterion D and Golden Rule(1) (NPPF 156(a))</u>

- NPPF 156(a): Affordable Housing

<u>(6) Infrastructure Assessment (Criterion D and Golden Rule(2) (NPPF 156(b))</u>

- NPPF 156(b): "necessary improvements to local or national infrastructure"

(7) Open Space Assessment (Criterion D and Golden Rule (3) (NPPF 156(c))

- NPPF 156(c): Accessible Green spaces

(8) Draft Policies Map (Boundary-Setting) (Criterion A (NPPF 155(a))

- NPPF 145[2]: "permanence in the long term"

- NPPF 149(b): "unnecessary to keep permanently open"

- NPPF 149(e): "not need to be altered at the end of the plan period"

- NPPF 149(f) "physical features that...are likely to be permanent"

(9) General Planning / Overview Statements (Criterion A (NPPF 155(a) and Criterion B (NPPF 155(b))

- NPPF 145[1] "Green Belt boundaries should only be altered where exceptional circumstances have been fully evidenced and justified"

CHAPTER FIVE

PLANNING APPLICATIONS

(1) Introduction

5.1. Grey Belt cases come in many different shapes and sizes, from a single structure to a major multi-hectare site. There is plainly no one size fits all approach. Nevertheless, the legislation and revised national policy now provide a framework which is intended to set common principles and consistent targets which every application must meet if it is to succeed.

5.2. This Chapter explores some overarching practical points, ahead of exploring the composition of Planning Statements and other supporting documentation in Chapter 6.

(2) A Decision-Taker-Centred Approach

5.3. Every Grey Belt case must be prepared, negotiated and presented with a consistent focus on the eventual decision-maker, and what *they* will regard as being the pivotal issues in the case.

5.4. There are four types of individuals who can determine whether permission should be granted for a Grey Belt development, with slightly different statutory roles and a different balance of professional and political influences:

(1) Local Planning Authority Officers (under delegated powers);

(2) Elected Councillors sitting on Planning Committees;

(3) Planning Inspectors (under delegated powers);

(4) The Secretary of State and Ministers of State within the Department (following recommendations from Planning Inspectors.)

5.5. The reforms in the Planning and Infrastructure Bill should increase the extent of delegation to Officers, and also alter the composition and expertise of Planning Committees over time. However, in very broad terms, the bigger the scheme, the more likely that the application or appeal will be elevated to the political level, to decision-takers that are politicians rather than officials.

5.6. National policy is not (purely) algorithmic and the decision-making process will always entail an element of planning judgement, subjectivity and/or discretion. This is of particular importance in Grey Belt cases, given the legacy of the strict VSC position under the current NPPF 153.

5.7. Grey Belt cases must therefore be prepared in a manner to persuade that "audience" : the final decision-maker. This places a very significant premium on clarity of messaging and tailoring the specific development, its benefits, adverse effects and mitigation measures. This requires early focus on the real points in issue.

5.8. This must be conveyed through the Planning Statement and any accompanying documentation (e.g. covering letters). However, it may also be reflected in design choices and other project decisions, for example the nature of the affordable housing offer, the provision of additional on-site benefits, the position as to certain types of s106 contribution and so on. Most successful cases will benefit from a positive approach, a determined effort to lead with the opportunity presented by the benefits of the scheme.

5.9. Grey Belt cases are already being granted planning permission on application at much higher rates than historic VSC cases prior to July 2024. There are at least three potential causes for this, and the application material should seek to understand these specific opportunities and "pressure points".

5.10. First, the national policy position is inherently much more supportive of a grant of permission, with the critical quality of being much easier to interpret and apply. The uncertainties of the Very Special Circumstances test (including the historic litigation over questions of openness and what might VSC comprise) have been replaced with a much more logical pathway, with much less room for debate.

5.11. Second, in the housing context, the changes to the standard method/Local Housing Need for the purposes of housing land supply have created far higher shortfalls. Critically, these are now made a mandatory material consideration by virtue of Criterion B (NPPF 155b), in extreme contrast to the uncertainty that existed before.

5.12. Third, it would appear that the Central Government message (a combination of the NPPF, the Written Ministerial Statements, letters to the Inspectorate and LPAs, Local Plan intervention and some limited call-in and recovery) has had a significant impact upon the broader consensus as to how applications should be approached. The picture will differ authority by authority, and develop with successive local elections. However, it is apparent that there is a considerably greater willingness to grant permission for schemes that would have faced significant opposition prior to the current national policy changes.

5.13. Where there are early signs that the application will not be supported locally, for whatever reason, it is vital that the application material is prepared and the negotiation undertaken in such a manner as to ensure that the appeal sets the narrowest possible target for the Inspector/Secretary of State.

(3) Scrutiny of the Current Development Plan

5.14. All Grey Belt applications should begin with a rigorous consideration of the current development plan position.

5.15. The development plan will remain a statutory starting point for the purposes of s38(6) PCPA, until the reforms under LURA ss93-94 come into force. The development plan and its policies must therefore be interpreted and applied correctly.

5.16. Moreover, for the purposes of Criterion B (NPPF 155b) and NPPF 11d in housing cases, it will often be necessary to show a shortfall in terms of housing land supply against the adopted housing requirement (or Local Housing Need if the plan has not been reviewed within the past 5 years). Criterion C (NPPF 155c) and all of the Golden Rules (NPPF 156a, b and c) also refer to important local standards that may be expressed in the development plan and must be either met or exceeded.

5.17. Even if the plan is out-of-date, it will likely contain important information in respect of its spatial strategy (e.g. the classification of large built-up areas, towns and villages for the purposes of Criterion A; the settlement hierarchy and distances for the purposes of locational sustainability). As part of the overall case for why the development plan should be accorded limited weight, it may also be necessary to highlight statements on the Green Belt which no longer sit well with the current national policy context.

(4) Tracking the Progress of the Emerging Local Plan

5.18. The progress of the emerging Local Plan will become of increasing importance over time in all Grey Belt cases. Indeed, what the emerging Local Plan's evidence says may become of greater significance than the existing development plan, with many applications looking to the Green Belt Assessment, Strategic Housing Market Assessment and other Local Plan evidence base documents and whether these support the case for early release ahead of plan adoption via NPPF 155.

5.19. All applicants will therefore need to have a very clear picture of where the emerging development plan has got to, and also what stage it will have reached at the point of determination, and in particular whether it can be convincingly demonstrated that there will be a demonstrable unmet need for the proposal at the point of decision under Criterion B. This may require targeted requests to the Local Planning Authority itself or a detailed monitoring strategy.

5.20. It is vital that the project timescale carefully takes on board when these documents will be published and how they can be factored into the determination phase. This will be of particular importance if there is any likelihood of a dispute with their findings, and a risk of refusal resulting in an appeal.

(5) Locational Sustainability

5.21. Whatever the state of the development plan (adopted or emerging), locational sustainability is a mandatory requirement under Criterion C, and may become a critical consideration in certain kinds of cases.

5.22. For those Grey Belt sites which are adjacent to existing larger settlements, the question of locational sustainability may be agreed with the LPA. However, in villages (which are excluded from consideration under the NPPF 143 purposes), LPAs may raise objections on the grounds of a lack of sustainability (Criterion C).

5.23. It is therefore important to look wider than the existing settlement hierarchy. Sustainability is a far broader concept than mere proximity to existing settlements, notably NPPF 110's recognition that the decision-maker must look to how the site can be made sustainable. As part of the boundary-setting and initial site survey work, it will be important to consider identifying arguments for how the site can be said to be not merely well-related to any existing development, but also well-connected.

5.24. The specific policy provisions in NPPF 110 and 115 shall be explored in Part II, Chapter 16.

(6) Site Boundaries and the Quantum/Footprint of Development

5.25. Key project decisions will involve (a) where to draw the application red line and (b) how much development to place within that area. A range of considerations will govern this: land ownership, development purpose, viability, and constraints (physical, environmental and technical) will all feed into that decision.

5.26. Careful thought must be applied to the site's overall size and the footprint of development within the site (Criterion A, Green Belt Purpose C). Care may need to be taken over the development's height and bulk (particularly if there is any intention to run a reserve Very Special Circumstances case, if the Grey Belt tests are not found to be met).

5.27. Another key consideration is the extent of existing enclosure, whether by natural forms (tree belts, hedgerows, topography and rivers) or man-made structures (other buildings, roads, railways, canals and other infrastructure), as well as how enclosure can be promoted on site through new planting (Criterion A and the Glossary Definition for Purposes A, B and D).

5.28. Given Golden Rule (3) (NPPF 156(c)), there will often be a need to retain at least a portion of the land free from development, ideally converted into public access use. Clear thinking on the appropriate red line boundary, and the extent of development within the site at the very outset will manifest itself in a clear narrative capable of presentation before all decision-takers.

5.29. The process of boundary-setting will ultimately need to be clearly articulated in the Planning Statement, supported as necessary by the Design and Access Statement.

5.30. As part of this overall exercise, a decision will also need to be made as to whether the application should seek outline or detailed planning permission. Both have their own respective practical and commercial advantages and drawbacks. For present purposes, there is nothing within either national policy, guidance or indeed any appeal decision to suggest that a Grey Belt application should be detailed, and not outline. It is critical, however, to ensure that if the application is in outline, then the combined conditions and S106 agreement make provision for the requisite benefits, for example, the accessible green space.

(7) Instruction of the Multi-Disciplinary Professional Team

5.31. Grey Belt cases will require the instruction of multiple experts across various disciplines, notably qualified landscape architects (alongside planners) to undertake Green Belt Assessment against the purposes, and transport/highways professionals to address locational sustainability. For smaller schemes, it may be possible to rely simply on planning evidence, but any greater number or scale would generally require separate qualified advice.

5.32. The integrated nature of the Golden Rules, in particular, will increase the need for joined-up working. It is therefore even more important to translate to all team members the particular rigour required in the Grey Belt tests (and any VSC reserve position), and the part played by each team member in tackling those.

(8) Use of Appeal Decisions

5.33. Appeal Decisions are an invaluable resource for understanding how the Grey Belt tests are being applied nationally at a given point in time. In Part II, we shall cover some of the early appeal decisions interpreting the Grey Belt tests.

5.34. However each case will turn very much on its own facts, and appeal decisions should always be used in a targeted, ancillary way, making sure that the application stands out in its own right.

5.35. Caution should be applied to decisions that pre-date the publication of the PPG on 27 February 2025, especially on the Glossary definition. As we shall explore in Chapter 9 onwards, the PPG provided new tests and a clearer structure.

5.36. The relevance of an appeal decision to a given case will also depend upon a number of factors, including (a) location: e.g. within the same LPA or within the same Green Belt? (b) the type of development; (c) the extent of need at that point; and (d) the extent to which the issue was contested and thus the fullness of the decision.

(9) Pre-Application Contact with Council

5.37. A decision will need to be made early as to whether to seek pre-application advice on a project. National policy supports pre-application, especially for larger schemes. Pre-application advice can be particularly useful in requiring the authority to define the boundaries of what may be acceptable, securing a steer on the likely progress of the application and confirmation matters that are not likely to be contested. It may also be used to good effect at appeal, in demonstrating a careful long-term approach by the applicant/appellant and demonstrating inconsistency within the LPA's position (where applicable).

(10) Officers' Reports

5.38. Following completion of all statutory consultation stages, either within the statutory window or after any agreed extensions of time,

Officers will either produce a Report to Committee or indicate that the decision will be made under delegated powers.

5.39. The structure of the Officer's Report will be governed by the LPA's own templates, the specific principal issues engaged by the application and any third party concerns. The Planning Statement will play a key role in structuring the Officer's consideration of the issues.

5.40. There is a considerable body of law on the content and detail of Officer's Reports, and the critical legal question as to whether the Report has covered key issues, or in the case of error/omission misled the Committee. In the early phases of Grey Belt policy, it is possible that situations will arise where it is alleged that the Officer's Report has failed to interpret the relevant national policy correctly. This shall be explored below in Chapter 8.

(11) The Committee Stage

5.41. If the application is due to be determined by a Planning Committee, it is advisable to secure the Report as early as possible, at least 7 days prior (a common LPA constitutional requirement) and (where applicable) issue a follow-up note to members. In a case of a recommendation to grant this can also assist with addressing or correcting any potential errors or further information to assist Councillors in determining the application.

5.42. Green Belt applications have always been politically controversial and with the long history of refusals historically prior to 2024, will require careful presentation and navigation before local politicians.

5.43. The majority of Planning Committees will allow a short period for public speaking, but often no longer than a few minutes. A presentation to Committee is likely to be very time limited. It is likely to be best focussed on the benefits that a scheme may bring, rather than other aspects of the case.

5.44. A careful note should be made of the Committee discussions to identify core themes and the precise basis for any grant or refusal, as this may be used in either (a) the defence of a grant of permission in a challenge by way of judicial review or (b) the preparation of an appeal against refusal of permission (e.g. identifying an error or misunderstanding on the part of the members).

(12) Decision Notices

5.45. Article 35(1)(c) of the DMPO sets out the main requirements for decision notices, notably in respect of refusal of permission:

(1)(a) where planning permission is granted subject to conditions, the notice must state clearly and precisely their full reasons—

(i) for each condition imposed; and

(ii) in the case of each pre-commencement condition, for the condition being a pre-commencement condition;

(b) where planning permission is refused, the notice must state clearly and precisely their full reasons for the refusal, specifying all policies and proposals in the development plan which are relevant to the decision;

5.46. Under Article 35(1)(b) any reasons for refusal must therefore be clearly specified. This is a crucial provision in terms of identifying the structure and focus of any appeal under section 78 TCPA.

(13) Summary

5.47. In the next Chapter, we shall examine the structure of effective Planning Statements and supporting documents, looking both to the grant of permission at first instance, and the later appeal process and the High Court challenge process (noting that the Grey Belt policy is drafted in a way that could reduce the incidence of both appeals and legal challenges).

CHAPTER SIX

PLANNING STATEMENTS AND OTHER DOCUMENTS

(1) The Development Management Procedure Order and Appeal Documents

6.1. The content and procedure for Grey Belt planning applications is governed chiefly by the Town and Country Planning (Development Management Procedure) (England) Order 2015 ("DMPO") and the Local Planning Authority's own arrangements for decision-making – whether under delegated powers by Planning Officers, or by Planning Committees.

6.2. Applications must be submitted in writing on the form published by the Secretary of State (Article 7(1) of the DMPO) and accompanied by "*(c)(i) a plan which identifies the land to which the application relates*" and *"(ii) any other plans, drawings and information necessary to describe the development which is the subject of the application*".

6.3. Article 9 DMPO specifies that all applications for major development must be accompanied by a Design and Access Statement explaining a number of design and access aspects of the development (see further below).

6.4. Under Articles 11 and 12 DMPO a local planning authority may specify that an applicant should provide certain particulars or evidence to be included with each application, divided into national and local requirements. There are currently no national requirements specific to Green Belt/Grey Belt, for example any requirement to include any specific document. Local requirements must be specified on an adopted "local list" published on the LPA's website less than 2 years prior to submission.

6.5. Under section 62(4A) TCPA and Article 11(3)(c) DMPO, any information must be "*(i) reasonable having regard, in particular, to the nature and scale of the proposed development; and (ii) about a matter which it is reasonable to think will be a material consideration in the determination of the application*".

6.6. In this Chapter, we shall consider the Planning Statement, Design and Access Statement, Landscape Visual Impact Assessment, and Green Belt Assessments.

(2) The Planning Statement

6.7. The Planning Statement is the most important document in any Grey Belt case, bringing together all of the analysis of the tests under NPPF 155-159, and related NPPF provisions. An effective Planning Statement will collect, in one single place, the conclusions of the many evidence base documents, accompanying reports, and any pre-application correspondence with the local authority. As observed in the previous Chapter, there is plainly no one size fits all approach, however every case will benefit from both a clear focus on the key tests, and an ability to marshal the many diverse sources of information that comprise a Grey Belt case.

6.8. The Planning Statement should be drafted from the applicant's perspective, but must be structured in a fashion that most assists the planning officer who will write the Report supporting the recommendation whether for the Committee or the delegated decision. If permission is refused, the Planning Statement will shape the Appeal Statement of Case, the Proof of Evidence and could form a focus of cross-examination at inquiry (e.g. in case of inconsistency). Equally, if there is a challenge to a grant by way of judicial review, it may also form part of the evidence before the court.

6.9. It is therefore essential that the Planning Statement is drafted carefully, with numbered paragraphs and headings, with clear cross-referencing to the separate parts of the supporting evidence. Above all, it should follow the NPPF policy pathway in the clearest possible order, addressing Grey Belt in its own right, and the other material considerations separately.

(3) Suggested Structure for a Planning Statement

6.10. The description below is simply an illustration, structured around a series of potential "Sections". These may be longer "Chapters" or shorter sections, but there must be clear sub-division and a clear structuring of the components so that an Officer's Report is guided to the key elements in the right order.

6.11. Each of the specific tests and applicable guidance will be examined in Part II, Chapters 9 to 21.

Section 1: Introduction

6.12. Grey Belt cases will likely benefit from a short overview statement of a couple of paragraphs' length, setting out the development description, but also providing a strong statement of the positive vision for the scheme and the site.

6.13. It is important to present the application as an opportunity and not merely as a question of box-ticking or entitlement (reflecting Grey Belt policy's continuing role as an exception to the VSC test and the relative novelty of the reforms).

6.14. For housing schemes, it will be advisable to set out early on that the scheme seeks to address the demonstrable unmet need established by a 5YHLS shortfall (Criterion B (NPPF 155(b)). For other types of development, the economic and social benefits may also be emphasised, with express references to the Government's wider statements, e.g. the 2024 Milestones for Mission-Led Government.

Section 2: Site and Context

6.15. Having set out the development description and introduction, it is then advisable to provide a separate section setting out the site's key features and immediate context, cross-referencing as necessary to the Design and Access Statement, the Landscape and Visual Assessment and any plans.

6.16. It is important to take time over setting out this immediate context, and the site's boundaries en route to assessment against Criterion A (155a and Glossary Definition) and description of locational sustainability for the purposes of Criterion C (NPPF 156(c)). A careful, detailed description will assist the Officer's Report and indeed any future Statement of Common Ground and Inspector's Decision Letter, if the case proceeds to appeal.

Section 3: The Development

6.17. Having situated the site/context, the development should be described in full within its own chapter, including all built form and any phasing.

6.18. At this stage, it is not necessary to cross-refer to the respective NPPF, PPG and development plan policy requirements, and how the development meets them. Those can be set out more effectively in later, individual sections. The objective is simply to list the key components of what will be built, ahead of that later policy analysis.

Section 4: Planning History

6.19. The planning history of the site is often best set out immediately after the development section, unless the application is directly connected to a previous permission. This ensures that the focus is upon the present application and not the history.

6.20. It will be necessary to differentiate the application from any previous refusals. However the relevance of such decisions will depend upon their age and the type of development applied for (e.g. if they pre-date 12 December 2024 and thus Grey Belt policy altogether).

Section 5: Development Plan

6.21. The development plan remains a mandatory statutory consideration under both s38(6) PCPA 2004 and the successor provisions under s38(5A-C) PCPA. It is therefore important to list all relevant development plan policies first, before addressing the national policy tests. There is no need to cite the full text of the relevant policies, merely the key components that are of particular relevance to the scheme.

6.22. At this point, it is generally advisable to itemise any policies that are considered to be out-of-date, either because of overall age or conflict with the terms of the current NPPF. A clear list of such policies is vital for the purposes of NPPF 11d(ii), as explained in Part II, Chapter 21.

6.23. This is often the most suitable section in which to present a brief history of the designation of the site as Green Belt, i.e. to demonstrate the age of the designation and any submissions to the effect that it has acted as an excessive constraint on growth over time, contributing to current shortfalls. Care should be taken to keep this strictly separate from the Glossary Definition analysis for the purposes of Criterion A (NPPF 155(a)).

Section 6: National Policy (General)

6.24. A separate chapter should then be provided on national policy in all its key forms, i.e. both the NPPF and any relevant PPG and Written Ministerial Statements.

6.25. At this point, it may be necessary to cross-refer to some of the recent history explored in Chapter 2 of this book, at least from the Second Written Ministerial Statement (12 December 2024) onwards.

Section 7: Grey Belt Assessment

6.26. Green Belt/Grey Belt issues are often best addressed first before addressing other parts of the development plan compliance and other main issues. That is because they will ordinarily go to the principle of development and therefore situate many of the other considerations.

6.27. Given the compartmentalised and somewhat intricate nature of the NPPF 155 and 156 tests, it is advisable to split up each section carefully, sub-dividing them into sections (or even whole chapters) which match the four-part structure of the Criteria. A constant focus should be the structure and clarity of the Officer's Report and any subsequent determination, to assist the decision-maker in following each step.

Criterion A: Previously Developed Land

6.28. Where a site is presented as PDL, a detailed survey should be presented of the layout and footprint of the site, especially the structures or surfaces relied on and any argument as to curtilage. Reference may also be necessary to the detailed planning history to confirm lawfulness.

Criterion A: Contribution to Green Belt Purposes

6.29. This is likely to be one of the most extensive sections of the Statement, requiring coordination of both the Application evidence and the PPG tests, and also analysis of both historical and emerging Green Belt Assessment work.

6.30. For most sites, a free-standing Green Belt Assessment should be drawn up by a qualified landscape architect (with careful discussion with the planning team), providing a systematic analysis against each of Purposes (a), (b) and (d), ahead of the wider NPPF 155(a) exercise, including any illustrative material (e.g. maps and photographs).

6.31. Historical Green Belt Assessment work for previous Local Plans may be both helpful and unhelpful for a contemporary case. The general position is likely to be that the assessment work is simply not up-to-date as it precedes the modern PPG approach. Therefore both the Planning Statement and the Green Belt Assessment should highlight and/or distinguish any relevant findings, and explain the weight to be accorded that exercise.

6.32. If a contemporary-era (2025 onwards) Green Belt Assessment has been completed then this can be cross-referenced. If there is any dispute with its findings, then this can be set out in full here.

Criterion A: "Strong Reason"/ Footnote 7 Policies

6.33. It should be confirmed early that no Footnote 7 policies form a basis for refusal. However it may be best to defer detailed analysis of the specific footnote 7 policies that are potentially engaged, for example in respect of heritage or flood risk matters, to later sections of the Statement. It is important not to break the flow of the Grey Belt analysis through all three stages to answer the overall NPPF 155(a) question.

Criterion A: Wider Green Belt

6.34. Addressing the final provision of NPPF 155(a) (that the development will not undermine the Green Belt purposes across the whole plan area) will necessarily incorporate parts of the analysis against Purposes (a), (b) and (d) above, but supplemented by the wider Green Belt analysis. This test is unlikely to be breached in the vast majority of cases.

Criterion B: Demonstrable Unmet Need

6.35. The Planning Statement will need to confirm demonstrable unmet need. In the housing context, this may be straightforward (e.g. where the authority has accepted that they are unable to demonstrate a 5YHLS) or much more complex and contested (e.g. where there is a dispute as to 5YHLS or there is an accepted 5YHLS but the development is of a particular type e.g. C2). If there is such a contest, then it may help to defer the specific numerical analysis to a later section of the Planning Statement or to a separate report (e.g. Older Persons Housing Needs Assessment). In other contexts, e.g. commercial / employment development or energy development, the same approach may be deployed, unless there is a clear-cut case on need demonstrated by national policy, the LPA's recent stance, or any appeal decisions.

Criterion C: Locational Sustainability

6.36. The Planning Statement will need to confirm that the Site is locationally sustainable, in direct accordance with NPPF 110 and 115, including by direct reference to any Transport Assessment / Statement submitted with the application. Just as for Criterion B, this may be relatively straightforward (in the case of sites that are adjacent to and/or close to services) or more complex (for sites which are further away). In any event, detailed reference will be necessary to the Transport Statement and any accompanying analysis, for example through walking cycling / public transport isochrones.

Criterion D: Golden Rules

6.37. Criterion D incorporates the Golden Rules, for major housing development only, defined as: "*development where 10 or more homes will be provided, or the site has an area of 0.5 hectares or more.*" Any site over 0.5ha will qualify as "major development."

Golden Rule (1): Affordable Housing

6.38. Given the specific nature of the tests and thresholds, the Statement may simply need to refer to the relevant affordable housing offer and the conclusion of a Section 106 Agreement – unless there is a significant dispute about the correct percentage to be applied. All references here to a Section 106 Agreement would apply to Unilateral Undertaking.

Golden Rule (2): Necessary Infrastructure

6.39. The Statement should list the contributions to be provided, cross-referenced to any Head of Terms or draft Section 106 Agreement.

Golden Rule (3): Accessible Green Space

6.40. Finally, the Statement should confirm the total accessible green space provided on site, or contributions to any off-site provision, again by reference to the Section 106 Agreement.

Very Special Circumstances as a Reserve Position

6.41. If a VSC case is to be run, then it is vital that the four stages are clearly demarcated (Green Belt harm, Non-Green Belt harm, Other Considerations, Overall Very Special Circumstances), with clear summary conclusions under each section. Key case law should be cited at the outset or in a specific separate section to draw the

Officer's attention to the key principles. All of these matters are addressed in further detail in Part II, Chapter 20.

VSC Stage 1: Green Belt Harms

6.42. The Planning Statement should refer to Definitional harm, and also quantify harm to openness: in both spatial and visual respects (ideally in separate sections) and then record harm to purposes, being clear as to which purposes and to what degree. This will need to be carefully compared to/considered in the light of the Grey Belt conclusions above, to avoid any contradiction or ambiguity.

6.43. Importantly, there should be no positive suggestion that the decision-taker might have reached the VSC analysis due to a finding of "strong contribution", unless there is a specific dispute with an LPA Green Belt Assessment that has been produced in accordance with the current PPG.

VSC Stage 2: Non-Green Belt Harms

6.44. The Planning Statement should then explain any non-Green Belt harm, but may simply list this and defer analysis to later specific sections.

VSC Stage 3: Other Considerations

6.45. The Planning Statement should list the Benefits (plus individual grading of the weight), and then address other Considerations: timing, alternatives, fallback (as applicable).

VSC Stage 4: Overall Very Special Circumstances

6.46. Finally, the Statement should summarise the Green Belt Harms (making clear that they have been accorded substantial weight in line with NPPF 153), add the non-Green Belt Harms, then list the other considerations with express reference to their individual weight and then explain why the Green Belt and other non-Green Belt harm is clearly outweighed.

Other Main Issues

6.47. The various other main issues, assessments of need, harm and other question of development plan compliance can follow, assuming that Grey Belt is considered to be the primary main issue, going to the principle of development.

The Presumption and the Planning Balance

6.48. All Grey Belt cases will finally need to explain the position on the presumption in favour of sustainable development, and how the tilted balance under NPPF 11d(ii) supports the grant of permission.

6.49. A clear conclusion should also be reached on Section 38(6) PCPA: whether the proposal is in accordance with the development plan considered as a whole, or if material considerations indicate that permission should be granted notwithstanding any conflict.

(4) Design and Access Statements

6.50. The Design and Access Statement is one of the few documents that is specifically mandated by the DMPO. Article 9 DMPO specifies the contents as follows:

(2) An application for planning permission to which this paragraph applies must, ... be accompanied by a statement ("a design and access statement") about—

(a) the design principles and concepts that have been applied to the development; and

(b) how issues relating to access to the development have been dealt with.

(3) A design and access statement must—

(a) explain the design principles and concepts that have been applied to the development;

(b) demonstrate the steps taken to appraise the context of the development and how the design of the development takes that context into account;

(c) explain the policy adopted as to access, and how policies relating to access in relevant local development documents have been taken into account;

state what, if any, consultation has been undertaken on issues relating to access to the (d) development and what account has been taken of the outcome of any such consultation; and

(e) explain how any specific issues which might affect access to the development have been addressed.

6.51. It is generally advisable to draw this up as a separate document from the Planning Statement in all but the very smallest Grey Belt developments (i.e. 1 or 2 units). A DAS should be proportionate, but applicants should take time over its composition and should not treat it as simply ancillary to the other evidence.

6.52. A DAS should be treated as a positive opportunity to provide a powerful visual illustration of the quality of the scheme and the depth and detail of the design process that has been followed. It should include illustrative sketches or photomontage work demonstrating how the development will appear in the landscape or relevant setting.

6.53. It can also show how the Green Belt issues have been considered (e.g. surrounding structures and vegetation). It may illustrate the different configurations of development that have been examined, en route to finalising the specific proposed site layout. It may also be used to demonstrate compliance with a number of the Grey Belt criteria, notably NPPF 156(c): publicly accessible green space.

(5) Landscape and Visual Impact Assessments

6.54. Many LPAs' local lists will require the submission of a Landscape and Visual Impact Assessment ("LVIA") (or equivalent Landscape Visual Appraisal (LVA)).

6.55. This should always be drawn up by a qualified landscape architect in accordance with the Guidelines on Landscape and Visual Impact Assessment ("GLVIA") specifically the current (3rd) edition.

6.56. The precise role of the LVIA needs to be carefully circumscribed, consistent with the core principles that (1) Green Belt is not a landscape designation, and merely a spatial designation and (2) Grey Belt cases do not involve assessments of openness, unless a VSC case is pursued as a reserve position.

6.57. However, it is advisable to seek common authorship of the LVIA and the Green Belt Assessment ("GBA") by the same individual landscape architect and/or their team. In practice, the LVIA and GBA site assessment and report-writing processes will inevitably inform each other.

6.58. In particular, the LVIA will be a key document for considering the footprint and physical extent of the development, including the extent of enclosure and interaction with existing built form, and potentially decisions made as to the extent of publicly accessible green space.

(6) Green Belt Assessments

6.59. The Green Belt Assessment can thus be understood as a document that sits alongside the Planning Statement, DAS and LVIA. It should contain a detailed assessment of the Green Belt harms, notably in respect of the development site's contribution to the purposes. As emphasised above, qualified landscape professionals are ordinarily the best-placed expert within the team to assess, map, illustrate and present on the Green Belt purposes, including in expert evidence at appeal.

6.60. A Green Belt Assessment should be firmly grounded in the text of the current PPG. It can explore historic assessments of the contribution made by the site to the Green Belt (in LPA Green Belt Assessments, earlier Officer's Reports and appeal decisions). It may seek to draw on or critique/distinguish earlier findings, for example, if it is to be argued that the parcels assessed on those occasions were too large and should have been sub-divided.

6.61. The document should contain a clear and systematic concluding section, potentially tabulated, providing a clear verdict of the contribution of the site against each of the Green Belt Purposes A, B and D, as well as the impact of the development on the Green Belt across the whole plan area for the purposes of Criterion A (NPPF 155(a)).

(7) Transport Assessment/Statement

6.62. A Transport Assessment/Statement should also be drawn up for any development generating "significant amounts of movement" (NPPF 118), and must be drawn up by a qualified highways/transport professional.

6.63. The transport statement should engage squarely with NPPF 110 and 115, defining the extent to which the Site is locationally sustainable. Express references will be necessary to all forms of sustainable transport that are available, especially if there is some contest in respect of overall locational sustainability.

(8) Section 106 Heads of Terms

6.64. Finally, during the Application phase, it will be necessary to confirm that all of the three Golden Rules are met by any necessary obligations under Section 106 of the Town and Country Planning Act 1990, notably affordable housing (on site or off-site contributions), any other necessary infrastructure contributions, and (where applicable) obligations that ensure public access to the accessible green space on site. This may be in the form of either an agreed Section 106 Agreement or a Unilateral Undertaking.

CHAPTER SEVEN

PLANNING APPEALS

(1) Introduction

7.1. Under Section 78 TCPA 1990, applicants may bring an appeal against either (a) a refusal of planning permission or (b) a failure to determine the application within the required time limit ("non-determination").

7.2. Section 78 appeals are determined by the Secretary of State. However, in the vast majority of cases the decision is taken on a delegated basis by Inspectors from the Planning Inspectorate. The Secretary of State retains a separate power to recover appeals for her own determination under s79 TCPA. Alongside this, she also retains a residual power to call in an application for her own determination under section 77 TCPA. The Secretary of State's decisions may be delegated to another Minister and in practice often are.

7.3. The appeals procedure is governed by various Inquiry, Hearing and Written Representations Rules, for example, the Town and Country Planning Appeals (Determination by Inspectors) (Inquiries Procedure) (England) Rules 2000 in respect of inquiries before Inspectors.

7.4. Guidance on Appeals is also offered in the Planning Inspectorate's Procedural Guide, which is regularly updated. This Chapter does not seek to exhaustively set out the various stages, but instead provides focussed advice relevant to Grey Belt appeals. All such cases will turn on their own specific facts and be shaped by their own main issues, however a number of common themes are apparent from contemporary practice in Grey Belt cases.

(2) Timing of Appeal Submission

7.5. All appeals must be brought within 6 months of the decision to refuse permission, or from the relevant expiry date for the purposes of non-determination.

7.6. This requirement is set by the Appeal Procedure Guidance rather than legislation. The 6 month deadline is enforced strictly, without any scope for extension.

7.7. A careful balance must be struck between (a) thorough preparation of the appeal documentation, which will often be extensive, (b) securing consideration early before various windows of opportunity close, for example, an increase in the 5YHLS figure above 5 years or submission/ examination/ adoption of the Local Plan and (c) securing Local Plan evidence base material which may assist (or disrupt) arguments for Grey Belt compliance.

7.8. The timescales for appeals to be heard through different formats fall outside the scope of this book, given their tendency to change quite significantly over time, depending on the rate of appeal submission and the Inspectorate's workload across all casework types (including plan examination work).

(3) The Format of the Appeal

7.9. The Planning Inspectorate, on behalf of the Secretary of State can decide one of three formats for a planning appeal: (1) inquiry; (2) hearing or (3) written representations.

7.10. The criteria applied by the Inspectorate have evolved over time, but the core considerations are (1) complexity; (2) the need for cross-examination and (3) public interest:

"*1. Written representations*

written representations would be appropriate if:

- the planning issues raised or, in an enforcement appeal, the grounds of appeal, can be clearly understood from the appeal documents and a site inspection (if required (A small number of appeals do not require a site visit and can be dealt with on the basis of the appeal documents))

- the issues are not complex and the Inspector is not likely to need to test the evidence by questioning or to clarify any other matters in an enforcement appeal the alleged breach, and the requirements of the notice, are clear

2. Hearing

a hearing would be appropriate if:

- the Inspector is likely to need to test the evidence by questioning or to clarify matters (for example where detailed evidence on housing land supply needs to be tested by questioning)

- the status or personal circumstances of the appellant are at issue (for example whether in traveller appeals the definition in Annex 1 of the Department for Levelling Up, Housing and Communities planning policy for traveller sites is met, or in agricultural dwelling appeals)

- there is no need for evidence to be tested through formal questioning by an advocate or given on oath

- the case has generated a level of local interest such as to warrant a hearing (Where the proposal has generated significant local interest a hearing or inquiry may need to be considered. In such circumstances the local planning authority should indicate which procedure it considers would be most appropriate taking account of the number of people likely to attend and participate at the event. We will take that advice into account in reaching the decision as to the appropriate procedure)

- it can reasonably be expected that the parties will be able to present their own cases (supported by professional witnesses if required) without the need for an advocate to represent them

- in an enforcement appeal, the grounds of appeal, the alleged breach, and the requirements of the notice, are relatively straightforward

3. Inquiry

an inquiry would be appropriate if:

- there is a clearly explained need for the evidence to be tested through formal questioning by an advocate (This does not preclude an appellant representing themselves as an advocate)

- the issues are complex (for example where large amounts of highly technical data are likely to be provided in evidence)

- the appeal has generated substantial local interest to warrant an inquiry as opposed to dealing with the case by a hearing (where the proposal has generated significant local interest a hearing or inquiry may need to be considered. In such circumstances the local planning authority should indicate which procedure it considers would be most appropriate taking account of the number of people likely to attend and participate at the event. We will take that advice into account in reaching the decision as to the appropriate procedure)

...

Note - It is considered that the prospect of legal submissions being made is not, on its own, a reason why a case would need to be conducted by inquiry. Where a party considers that legal submissions will be required (and are considered to be complex such as to warrant being made orally), the Inspectorate requires that the matters on which submissions will be made are fully explained – including why they may require an inquiry – at the outset of the appeal or otherwise at the earliest opportunity."

7.11. Many Grey Belt Appeals will involve both (a) a degree of complexity and (b) public interest, and therefore appellants should always consider whether to apply for *at least* a hearing, rather than written representations. This will allow a much greater degree of procedural control.

7.12. At the time of writing, there is presently little difference in timescales between hearings and inquiries. The key consideration will generally be the procedural control afforded in the inquiry format and the likely far greater cost of the inquiry process.

7.13. For larger schemes (100+ homes), an inquiry will be essential and there should be little dispute about this format. For smaller schemes (<100 homes), it may however be difficult to secure a hearing without specifying clearly which of the principles are engaged.

(4) Appeal Strategy and the Decision-Taker Centred Approach

7.14. A planning appeal is a project in its own right, of at least 6-12 months duration. Preparation for the appeal begins at the application stage, especially where the LPA give an early indication that there will be a delegated refusal or a recommendation for refusal. It will help to ensure that the Decision Notice Reasons for Refusal are as narrow as possible.

7.15. Once an appeal is likely, it is vital to shape the case towards the likely decision-taker: normally the Inspector, but potentially the Secretary of State.

7.16. As explored in Chapter 5 and 6, the hallmarks of successful Grey Belt cases (and those with a reserve VSC position) include (a) clear structure and (b) a positive approach to the development. An

Inspector's reasoning on the Grey Belt tests need not be extensive, and may extend to just a few paragraphs. It is instructive, for example, to note appeal decisions where the purposes are dealt in just a sentence each,[39] and to examine the brevity of the Secretary of State's own reasoning in recovered appeals.[40]

7.17. An appeal case should therefore begin with a clear view to its end-point, with detailed consideration of the components of the Decision Letter, and the precise steps needed to reach positive conclusions.

(5) Statements of Case

7.18. A Statement of Case is the central document in which the key planning arguments must be marshalled and presented. Because an inquiry is not guaranteed and a hearing may be ordered instead, it is essential that the Statement of Case is sufficiently full to cover all main planning arguments.

7.19. The Statement of Case should adopt a similar format to the Planning Statement (in the previous Chapter), save that it should expressly focus on the Reasons for Refusal and the specific text of the underlying Officer's Report. Reference may be made to Article 35(1)(b) DMPO and the understanding that the reasons for refusal are therefore full and cite all relevant policies.

(6) Statements of Common Ground

7.20. A Statement of Common Ground must be submitted in draft with all appeals that are to proceed by way of inquiry and hearing. An SoCG is a statutory requirement under Town and Country Planning (Inquiries Procedure) (England) Rules 2000, Rule 14 and

---

39 3354772 – Northaw (25 March 2025), DL15

40 3345318 – Tatton Services (5 March 2025), DL32-37

the Town and Country (Hearings Procedure) (England) Rules 2000, Rule 6(A).

7.21. Under the Rules, an SoCG should "*contain agreed factual information about the proposal, which is the subject of the application or appeal*". However the scope and format of such documents has expanded somewhat over time beyond mere "factual information", such that the process of agreement of an SoCG may form a critical part of identifying the precise case that is to be met at the inquiry or hearing. The Planning Inspectorate has published a short guide to SoCGs and a draft template online.

7.22. The draft SoCG should be carefully composed to identify the key dividing lines between the parties on Grey Belt matters. This should include a bespoke section for each of the headings under NPPF 155 and 156, and allied NPPF paragraphs.

7.23. Whilst specific itemisation of Green Belt harms may be too contested to reach full agreement, appellants should still look to seek agreement with the LPA on the maximum number of factors possible. This may include agreement on weight to be accorded to the development plan and its constituent policies, or on the factual components which make up the benefit (e.g. the scale of the need).

(7) Agreeing Grey Belt Status

7.24. As part of the SoCG process, it may be worth exploring whether Grey Belt status can be agreed (both the Glossary definition and the broader Criteria A-D). This is the case for a considerable number of the early appeal decisions, which were transition cases.[41]

[41] 3342701 Colney Heath (3 February 2025), DL16; 3346228 – Hadlow (21 February 2025), DL4 and 36; 3350890 – Burcot Farm (4 March 2025), DL4-5; 3353896 – Sevenoaks (2 April 2025)

(8) Appeal Start Date and Inspector Identity

7.25. Once the appeal is registered and a start date given, the Planning Inspectorate will issue a start letter with the Inspector's name and key dates. In contemporary appeal practice, it is recommended to gather recent decisions by the Inspector (using one of the commercially available Appeals databases). This research exercise will assist in understanding how they have dealt with similar issues. The decisions should be shared with the appeal team. Every case will turn on its own facts, of course. However, early focus on the nature of the decision-taking process and how the Decision Letter is drawn up will help the whole team to understand its target and the nature of the evidence required.

7.26. It is also advisable to keep a regular check for appeal decisions within the LPA administrative area, and even where applicable neighbouring LPAs within the same Green Belt area. Decisions of all scales, including written representations decisions on smaller schemes and different types of development may provide useful insights into how the Grey Belt tests are being applied – even if the appeal case will seek to distinguish certain findings.

(10) Proofs of Evidence

7.27. Evidence at inquiry is presented in the format of Proofs of Evidence, formal documents setting out all aspects of a given subject area.

7.28. In most Grey Belt cases it will be necessary to call witnesses in respect of at least (1) Planning and (2) Landscape and Green Belt purposes (together) and then (3) a specialist witness on the specific type of unmet need – e.g. Market Housing, Affordable Housing and Employment Land and (4) where contested, an expert on transport/locational sustainability matters.

(11) Core Documents

7.29. The bulk of the documentary evidence for Grey Belt appeals will consist of Core Documents, arranged in the following general "CD Volume" headings:

- CD1 Application Documents and Plans

- CD2 Additional/Amended Reports and/or Plans submitted after validation

- CD3 Committee Report and Decision Notice

- CD4 The Development Plan

- CD5 Emerging Development Plan

- CD6 Relevant Appeal Decision

- CD7 Relevant Judgements

- CD8 Other

7.30. Green Belt Assessments at the Local Plan level should be included in the Development Plan or Emerging Development Plan CD Volume, and these will form an important part of the consideration of Grey Belt land qualification for the purposes of NPPF 155a. Similarly evidence base on housing need, transport, local sustainability, affordable housing and open space may be included in this section.

7.31. It is possible to include bespoke chapters on any relevant topic, for example Economic Benefits, including relevant Government Reports and economic data.

(12) Rule 6 Parties and Third Parties

7.32. Third parties including members of the public may apply to become full parties to the appeal, formally termed a "Rule 6 Party" under the Town and Country Planning (Inquiries Procedure) (England) Rules 2000. A Rule 6 Party may instruct a legal representative and cross-examine the Appellant's witnesses.

7.33. However this is a more formal status and many objectors may simply choose to appear at the inquiry or hearing and make shorter submissions. Because of the higher profile of Green Belt and Grey Belt cases, Rule 6 participation is not uncommon, but is by no means a given.

(13) Case Management Conferences

7.34. Ahead of an inquiry, the appointed Inspector will hold a Case Management Conference ("CMC") circa 8-12 weeks prior to the appeal event start date to discuss matters of procedure, including deadlines for submission of evidence. This is a key opportunity to settle points of procedure, e.g. running order of witnesses, supplementary SoCGs. The merits of the case are not discussed. Green Belt and Grey Belt matters will ordinarily be identified as a main issue at this stage.

(14) Inquiry Procedure

7.35. Inquiries are multi-day proceedings, often around 4 days but very rarely more than 15-20 sitting days, save in the very largest schemes. Witnesses will generally be called on a topic-by-topic basis in accordance with the identified main issues, with Planning witnesses heard last.

7.36. Following opening submissions, Inquiries are now generally structured on a topic by topic basis, whereby the LPA witness gives evidence first, followed directly after by the corresponding

Appellant's witness. Green Belt/Grey Belt evidence may be the subject of formal evidence (i.e. cross-examination), or may be heard by way of round-table sessions. Closing submissions are presented formally in written form, but generally read out in full. The LPA closes first, followed by the Appellant.

(15) Hearing Procedure

7.37. Hearings are Inspector-led and normally last no longer than 1 day. An Appeal team should bring individual experts to cover all reasons for refusal who will address the Inspector's questions in accordance with a pre-notified agenda.

(16) Site Visits

7.38. Inspectors will generally visit the Site informally prior to an inquiry event. For an inquiry, they will schedule a post-inquiry visit after the evidence has been heard. Parties should agree an itinerary prior to the site visit, including the selection of key viewpoints to identify questions of contribution to Green Belt purposes.

(17) Post-Inquiry Submissions

7.39. If a matter arises after the inquiry which could not reasonably have been raised with the Inspector at the time, then a party can apply to submit this and engage in post-inquiry representations. The discretion to hear post-inquiry submissions is exercised extremely sparingly.

(18) Call-In Inquiries

7.40. Section 77 TCPA 1990 confers the Secretary of State the power require applications of identified types to be referred to them directly prior to a grant of permission. The criteria are set out in the Written Ministerial Statement of 26 October 2012, including: "*The Secretary of State will, in general, only consider the use of his call-*

in powers if planning issues of more than local importance are involved. Such cases may include, for example, those which in his opinion: [1] *may conflict with national policies on important matters;* [2] *may have significant long-term impact on economic growth and meeting housing needs across a wider area than a single local authority;* [3] *could have significant effects beyond their immediate locality;...*"

7.41. Call-in inquiries follow a very similar procedure to recovered appeals with the sole difference being that the LPA is normally not in opposition to the scheme and therefore will take a supportive role.

7.42. The power has been used relatively sparingly, on just 198 occasions between 2010/11 and 2022/23. However Green Belt cases have historically been one of the major targets for call-in. Once the decision is made to call in the application, the case is referred to the Planning Inspectorate.

(19) Recovered Appeals

7.43. Under Section 79, the Secretary of State also has the power to recover an appeal following its issue. The criteria are set out in the PPG,[42] including the following:

"The Secretary of State will consider recovery in line with the criteria below, set out in a Parliamentary Statement on 30 June 2008. There may be other cases which merit recovery because of the particular circumstances:

- *Proposals for development of major importance having more than local significance.*

- *Proposals giving rise to substantial regional or national controversy.*

42 PPG Reference ID: 16-005-20160713

• Proposals which raise important or novel issues of development control, and/or legal difficulties.

• Proposals for significant development in the Green Belt…."

A recovered appeal will be determined via written representations, a hearing or an inquiry in the same way as other planning appeals. Where an appeal case has been recovered, the Inspector will not make the decision but instead will write a report and include a recommendation to the Secretary of State who will make the decision.

7.44. If an appeal is recovered then the Inspector will issue a report recommending whether the Secretary of State should grant or refuse permission, with the final decision being set out in a formal Decision Letter in the Secretary of State's name

7.45. Recovered decisions are made on the basis of the Inspector's recommendation. However, they are fundamentally political decisions, signalling the Government's position on certain key issues. Government is aware that such decisions may be scrutinised widely for clues as to the approach to various national policy considerations and questions of policy interpretation. It is therefore necessary to carefully address the entire national policy position: as set out within the NPPF, Written Ministerial Statements, other speeches and indeed other recovered decisions.

7.46. Whilst historic Green Belt cases may have been called in or recovered simply on account of their location in the Green Belt (and associated local political pressure), the Secretary of State's position under the current administration is characterised by an increased interest in what the development itself provides. An application headed for a political determination at this level will need to demonstrate policy-compliance. However, it may also need to demonstrate a commitment to go beyond the normal thresholds, in terms of the scale and range of the benefits.

7.47. Extensive reference will be necessary to the current Government's priorities, as explained in the NPPF and the WMS including the twin objectives of (1) delivering 1.5 million homes across the full Parliament and (2) delivering significant economic growth. Drilling down into the detail, Ministers will evidently wish to see major contribution to affordable housing, improved local infrastructure and a genuine commitment to provide high-quality living environments for the community.

7.48. On larger schemes, it is therefore essential to ensure that there is a political strategy alongside the planning strategy to make the application not merely acceptable to Officers and Inspectors but strike a real chord with the Government's leading politicians, as advised by their own civil servants and special advisers.

7.49. The Government have committed to the publication of decisions determined under recovered powers within the same timescales as conventional applications, i.e. 13 weeks from the receipt of the Inspector's Report providing the underlying recommendation. This follows extraordinary delays in the 2010s of up to four years between closure of inquiry and the final decisions in certain cases. Given the much shorter timescales, the need for post-inquiry representations to the Secretary of State will hopefully be much reduced. However, such representations were a regular feature under the previous Government, to address changes in national policy, progress of Local Plans and other intervening circumstances.

(20) Decision Letter Checking and Prospective Legal Challenge

7.50. Once the Inspector or Secretary of State's Decision Letter is received, it is important to check this thoroughly, even if permission has been granted.

7.51. Key areas to check include (a) the description of development; (b) the conditions; (c) planning obligations and then the core findings on development plan accordance.

7.52. Any legal challenge under s288 must be brought within 6 weeks, and thus if a challenge is to be issued (or defended against) then preparations will need to start as early as possible. The general procedural and substantive framework of legal challenges is the subject of the next chapter.

CHAPTER EIGHT

JUDICIAL REVIEW AND STATUTORY REVIEW

(1) Introduction

8.1. This Chapter concerns two types of legal challenge that are heard by the Planning Court (part of the King's Bench Division of the High Court), and the appellate courts (the Court of Appeal and the Supreme Court):

(1) Judicial review challenges to decisions to grant permission by LPAs at first instance;

(2) Statutory review challenges under s288 of the Town and Country Planning Act 1990 ("TCPA") against decisions of the Secretary of State or Planning Inspectors under delegated powers, following appeals under s78 TCPA

8.2. The purpose of this chapter is to explain (1) the key procedural stages in such challenges (including timescales) and (2) general principles about grounds of challenge, including significant limitations on the court's jurisdiction to address only errors of law.

8.3. There is considerable procedural overlap between Judicial Review and Section 288 procedures, with only very focussed differences. However, each has a different substantive target, with an attendant body of case law.

8.4. We shall begin by setting out the full procedure for Judicial Review, and then supplement this by reference to the bespoke elements of Statutory Review under s288 TCPA.

(2) Identifying Potential Challengers/Challenge Points for Judicial Review

8.5. A judicial review can only be brought by a person with a "sufficient interest" in the decision.[43] This test is not applied strictly by the courts, and will ordinarily be satisfied (for example) by residence in the general area, or the submission of an objection to the application.

8.6. It is therefore necessary to examine representations made by residents, members of the public, community groups, parish/town councils and occasionally commercially interested parties (e.g. businesses in the same sector), to identify early if these raise any allegations of an arguable error of law in the approach being taken to an application – prior to the decision.

(3) Limitation and the Pre-Action Protocol on Judicial Review

The Six Week Limitation Period

8.7. The deadline for challenges by judicial review is six weeks from the date of the decision, however such claims must also be brought "promptly.[44] The court will not extend time beyond the six weeks save in only the rarest of circumstances.

Pre-Action Protocol for Judicial Review

8.8. Claimants are expected to comply with the Pre-Action Protocol for Judicial Review, whereby they set out their prospective grounds of challenge and the proposed remedy (ordinarily a quashing order, which would remove the decision to grant permission, and effectively require it to be redetermined).

---

43 Section 31(3) of the Senior Courts Act 1981

44 CPR r54.5(1)(a)

8.9. A prospective claimant should write to both the LPA and the applicant for planning permission (through their appointed agents, or where known, any instructed solicitors).

8.10. The Pre-Action Protocol for Judicial Review expects prospective claimants to write to the defendant as soon as possible, and ordinarily to allow them 2 weeks to respond. This document is known as a Pre-Action Protocol Letter ("PAPL").

8.11. Accordingly, the first point at which a defendant or an applicant may hear about a legal challenge may be somewhere between 1 and 5 weeks within the challenge period. Solicitors should be instructed as soon as possible on receipt of any Pre-Action Protocol Letter. Due to professional rule constraints on barristers' conduct of litigation, a Pre-Action Protocol Response would generally need to be issued by an instructed solicitor, but may be drafted by a barrister.

(4) Submission of Claim and the Acknowledgement of Service

8.12. Most claimants will notify defendants and interested parties at the point of submission of the claim, and then formally serve (i.e. send) the claim form, the Statement of Facts and Grounds, and the claim bundle.

8.13. The defendant and interested party's response is due within 21 days of the date of service,[45] comprising an Acknowledgement of Service Form and a Summary Grounds of Defence.

8.14. It is vital that any interested party and their legal representative liaise early with the defendant LPA to agree common positions on the grounds and discuss any evidence to be produced, including

---

45 CDR r. 54.8(2)(a)

any short witness statement to cover narrow evidential points, or to exhibit documents omitted from the claimant's claim bundle.

(5) The Permission Requirement

8.15. All claims for judicial review must be granted permission (also termed "leave") by the Planning Court before they are allowed to proceed.[46] The test applied is simply whether the claim is "arguable". This is not intended as an especially high threshold, but will depend on a number of factors, e.g. the novelty of the question of law/interpretation or whether it is relatively settled through various other cases.

8.16. The Courts will only grant permission for and ultimately uphold claims which concern legal errors in a decision. They cannot determine pure disputes with the planning merits of a decision. Any such challenges will often be filtered out at the permission stage.

8.17. The first consideration is on the papers only. If permission is refused, then the claimant has the right to seek a renewal hearing within 7 days.[47]

8.18. A renewal hearing will then be listed within 1-2 months of the date of the order refusing permission.

8.19. Renewal hearings are scheduled for 30 minutes, subject to requests for extension. The parties should file and serve skeleton arguments.

8.20. Defendants have the option to argue that the claim is totally without merit, restricting the right to a renewal hearing. This decision can only be appealed to the Court of Appeal.

---

46 Section 31(3) of the Senior Courts Act 1981

47 CPR 54.12(3) and (4)

(6) Steps Following Permission

8.21. If permission is granted (on the papers or following a hearing), then the court will set out key future dates in an Order.

8.22. Ordinarily, the next step will be the filing and service of Detailed Grounds of Defence and any additional evidence by the defendant and interested party, within 35 days.[48]

8.23. Again, this is a crucial stage for cooperation between defendant and interested party. Both should share draft detailed grounds and witness statements, and even meet to discuss case strategy.

8.24. It may be helpful for the defendant LPA to submit a witness statement from the case officer, or another officer with direct involvement in the case. Interested parties' own employees or consultants may also submit witness statements explaining factual matters or appending documents. Cross-examination in judicial review proceedings is extremely rare, and thus such documents almost always form the entirety of the witness' evidence.

8.25. In the run-up to the substantive hearing, further steps include work on the hearing bundle, exchange of skeleton arguments and the agreement of authorities (i.e. legislation and cases).

(7) Substantive/Final Hearing

8.26. Following the grant of permission, the substantive/final hearing may be listed within circa 4-6 months.

8.27. Substantive or final hearings in judicial review proceedings are often listed for no more than 1 to 2 days.

---

48 CPR 54.14(1)

8.28. The High Court will hear from the Claimant first, then the Defendant, then the Interested Party. The Claimant then has a right of reply.

8.29. Judgement will ordinarily be reserved, i.e. handed down in writing at later date, between 1 to 3 months from the date of substantive hearing.

(8) Remedy and Costs

Remedy

8.30. The standard remedy is a quashing order where a legal error is upheld. The court has some discretion in this respect and may simply issue a declaration, however this is relatively rare.

8.31. Where the court considers that it is "*highly likely that the outcome for the applicant would not have been substantially different if the conduct complained of had not occurred*", then the relief may be refused.[49] This is however exercised very sparingly and would require a relatively minor error.

8.32. A quashing order renders the decision void such that it must be taken again by the LPA, albeit informed by the court's judgment.

Costs

8.33. The losing party will be ordered to pay the winning party's costs, subject to any protective costs order ("PCO") in place.[50]

---

49 Section 31(2A) of the Senior Courts Act 1981

50 CPR rr.46.24-28

8.34. An Interested Party can ordinarily claim its costs of the submission of the Acknowledgement of Service phase, but not the substantive hearing.

(9) Appeals to the Court of Appeal and Supreme Court

8.35. Appeals from the Planning Court are heard by the Court of Appeal (Civil Division) subject to a strict filter on leave to appeal: *"(a) the appeal would have a real prospect of success; or (b) there is some other compelling reason for the appeal to be heard."*[51]

8.36. Appeals to the UK Supreme Court are subject to an even stricter permission stage and thus are very rare indeed: where there is "*a point of law of general public importance*" and if it appears to the Supreme Court "*that the point is one that ought to be considered by the Court.*"

(10) Statutory Review: Key Differences

8.37. Statutory review under s288 follows an almost identical pathway to judicial review, save for four key differences.

8.38. First, a claim under s288 may relate to both a grant and a refusal of permission. A s288 claim will be defended by the Government Legal Department on behalf of the defendant Secretary of State. They therefore bring a particular experience and expertise to the defence process. If the claimant is the LPA, then the appellant will be the 2nd defendant and the appellant should therefore seek to make early contact with GLD, especially prior to the Acknowledgement of Service. If the appellant is the claimant, the position is reversed.

8.39. Second, a claimant will only have standing to bring the claim if they are a "person aggrieved" – i.e. a full participant in the appeal

---

[51] CPR r. 52.6(1)(a)-(b)

proceedings. This would ordinarily need to be the appellant, the LPA or an individual who actively submitted representations and ordinarily attended the inquiry.

8.40. Third, the six-week deadline is fixed and cannot be extended in any circumstances at all (save for narrow provisions on bank holidays and court opening times that fall beyond the scope of this book).

8.41. Fourth, there is no Pre-Action Protocol requirement for s288 challenges. Such letters are however increasingly used to seek early consent to judgment or to notify the Secretary of State's legal representatives of the need for disclosure, but there is no formal requirement to do so.

8.42. Statutory reviews under s288 TCPA (and parallel challenges to enforcement appeals under s289 TCPA) have historically been the largest and most significant area of Green Belt jurisprudence. Such challenges, by their nature, involve a detailed consideration of the policy by the Planning Inspector (or the Secretary of State) and they are defended by the Secretary of State's legal representatives. They therefore represent a very important reference point for the interpretation of the contested terms.

(11) Judicial Review Grounds of Challenge

8.43. The total number of judicial review claims each year is hard to measure, as there is limited data provided by the Ministry of Justice and HMCTS.

8.44. Green Belt cases have however been an area of significant litigation. The Courts have determined cases involving Green Belt policy for at least six decades, stretching back to some of the earliest cases considering Circular 42/55. However most of these have related to challenges on the interpretation of the exceptions to Very Special Circumstances.

8.45. Judicial review challenges have often been brought on the basis that the Officer's Report incorrectly applies some aspect of the Green Belt policy. In the Grey Belt context, a potential ground of challenge could be an allegation that the decision-maker has incorrectly interpreted the wording of a policy provision, for example a given term within national planning policy.

8.46. The total number of challenges that are granted permission may be affected by the comparative simplicity of the policy and the absence of some of the textual ambiguity that has characterised historic Green Belt policy.

8.47. The UK Supreme Court's judgment in *Tesco Stores Ltd v Dundee City Council* [2012] UKSC 13, [17]-[20] marked the start of much of the policy-related litigation in the modern era. The judgment was handed down on 21 March 2012 just one week prior to the publication of the first edition of National Planning Policy Framework (27 March 2012). It was not the first judgement to confirm that the courts could provide an objective interpretation for policy. However, as an appellate judgement at the highest level, it clarified the width of the courts' jurisdiction and prompted a surge of litigation concerning the NPPF through the first half of the 2010s, which continued at a steady level up to the 2020s. The courts have, however, been generally protective of LPA's interpretation of policy, only upholding claims where there is a clear error in the exercise undertaken.

8.48. The leading case on Officer's Reports remains *R(Mansell) v Tonbridge and Malling* [2017] EWCA Civ 1314, [41]-[42]:

> *41. The Planning Court—and this court too—must always be vigilant against excessive legalism infecting the planning system. A planning decision is not akin to an adjudication made by a court: see para 50 of my judgment in the East Staffordshire case. The courts must keep in mind that the function of planning decision-making has been assigned by Parliament, not to judges, but—at local level—to elected*

councillors with the benefit of advice given to them by planning officers, most of whom are professional planners, and—on appeal—to the Secretary of State and his inspectors. They should remember too that the making of planning policy is not an end in itself, but a means to achieving reasonably predictable decision-making, consistent with the aims of the policymaker. Though the interpretation of planning policy is, ultimately, a matter for the court, planning policies do not normally require intricate discussion of their meaning. A particular policy, or even a particular phrase or word in a policy, will sometimes provide planning lawyers with a "doctrinal controversy". But even when the higher courts disagree as to the meaning of the words in dispute, and even when the policy-maker's own understanding of the policy has not been accepted, the debate in which lawyers have engaged may turn out to have been in vain—because, when a planning decision has to be made, the effect of the relevant policies, taken together, may be exactly the same whichever construction is right: see para 22 of my judgment in the East Staffordshire case [2018] PTSR 88 . That of course may not always be so. One thing, however, is certain, and ought to be stressed. Planning officers and inspectors are entitled to expect that both national and local planning policy is as simply and clearly stated as it can be, and also—however well or badly a policy is expressed—that the court's interpretation of it will be straightforward, without undue or elaborate exposition. Equally, they are entitled to expect—in every case—good sense and fairness in the court's review of a planning decision, not the hypercritical approach the court is often urged to adopt.

42. The principles on which the court will act when criticism is made of a planning officer's report to committee are well settled. To summarise the law as it stands:

(1) The essential principles are as stated by the Court of Appeal in R v Selby District Council, Ex p Oxton Farms [2017] PTSR 1103: see, in particular, the judgment of Judge LJ. They have since been confirmed several times by this court, notably by Sullivan LJ in R (Siraj) v Kirklees Metropolitan Borough Council [2011] JPL 571, para 19,

and applied in many cases at first instance: see, for example, the judgment of Hickinbottom J in R (Zurich Assurance Ltd (trading as Threadneedle Property Investments)) v North Lincolnshire Council [2012] EWHC 3708 (Admin) at [15].

(2) The principles are not complicated. Planning officers' reports to committee are not to be read with undue rigour, but with reasonable benevolence, and bearing in mind that they are written for councillors with local knowledge: see the judgment of Baroness Hale of Richmond JSC in R (Morge) v Hampshire County Council [2011] PTSR 337, para 36 and the judgment of Sullivan J in R v Mendip District Council, Ex p Fabre [2017] PTSR 1112 , 1120. Unless there is evidence to suggest otherwise, it may reasonably be assumed that, if the members followed the officer's recommendation, they did so on the basis of the advice that he or she gave: see the judgment of Lewison LJ in R (Palmer) v Herefordshire Council [2017] 1 WLR 411, para 7. The question for the court will always be whether, on a fair reading of the report as a whole, the officer has materially misled the members on a matter bearing upon their decision, and the error has gone uncorrected before the decision was made. Minor or inconsequential errors may be excused. It is only if the advice in the officer's report is such as to misdirect the members in a material way—so that, but for the flawed advice it was given, the committee's decision would or might have been different—that the court will be able to conclude that the decision itself was rendered unlawful by that advice.

(3) Where the line is drawn between an officer's advice that is significantly or seriously misleading—misleading in a material way—and advice that is misleading but not significantly so will always depend on the context and circumstances in which the advice was given, and on the possible consequences of it. There will be cases in which a planning officer has inadvertently led a committee astray by making some significant error of fact (see, for example R (Loader) v Rother District Council [2017] JPL 25), or has plainly misdirected the members as to the meaning of a relevant policy: see, for example, R (Watermead Parish Council) v Aylesbury Vale District Council

[2018] PTSR 43. There will be others where the officer has simply failed to deal with a matter on which the committee ought to receive explicit advice if the local planning authority is to be seen to have performed its decision-making duties in accordance with the law: see, for example, R (Williams) v Powys County Council [2018] 1 WLR 439. <u>But unless there is some distinct and material defect in the officer's advice, the court will not interfere.</u>

8.49. *Mansell* has been applied in many cases involving allegations that an Officer's Report to Committee has failed correctly to cite or interpret some aspect of national policy or the development plan. As the judgment makes clear, a high threshold will be applied to such challenges: there must be a "distinct and material defect".

<u>(12) Statutory Review Grounds of Challenge</u>

8.50. Similar to judicial review, most s288 challenges will concentrate on an error or gap in the reasoning within the Inspector's Report or the Secretary of State's Decision Letter. The key principles for challenges to Inspector's decisions were explored by the Court of Appeal in St *Modwen v SSCLG* [2017] EWCA Civ 1643, [6]-[7] (endorsing an earlier summary in *Bloor Homes East Midlands Ltd. v Secretary of State for Communities and Local Government* [2014] EWHC 754 (Admin), [19]).

8.51. The Court of Appeal explained both the limits of court's role where a decision-maker (specifically a Planning Inspector) has reached a planning judgement and the scope for a challenge where there has been a genuine error in respect of the interpretation of policy:

6. In my judgment at first instance in Bloor Homes East Midlands Ltd. v Secretary of State for Communities and Local Government [2014] EWHC 754 (Admin) (at paragraph 19) I set out the "seven familiar principles" that will guide the court in handling a challenge under section 288. This case, like many others now coming before the

Planning Court and this court too, calls for those principles to be stated again – and reinforced. They are:

"(1) <u>Decisions of the Secretary of State and his inspectors in appeals against the refusal of planning permission are to be construed in a reasonably flexible way</u>. Decision letters are written principally for parties who know what the issues between them are and what evidence and argument has been deployed on those issues. <u>An inspector does not need to "rehearse every argument relating to each matter in every paragraph"</u> (see the judgment of Forbes J. in Seddon Properties v Secretary of State for the Environment (1981) 42 P. & C.R. 26, at p.28).

(2) <u>The reasons for an appeal decision must be intelligible and adequate, enabling one to understand why the appeal was decided as it was and what conclusions were reached on the "principal important controversial issues".</u> An inspector's reasoning must not give rise to a substantial doubt as to whether he went wrong in law, for example by misunderstanding a relevant policy or by failing to reach a rational decision on relevant grounds. But the reasons need refer only to the main issues in the dispute, not to every material consideration (see the speech of Lord Brown of Eaton-under-Heywood in South Bucks District Council and another v Porter (No. 2) [2004] 1 W.L.R. 1953, at p.1964B-G).

(3) <u>The weight to be attached to any material consideration and all matters of planning judgment are within the exclusive jurisdiction of the decision-maker.</u> They are not for the court. A local planning authority determining an application for planning permission is free, "provided that it does not lapse into Wednesbury irrationality" to give material considerations "whatever weight [it] thinks fit or no weight at all" (see the speech of Lord Hoffmann in Tesco Stores Limited v Secretary of State for the Environment [1995] 1 W.L.R. 759, at p.780F-H). And, essentially for that reason, an application under section 288 of the 1990 Act does not afford an opportunity for a review of the planning merits of an inspector's decision (see the judgment of

Sullivan J., as he then was, in Newsmith v Secretary of State for Environment, Transport and the Regions [2001] EWHC Admin 74, at paragraph 6).

(4) Planning policies are not statutory or contractual provisions and should not be construed as if they were. The proper interpretation of planning policy is ultimately a matter of law for the court. The application of relevant policy is for the decision-maker. But statements of policy are to be interpreted objectively by the court in accordance with the language used and in its proper context. A failure properly to understand and apply relevant policy will constitute a failure to have regard to a material consideration, or will amount to having regard to an immaterial consideration (see the judgment of Lord Reed in Tesco Stores v Dundee City Council [2012] P.T.S.R. 983, at paragraphs 17 to 22).

(5) When it is suggested that an inspector has failed to grasp a relevant policy one must look at what he thought the important planning issues were and decide whether it appears from the way he dealt with them that he must have misunderstood the policy in question (see the judgment of Hoffmann L.J., as he then was, South Somerset District Council v The Secretary of State for the Environment (1993) 66 P. & C.R. 80 , at p.83E-H).

(6) Because it is reasonable to assume that national planning policy is familiar to the Secretary of State and his inspectors, the fact that a particular policy is not mentioned in the decision letter does not necessarily mean that it has been ignored (see, for example, the judgment of Lang J. in Sea Land Power & Energy Limited v Secretary of State for Communities and Local Government [2012] EWHC 1419 (QB) , at paragraph 58).

(7) Consistency in decision-making is important both to developers and local planning authorities, because it serves to maintain public confidence in the operation of the development control system. But it is not a principle of law that like cases must always be decided alike. An

inspector must exercise his own judgment on this question, if it arises (see, for example, the judgment of Pill L.J. in Fox Strategic Land and Property Ltd. v Secretary of State for Communities and Local Government [2013] 1 P. & C.R. 6, at paragraphs 12 to 14, citing the judgment of Mann L.J. in North Wiltshire District Council v Secretary of State for the Environment [1992] 65 P. & C.R. 137 , at p.145)."

7. <u>Both the Supreme Court and the Court of Appeal have, in recent cases, emphasized the limits to the court's role in construing planning policy</u> (see the judgment of Lord Carnwath in Suffolk Coastal District Council v Hopkins Homes Ltd. [2017] UKSC 37, at paragraphs 22 to 26, and my judgment in Mansell v Tonbridge and Malling Borough Council [2017] EWCA Civ 1314 , at paragraph 41). More broadly, though in the same vein, this court has cautioned against the dangers of excessive legalism infecting the planning system – a warning I think we must now repeat in this appeal (see my judgment in Barwood Strategic Land II LLP v East Staffordshire Borough Council [2017] EWCA Civ 893, at paragraph 50). There is no place in challenges to planning decisions for the kind of hypercritical scrutiny that this court has always rejected – whether of decision letters of the Secretary of State and his inspectors or of planning officers' reports to committee. The conclusions in an inspector's report or decision letter, or in an officer's report, should not be laboriously dissected in an effort to find fault (see my judgment in Mansell, at paragraphs 41 and 42, and the judgment of the Chancellor of the High Court, at paragraph 63).

8.52. These principles have been applied in many subsequent challenges to Inspectors' and Secretary of State's decisions, including in the Green Belt.

(14) Summary

8.53. There have been many High Court and Court of Appeal cases (and one Supreme Court case) concerning various aspects of Green Belt policy, especially in the past 13 years since the NPPF was first published.

8.54. As explored above, Grey Belt policy no longer contains the same extent of ambiguities, controversies and interpretative complexities, as the broader category of "not inappropriate" development and indeed Very Special Circumstances itself.

8.55. There is no single way to avoid legal challenge to a decision-maker's grant of permission (whether by an Officer, Committee or Inspector). However, the clear presentation of the application material, targeted references to the main case law on certain core points, and a proactive approach to third party objections will all assist the exercise.

8.56. Fundamentally, the best route is a rigorous description and application of specific Grey Belt policy tests and to provide a practical planning assessment, backed up by relevant technical evidence and other information as appropriate. This is the essence of an exercise of planning judgement, with which the courts will not readily interfere. It is to those individual provisions that we shall now turn in Part II.

PART II

THE POLICY TESTS

CHAPTER NINE

GREEN BELT PURPOSE A

(1) Introduction

9.1. Chapters 9 through to 13 consider each stage of NPPF 155a (termed here Criterion A).

9.2. Chapters 9, 10 and 11 specifically examine the gateway test in the Glossary Definition. To qualify as Grey Belt land, the application site cannot make a "strong contribution" to the purposes listed in NPPF 143(a), (b) and (d) (termed here Purposes A, B and D):

[Criterion A]

155. The development of homes, commercial and other development in the Green Belt should also not be regarded as inappropriate where all the following apply:

a. ***The development would utilise grey belt land*** *and would not fundamentally undermine the purposes (taken together) of the remaining Green Belt across the area of the plan;*

[The Glossary Definition]

For the purposes of plan-making and decision-making, 'grey belt' is defined as land in the Green Belt comprising previously developed land and/or any other land that, ***in either case, does not strongly contribute to any of purposes (a), (b), or (d) in paragraph 143.***

[Purposes A, B and D]

143. Green Belt serves 5 purposes:

(a) to check the unrestricted sprawl of large built-up areas;

(b) to prevent neighbouring towns merging into one another;

…

(d) to preserve the setting and special character of historic towns; and

9.3. As explored in Chapter 2, the test of "does not strongly contribute" was chosen in place of "makes a limited contribution" (to all five purposes) in the original 2024 consultation text. The "limited contribution" threshold was clearly considered too low, excluding too wide a range of sites. Government's intention is plainly that the threshold for exclusion from the Grey Belt definition should be a high one.

9.4. The Government however recognised that the test of "strong contribution" would require more detailed exposition in Planning Practice Guidance to ensure "a more consistent approach to assessing Green Belt Land".[52] That guidance was published on 27 February 2025.

9.5. Following the judgment in *Mead Realisations v Secretary of State for Housing, Communities and Local Government* [2025] EWCA Civ 32, the PPG enjoys equivalent status to the NPPF text and should not be regarded as in any way subordinate. It sits alongside the NPPF text and requires careful interpretation and application, noting that many of the terms involve planning judgement, informed by the input of qualified landscape professionals.

52 NPPF Consultation Response (12 December 2024), Response to Q3

9.6. A Grey Belt development need only "utilise" Grey Belt land. The development does not necessarily need to be entirely within Grey Belt land, and may, for example, be either partly inside a settlement boundary (and thus outside the Green Belt in that respect) or even hypothetically on greenfield land outside the Green Belt. However, if any component is located on Green Belt which does not qualify as Grey Belt, then this will either require another Green Belt exception or Very Special Circumstances. Such mixed Grey Belt/VSC cases are, however, likely to be rare. In this Chapter and the whole of Part II, the assumption shall be made that the whole site is presented as Grey Belt, and if it falls outside the Grey Belt definition then a VSC case may be presented as a reserve position (see Chapter 20).

(2) The Planning Practice Guidance: General Principles

9.7. Before examining the PPG's Table for the Purposes A, B and D,[53] it is important to reflect on the broader PPG text that prefaces it, explaining what kinds of evidence base LPAs should now produce.

9.8. The PPG explains that LPAs should carry out a new LPA-wide Green Belt Assessment in its initial paragraphs. The expectation is that LPAs should commence the process of Green Belt Assessment in line with the PPG as soon as practical:

> ***Scope of guidance***[54]
>
> *This guidance sets out:*
>
> - *the considerations involved in assessing the contribution Green Belt land makes to Green Belt purposes, where relevant to identifying grey belt land*

[53] Paragraph: 005 Reference ID: 64-005-20250225

[54] PPG Chapter on Green Belt – Top paragraph (unnumbered)

- the considerations involved in determining whether release or development of Green Belt land would fundamentally undermine the remaining Green Belt in the plan area;

- guidance for considering proposals on potential grey belt land

- guidance on identifying sustainable locations when considering the release or development of Green Belt land

- updated guidance on how major housing development on land which is released from the Green Belt through plan making, or on sites in the Green Belt, should contribute to accessible green space

- updated guidance on how to consider the potential impact of development on the openness of the Green Belt

Assessing Green Belt to identify grey belt land

This guidance is relevant to those authorities performing a review of Green Belt boundaries to meet housing or other development needs (either prior to or as part of the plan making process), those authorities otherwise required to determine whether land constitutes grey belt in decision making, and others seeking to identify grey belt land.

Where grey belt is identified, it does not automatically follow that it should be allocated for development, released from the Green Belt or for development proposals to be approved in all circumstances. The contribution Green Belt land makes to Green Belt purposes is one consideration in making decisions about Green Belt land. Such decisions should also be informed by an overall application of the relevant policies in the National Planning Policy Framework (NPPF).

Why should authorities assess their Green Belt to identify grey belt land?[55]

As set out in national policy, the review and alteration of Green Belt boundaries should take place, where necessary, as part of the plan making process. In doing so, we expect authorities to identify grey belt land to inform this review and the prioritisation detailed in paragraphs 147 and 148 of the NPPF.

National policy also requires authorities to identify, where necessary, whether land is grey belt for the purpose of considering applications on Green Belt land. Where land is identified as grey belt land, any proposed development of that land should be considered against paragraph 155 of the NPPF, which sets out the conditions in which development would not be inappropriate on grey belt land.

How should authorities assess their Green Belt to identify grey belt land?[56]

In order to identify grey belt land, authorities should produce a Green Belt assessment, either as part of the review of Green Belt boundaries during the preparation or updating of a local plan, or at another relevant point. This assessment should be informed by the guidance below.

We expect most Green Belt assessments to be undertaken by local authorities or appropriate groups of local authorities. Green Belt assessments should also inform the preparation of Spatial Development Strategies where these will be setting the strategic context for land release.

55 Paragraph: 001 Reference ID: 64-001-20250225

56 Paragraph: 002 Reference ID: 64-002-20250225

When updating or preparing plans, authorities will need to consider whether any existing Green Belt assessment remains up to date.

9.9. The latter sub-paragraph is important. All pre-December 2024 Green Belt Assessments will have been produced under the older NPPF, without the assistance of the current PPG, and are accordingly subject to significant limitations. Whilst certain findings may be relevant, almost no such assessments can be considered truly "up to date" in a complete sense. The pre-2024 GBA will not have adopted all elements of the updated PPG guidance, notably the specific illustrative features of the three-stage Strong, Moderate, Weak/None scale. They will often be based on larger or differently configured parcels beyond an application site's boundaries.[57]

9.10. Accordingly, every application now needs to be accompanied by a site-specific Green Belt Assessment which systematically applies the tests, until such point as the LPA's first contemporary, post-2024 Green Belt Assessment is published.

9.11. The PPG later continues:

Proposals on grey belt land

How can Green Belt assessments be used in the development management process?[58]

An assessment of Green Belt will (alongside other considerations) inform the determination of applications which involve reaching a judgement as to whether proposals utilise grey belt land and whether

57 3345053 – Fobbing (24 February 2025), DL8: "one small part of the wider parcel"

58 Paragraph: 009 Reference ID: 64-009-20250225

development of the site would fundamentally undermine the purposes of the remaining Green Belt across the plan area.

Where grey belt sites are not identified in existing plans or Green Belt assessments, it is expected that authorities should consider evidence, in light of this guidance, on:

- *whether* ***the site*** *strongly contributes to the Green Belt purposes a, b or d; and*

- *whether the application of policies to areas and assets of particular importance identified in footnote 7 to the NPPF (other than Green Belt) provide a strong reason to restrict development; and*

- *whether development of the site would fundamentally undermine the purposes of the remaining Green Belt across the plan area, as set out in national policy and this guidance.*

9.12. The PPG refers expressly to "the site", i.e. the whole land within the red line boundary of the application. Although this is relatively clear from the NPPF Glossary definition, this makes clear that the test is not focussed purely on the "built footprint".

9.13. A finding of "strong contribution" against any of the purposes would be sufficient to disqualify the site. This reflects that there has never historically been any hierarchy between the five purposes, and this remains the case for the reduced category of three purposes.

9.14. Express guidance is set out for the Glossary definition exercise in an extensive Table at the current PPG paragraph 005, as follows. This is termed "the PPG Table" in this Chapter and later Chapters of this book:

How should the contribution land makes to the relevant Green Belt purposes be assessed?[59]

When making judgements as to whether land is grey belt, authorities should consider the contribution that assessment areas make to Green Belt purposes a, b, and d. Considerations for informing these judgements are set out below:...

9.15. Under each PPG element, there are a number of terms that are ambiguous or may give rise to differences of view. It is important therefore to adopt a rigorous approach, to consider the purpose in full and how the words should be interpreted in a straightforward fashion, consistent with the overarching purpose of Grey Belt policy, within wider Green Belt policy.

(3) The PPG Table: Purpose A

9.16. Purpose A (NPPF 143(a)) is "*(a) to check the unrestricted sprawl of large built-up areas*".

9.17. In common with all of the purposes, none of the terms are defined in the NPPF nor in any legislation or guidance beyond the PPG itself.

9.18. The PPG Table provides, with numbered square brackets added for ease of reference:

Purpose A – to check the unrestricted sprawl of large built up areas

This purpose relates to the sprawl of large built up areas. Villages should not be considered large built up areas.

[59] Paragraph: PPG 005 64-006-20250225

Contribution

Strong

[Illustrative features]

[1] *Assessment areas that contribute strongly are* [a] *likely to be free of existing development, and* [b] *lack physical feature(s) in reasonable proximity that could restrict and contain development.*

They are also likely to include all of the following features:

- [c] *be adjacent or near to a large built up area*

- [d] *if developed, result in an incongruous pattern of development (such as an extended "finger" of development into the Green Belt)*

Moderate

[Illustrative features]

[2] *Assessment areas that contribute moderately are likely to be adjacent or near to a large built up area, but include one or more features that weaken the land's contribution to this purpose a, such as (but not limited to):*

- [a] *having physical feature(s) in reasonable proximity that could restrict and contain development*

- [b] *be partially enclosed by existing development, such that new development would not result in an incongruous pattern of development*

- [c] *contain existing development*

- [d] *being subject to other urbanising influences*

Weak or None

[Illustrative features]

[3] *Assessment areas that make only a weak or no contribution are likely to include those that:*

- [a] *are not adjacent to or near to a large built up area*

- [b] *are adjacent to or near to a large built up area, but containing or being largely enclosed by significant existing development*

Large Built-Up Area

9.19. The PPG does not expressly identify what qualifies as a "large built-up area", simply that "villages" are excluded.

9.20. The paradigm example of a "large built-up area" is a city: e.g. London or one of the major cities that form the urban centre of the 16 main Green Belts: Manchester, Birmingham, Leeds etc.

9.21. The primary area of difficulty relates to "towns". The three key determining factors are likely to be (1) the physical scale of the town; (2) the size of its population and (3) whether there is any express description of the town's status in the development plan and any historic Green Belt Assessments undertaken for that LPA, which will have considered this purpose, and (4) where applicable, any historic appeal decisions.

9.22. A large town, with a significant population (e.g. in excess of 100,000 population) and with an extensive spatial area, which is also identified within the adopted development plan at the top of the settlement hierarchy will plainly satisfy the test.

9.23. At the other end, if a settlement (1) does not cover a wide area; (2) has a population well below 100,000 and (3) has never been referred to as a large built-up area in the development plan, or any historic GBA work, then the purpose is unlikely to be engaged.

9.24. The two earliest decisions to grapple with the test (heard prior to the PPG) used existing Green Belt Assessments and effectively placed the threshold as low as 10,000.[60] However, such a figure would seem somewhat at odds with the distinct term "town" used for Purpose B. Ultimately the term "large" must be given its proper effect.

9.25. In practice, however, the exclusion of the purpose altogether may be less important in this context – given the height of the threshold for a strong contribution. The critical question is whether there will be "unrestricted sprawl".[61]

Unrestricted Sprawl

9.26. The term "sprawl" has never previously been defined in the NPPF and PPG. It has however been the subject of much debate at appeal historically. The PPG represents an important break with this past in terms of definitional precision. The test must now be read squarely against each element of the PPG Table. Although the PPG refers to "illustrative features", these are likely to be regarded as a near-complete definition of what amounts to a strong contribution against this objective.

9.27. The gradation is also important. The single question is whether the site/land makes a "strong contribution" to the purpose. The degree

---

60 3347882 – Beaconsfield (24 February 2025), DL13-14 (Beaconsfield population: 12,000 found to be a large built-up area); 3347530 – Bagshot (12 March 2025, but heard on 6 and 27 January 2025), DL11: (Bagshot population: 6,000 found not to be a large built-up area)

61 3346228 – Hadlow (21 February 2025), DL18

of contribution below strong is unimportant, provided that the Site goes on to qualify as Green Belt development in all respects.

[1][a] Free from Existing Development

9.28. The first test in [1][a] requires a simple assessment of the extent of the existing built form within the site. To score "strongly" a site must be "likely to be free of existing development". The test is "likely to" which would appear to envisage some small measure of flexibility, e.g. to allow for relatively small structures within the site, however this conclusion will not be readily drawn.

9.29. If the site "contains existing development" then it will ordinarily score moderately ([2][c]) or "contains significant existing development" ([3][b]) then it will score weakly or not at all.

9.30. This initial test is replicated in the PPG Table for Purposes B and D below, and is thus a recurrent theme. It is however just one component of the test and insufficient to determine the extent of contribution in its own right. The next test (considered below) is connected by "and" thus must be applied cumulatively.

[1][b] Lack physical feature(s) in reasonable proximity that could restrict and contain development

9.31. The second test in [1][b] is one of the more complex to apply, i.e. deciding what kind of physical feature will qualify as "restricting" and constraining" development and what the true effect of that physical feature is within the instant case/physical context. If the site has such physical feature(s) in reasonable proximity then it will score moderately ([2[[a]).

9.32. It is submitted that the test should be applied relatively broadly to include both man-made features (roads, railways, canals) and natural features (rivers, large hedgerows, banks of trees, banks, forests, even topography). Importantly, there is no "visual" component under Purpose A, and therefore the fact that the feature may be lower-lying (e.g. roads, canals) does not prevent it from having the practical effect of restricting growth beyond a specific line on the ground.

9.33. It is important to note that the test does not expressly refer to opportunities for new landscaping to be placed within the site at the edge of the development to give rise to the same effect. That component is picked up under the overarching NPPF 155(a) exercise that looks to the effect of the development, and in a more indirect way under NPPF 156(a) and the definition of accessible green space.

[1][c] Adjacent to or Near Built Up Area

9.34. The third test [1][c] is more straightforward than the second. The site must be "adjacent" or "near" the large built-up area. The test would appear to be a relatively low threshold and will ordinarily require proximity, e.g. measured in hundreds of metres, not kilometres.

9.35. If the large built-up area is not proximate, then the site will not contribute to the purpose at all ([3][a]).

[1][d] If developed, result in an incongruous pattern of development (such as an extended "finger" of development into the Green Belt)

9.36. The fourth criterion is unusually worded. It is juxtaposed with both [2][b] "*be partially enclosed by existing development, such that new development would not result in an incongruous pattern of development*" and [3][b] "*largely enclosed by significant existing development*"

9.37. The strong contribution and "incongruous" label is ostensibly a high threshold. Even partial enclosure (e.g. on just one side) would be enough to score a merely moderate contribution.

[2][d] Being subject to other urbanising influences

9.38. The Moderate contribution score provides one more option to remove the site from "strong contribution": "*urbanising influences*". This may denote forms of development that may not fully enclose, but nonetheless impose an "urbanising" effect, e.g. a motorway or a tall building, which essentially ensure that "urban form" exerts a clear landscape effect on the site. The term may extend wider still, to include a single line of development along one side of the site.

(4) Checklist

9.39. Throughout Part II, various checklist questions shall be provided by way of summary to the chapters. The lists of questions are by no means exhaustive. They are simply key points to reflect on and address in the Planning Statement, the Green Belt Assessment and related evidence documents.

9.40. The list below is a potential checklist to assist in confirming that the Site does not make a "strong contribution" to Purpose A:

Preliminary Question: Is there a relevant large built-up area in proximity to the Site?

[NB Although this question is strictly addressed last (see Q3), this is the gateway question and may be capable of being ruled out early]

- What is the nearest settlement's physical size?

- What is its population?

- Does the development plan refer to the scale and nature of the settlement?

- Have historic Green Belt Assessments recorded this as a large built-up area?

- Have historic appeal decisions recorded it as such?

Q1: Does the Site have any existing development within it?

- Are there any structures on site? If so, how many?

- What is the extent of coverage of those structures across the site?

- What is the current lawful use of the site and does this include large amounts of activity (e.g. vehicle movements across the site)?

Q2: Does the Site have physical feature(s) in reasonable proximity that could restrict and contain development?

- What physical features are located at the site's boundaries, or within the site?

- Are there man-made, permanent features (e.g. roads, railways, canals)?

- Are there natural features (e.g. woods, rivers, large hedgerows)?

- Does the immediate/local topography enclose the site (e.g. slopes, ridges)?

Q3: Is the Site adjacent to or near a large built-up area?

- What is the relevant built-up area? (see the Preliminary Question above)

- How far is the boundary of the site from the boundary of the large built-up area?

CHAPTER TEN

GREEN BELT PURPOSE B

(1) The NPPF Text

10.1. Purpose B / NPPF 143(b) is "*to prevent neighbouring towns merging into one another*".

(2) The PPG Table

10.2. The PPG Table provides:

Purpose B – to prevent neighbouring towns merging into one another

This purpose relates to the merging of towns, not villages.

Contribution

Strong

[*Illustrative Features*]

[1] *Assessment areas that contribute strongly are likely to be* [a] *free of existing development and include all of the following features:*

- [b] *forming a substantial part of a gap between towns*

- [c] *the development of which would be likely to result in the loss of visual separation of towns*

Moderate

[*Illustrative Features*]

[2] *Assessment areas that contribute moderately are* [a] *likely to be located in a gap between towns, but include one or more features that weaken their contribution to this purpose, such as (but not limited to):*

- [b] *forming a small part of the gap between towns*

- [c] *being able to be developed without the loss of visual separation between towns. This could be (but is not limited to) due to the presence or the close proximity of structures, natural landscape elements or topography that preserve visual separation*

Weak or None

[*Illustrative Features*]

[3] *Assessment areas that contribute weakly are likely to include those that:*

- [a] *do not form part of a gap between towns, or*

- [b] *form part of a gap between towns, but only a very small part of this gap, without making a contribution to visual separation*

Towns

10.3. The second purpose expressly refers to "towns" and must be interpreted in a distinct manner from the first purpose. Importantly it can cover any two towns at any scale.

10.4. The PPG now makes expressly clear that the purpose does not include "villages", even larger villages or collections of smaller villages that have already largely coalesced.

10.5. The most important question will therefore often be whether the town is referred to as a "town" within the development plan, alongside any historic Green Belt Assessment work and Appeal Decisions. Early reference has been made to a House of Commons Library Paper,[62] which used an adjusted version of the taxonomy developed by the Centre for Towns (NB across the whole UK, including Wales and Scotland):

> *12 Core Cities: twelve major population and economic centres (e.g. London, Glasgow, Sheffield)*
>
> *24 Other Cities: other settlements with a population of more than 175,000 (e.g. Leicester, Portsmouth, Aberdeen)*
>
> *119 Large Towns: settlements with a population between 60,000 and 174,999 (e.g. Warrington, Hemel Hempstead, Farnborough)*
>
> *270 Medium Towns: settlements with a population between 25,000 and 59,999 (e.g. Gravesend, Jarrow, Exmouth)*
>
> *674 Small Towns: settlements with a population between 7,500 and 24,999 (e.g. Falmouth, New Romney, Holbeach)*
>
> *6,116 Villages and small communities: settlements with a population of less than 7,500 (e.g. Chapel-en-le-Frith, Cottenham, Menai Bridge)*

10.6. On this analysis, 7,500 population is the key dividing line between "town" and "village". This Paper carries no formal status, indeed some defined cities are referred to as "large towns" (e.g. the City of St Albans). It was based on over 200,000 Census Output Areas to

[62] City & Town Classification of Constituencies & Local Authorities (21 June 2018) https://commonslibrary.parliament.uk/research-briefings/cbp-8322/

Built-up-areas and Built-up-area subdivisions, geographies developed by the Office for National Statistics, and accordingly should be revisited today.

10.7. Again, the earliest decisions have confirmed that figures as high as 6,000 can still be a village, where the development plan refers to as such.[63]

Merging Into One Another

10.8. The verb "merging" has conventionally been addressed in a similar manner to the noun "coalescence", with much discussion about the extent of both physical merger (normally measured in overhead, plan form) and the perception of merger (assessed from relevant vantage points on the ground).

10.9. As with Purpose A, the PPG now sets what should be considered a near-definitive list of how the test should be applied. The PPG is best understood as a search for a more objective standard, i.e. focussed on a much clearer-cut approach: emphasising both total distance and the extent of visibility/screening.

10.10. The test is again cumulative: "include all of the following features", so visual factors cannot be excluded.

[1][a] Free from Existing Development

10.11. The first element echoes that for Purpose A, and is to be assessed in largely the same way: i.e. identification of any relevant structures within the Site itself.

63 3347530 – Bagshot (12 March 2025), DL11-14: Bagshot designated a "large village" in the development plan

[1][b] Substantial Part of a Gap Between Towns

10.12. To make a strong contribution, the land itself must form "a substantial part of a gap between towns".

10.13. The test is focussed on the physical extent of the full distance in plan form, not questions of perception (which are picked up later). A plan form approach that measures the nearest point to the next town is therefore appropriate.

10.14. The exact measurement and proportion/percentage is not specified, understandably given the enormous variation in gap distances, and the varied configuration of settlements. However, the word "substantial" must be given its proper effect in the context, i.e. the site must extend over a significant portion of the gap.

10.15. The "substantial part" is to be contrasted with [2][b] "a small gap part of gap between towns". This does not mean that anything above "small" will automatically be "substantial" and make a "strong contribution". The test must be applied in the round, alongside the other tests. The "strong" contribution is intended to be a high threshold and unless it can definitively be shown that the site forms a "substantial" part of the gap, then a Moderate finding is merited.

[1][c] Loss of visual separation

10.16. The second test will only be met where there would be a loss of visual separation. The test is "visual separation" which requires careful regard to the relevant viewpoints. These should ordinarily be public viewpoints (rather than within the site itself or merely private viewpoints), in line with the general principle that there is no right to a view. Any case for strong contribution built purely on private viewpoints would tend to suggest that the relevant site is in fact relatively enclosed.

10.17. The Moderate description list at [2][c] is important. It is not an exhaustive list ("*such as (but not limited to)*"), but nonetheless prioritises the main likely features that will enclose the site or break up any sense of the development impacting the visual separation. Each of the elements must "preserve visual separation".

10.18. "Structures" again suggests man-made built form, the paradigm example being buildings, with a clear visible presence and/or a screening effect. However, lower-lying structures may still aid in preserving visual separation, for example a road with vehicular traffic, a railway (with associated fencing and embankment) or even a canal (with barges and embanked edges). All of these cannot be built upon and may be perceived from relevant vantage points as containing features within the gap.

10.19. "Natural landscape elements" denotes the obvious vegetation types: forests/woods/treelines, however equally a river of a sufficient width (including with river traffic) could also serve to preserve visual separation.

10.20. "Topography" denotes any rise and fall in the ground which may preserve visual separation.

10.21. This aspect of the test will ordinarily benefit from qualified landscape evidence, especially to identify the relevant Zone of Theoretical Visibility ("ZTV") of the development, and thereafter representative viewpoints towards the development. Whilst the LVIA exercise is formally targeted at landscape assessment and the question of visual effects of the development, this is the most established and simplest existing mechanism to assess the extent of "visual separation".

[3][a] and [b] Very Small Part of Gap / No Contribution to Visual Separation

10.22. Where a development is of a relatively small scale, or the gap is large, there will either a weak or no contribution to the purpose. This is likely to apply to quite a wide range of sites, especially where the sites are already very enclosed.

(3) Checklist

10.23. The list below is a potential checklist to exclude a "strong contribution". Again, it is an illustrative list, not exhaustive and can plainly be expanded depending upon the number and range of issues:

Preliminary Question: What are the relevant two (or more) "towns"?

- What are the settlements' physical size?

- What is their population?

- Does the development plan refer to the settlements as "towns" or "villages", even "larger villages"?

- Have historic Green Belt Assessments recorded them as towns?

- Have historic appeal decisions recorded them as towns?

Q1: Does the Site have any existing development within it?

[As for Purpose A]

- What are the structures on site?

- What is the extent of coverage of those structures across the site?

- What is the current lawful use of the site (e.g. vehicle movements across the site)

Q2: Does the Site form part of a substantial gap between the towns?

- What is the relevant gap's distance from one town boundary to the next town boundary?

- What is the relevant gap from the site's edge to the nearest town built edge?

- What proportion of the gap does the appeal site represent in percentage or distance terms?

Q3) Would the development of the Site cause a loss of visual separation?

- What are the main viewpoints towards the site?

- Can both towns be seen from any single viewpoint?

- What physical features are located at the site's boundaries, or in proximity, which screen or limit visibility towards the site?

- Are there man-made, permanent structures which preserve visual separation (e.g. buildings, bridges, roads, railways, canals)?

- Are there any natural landscape elements which preserve visual separation (e.g. woods, rivers, large hedgerows)?

- Does the topography preserve visual separation (e.g. slopes, ridges, valleys)?

CHAPTER ELEVEN

GREEN BELT PURPOSE D

(1) The NPPF Text

11.1. Purpose D / NPPF 143(d) is *"to preserve the setting and special character of historic towns"*.

(2) The PPG Table

11.2. The PPG Table provides:

Purpose D – to preserve the setting and special character of historic towns

This purpose relates to historic towns, not villages. Where there are no historic towns in the plan area, it may not be necessary to provide detailed assessments against this purpose.

Contribution

Strong

[Illustrative Features]

[1] *Assessment areas that contribute strongly are* [a] *likely be free of existing development and to include all of the following features:*

- [b] *form part of the setting of the historic town*

- [c] *make a considerable contribution to the special character of a historic town. This could be (but is not limited to) as a result of being within, adjacent to, or of significant visual importance to the historic aspects of the town*

Moderate

[Illustrative Features]

[2] *Assessment areas that perform moderately are* [a] *likely to form part of the setting and/or contribute to the special character of a historic town but include one or more features that weaken their contribution to this purpose, such as (but not limited to):*

- [b] *being separated to some extent from historic aspects of the town by existing development or topography*

- [c] *containing existing development*

- [d] *not having an important visual, physical, or experiential relationship to historic aspects of the town*

Weak or None

[Illustrative Features]

[3] *Assessment areas that make no or only a weak contribution are likely to include those that:*

- [a] *do not form part of the setting of a historic town*

- [b] *have no visual, physical, or experiential connection to the historic aspects of the town*

Historic Towns

11.3. There is no fixed list of historic towns, and national policy has never clearly identified whether the term is solely concerned with heritage value or whether it might have a broader meaning connoting the age of the settlement itself.

11.4. The word "historic" was first added in Planning Policy Guidance 2 (PPG2) (1988), evidently as an indicator that the category of towns relying upon "special character" needed to be narrower. The Department of the Environment analysis (1993) identified the origins in the designation of Green Belts around Chester, York, Oxford and Cambridge in the 1950s, and then latterly Harrogate and Lancaster in the 1980s.[64]

11.5. The term is therefore not strictly limited to "towns", but can cover settlements which are formally "cities". However, importantly, the whole town must be considered "historic", it is not sufficient merely for there to be a conservation area over part of the area.

[1][a] Free of Existing Development

11.6. The PPG again continues to include a requirement that the site be free of existing development, underscoring the importance of this element.

11.7. This test is repeated for Moderate Contribution, whereby [2][c] "*containing existing development*" may disqualify the site from "strong contribution".

[1][b] Setting of a Historic Town

11.8. The first question to be determined is whether the site actually falls within the relevant setting of the historic town. Qualified heritage evidence will almost invariably be necessary, if there is any allegation that there is a historic town in proximity.

---

64 Department of the Environment, The Effectiveness of Green Belts (1993), p18 [2.26]

11.9. The NPPF Glossary defines the terms "setting of a heritage asset" and "significance", with particular regard to the separate contexts of s66(1) and 72(1) of the Planning (Listed Buildings and Conservation Areas) Act 1990:

Setting of a heritage asset

The surroundings in which a heritage asset is experienced. Its extent is not fixed and may change as the asset and its surroundings evolve. Elements of a setting may make a positive or negative contribution to the significance of an asset, may affect the ability to appreciate that significance or may be neutral.

Significance (for heritage policy)

The value of a heritage asset to this and future generations because of its heritage interest. The interest may be archaeological, architectural, artistic or historic. Significance derives not only from a heritage asset's physical presence, but also from its setting. For World Heritage Sites, the cultural value described within each site's Statement of Outstanding Universal Value forms part of its significance.

11.10. In *Catesby Estates Ltd and SSCLG v Steer* [2018] EWCA Civ 1697, [24]-[30] the Court of Appeal confirmed that "*the effect of development on the setting of a listed building is not necessarily confined to visual or physical impact*" and that there is no "*single approach*" to setting.

11.11. However, the PPG expressly refers to land "*not having an important visual, physical, or experiential relationship*" in the Moderate category [2][d]. Accordingly the extent of visual or physical relationship with the historic town are very important features in determining whether the land falls within the setting. In any event, it is submitted that if there is no visual relationship at all, it will ordinarily be very difficult to establish the necessary strong contribution in any event.

[1][c] Considerable Contribution to Special Character

11.12. The land forming the Site must make a "*considerable contribution to the special character*" of the historic town if it is to make a strong contribution.

11.13. The test is helpfully clarified with an inclusive, physical description: "*This could be (but is not limited to) as a result of being within, adjacent to, or of significant visual importance to the historic aspects of the town*".

11.14. Development that is literally within, or adjacent to the edge of the historic town may therefore make the necessary "considerable contribution". Otherwise, the land must be of "*significant visual importance to the historic aspects*", i.e. a clear visual connection.

11.15. The Moderate elements record all the elements that may disrupt this: including [2][b] "*being separated to some extent from historic aspects of the town by existing development or topography*" and [2][d] "*not having an important visual, physical, or experiential relationship to historic aspects of the town.*"

11.16. There are a number of layers/stages to the test, however, the fundamental questions remain somewhat similar to those encountered under Purpose B above – a physical measure of the distance from the site to the relevant historic town and the extent to which the site can be seen in the context of the historic town. If the Site is not proximate to the historic town, or is otherwise separated by intervening features, then the necessarily high threshold of strong contribution will not be met.

(3) Checklist

11.17. The list below is a potential checklist to exclude a "strong contribution" under this purpose:

Preliminary Question: Is there a relevant "historic town"?

- Is the site in proximity to a town (or historic city)?
- What is the town's age?
- What is the extent of the Conservation Areas within the town and where are they located?
- Is there an extensive number of listed buildings, and where are they located?
- Does the development plan recognise it as a "historic town"?
- Have historic Green Belt Assessments recorded it as a "historic town"?
- Have historic appeal decisions recorded to it as a "historic town??

Q1: Does the Site have any existing development?

[As for Purposes A and B]

- What are the structures on site?
- What is the extent of coverage of those structures across the site?
- What is the current lawful use of the site (e.g. vehicle movements across the site)

Q2: Does the Site fall within the setting of the historic town?

- Is the site within the boundary of the historic town?

- Is the site adjacent to the edge of the historic town?

- Is the site visible alongside the historic town in public vantage points?

- Does the site have any physical or experiential relationship with historic aspects of the town?

<u>Q3) Does the Site make a considerable contribution to the special character of the historic town?</u>

- What is the special character of the historic town as recorded in the development plan, other guidance or within any relevant Heritage Assessment / Conservation Area assessment?

- Is the site separated from historic aspects of the town by existing development?

- Is the site separated from historic aspects of the town by topography?

- Does the site have any important visual, physical, or experiential relationship to historic aspects of the town?

CHAPTER TWELVE

PREVIOUSLY DEVELOPED LAND

(1) The NPPF Text

12.1. The NPPF Glossary Text refers to Previously Developed Land as follows:

For the purposes of plan-making and decision-making, 'grey belt' is defined as land in the Green Belt comprising previously developed land and/or any other land that, in either case, does not strongly contribute to any of purposes (a), (b), or (d) in paragraph 143.

12.2. As explored in Chapter 9, PDL status is not essential for Grey Belt status. What really matters is the absence of a "strong contribution" against Purposes A, B and D.

12.3. However, in the early days of the Grey Belt concept (in the Labour Manifesto), this aspect of the Grey Belt definition was in effect the poster child of the re-branding exercise, with much emphasis upon abandoned petrol stations and car parks.

12.4. After the Election, the Government acknowledged that the extent of previously developed land in the Green Belt that is not already subject to a planning application/planning permission or otherwise designated in existing development plan documents is relatively small. As the Second Written Ministerial Statement (12 December 2024) observed: "*we know that there are simply not enough sites on brownfield land registers to deliver the volume of homes that the country needs each year, let alone enough that are viable and in the right location*".

12.5. The Previously Developed Land definition has at least three main parts, the two qualifying elements listed as [1] and [2] below, i.e. [1] permanent structure and [2] fixed surface infrastructure, plus at [3] the long list of excluded types of land, listed as [3][a]-[d] below:

[1] *Land which has been* [a] *lawfully developed and* [b] *is or was occupied by a permanent structure and* [c] *any fixed surface infrastructure associated with it,* [d] *including the curtilage of the developed land (although it should not be assumed that the whole of the curtilage should be developed).*

[2] *It also includes* [a] *land comprising large areas of fixed surface infrastructure such as large areas of hardstanding* [b] *which have been lawfully developed.*

[3] *Previously developed land excludes:*

[a] *land that is or was last occupied by agricultural or forestry buildings;*

[b] *land that has been developed for minerals extraction or waste disposal by landfill, where provision for restoration has been made through development management procedures;*

[c]*land in built-up areas such as residential gardens, parks, recreation grounds and allotments; and*

[d] *that was previously developed but where the remains of the permanent structure or fixed surface structure have blended into the landscape.*

12.6. These shall be considered in detail below.

12.7. Two further points arise from the NPPF. There has long been a recognised exception for previously developed land under what is currently NPPF 154(g): "*the partial or complete redevelopment of previously developed land*" subject to the control that such development cannot "*cause substantial harm to the openness of the Green Belt*". The obvious limitation of this exception is the uncertainty that attaches to the "substantial harm" label, and its restriction of the size of development that can come forward.

12.8. The NPPF contains strong support for the development of PDL, at NPPF 89, 124 and 125. NPPF 125(c) is particularly notably in conferring <u>substantial</u> weight to the value of the use of suitable brownfield land:

89. Planning policies and decisions should recognise that sites to meet local business and community needs in rural areas may have to be found adjacent to or beyond existing settlements, and in locations that are not well served by public transport. In these circumstances it will be important to ensure that development is sensitive to its surroundings, does not have an unacceptable impact on local roads and exploits any opportunities to make a location more sustainable (for example by improving the scope for access on foot, by cycling or by public transport). <u>The use of previously developed land, and sites that are physically well-related to existing settlements, should be encouraged where suitable opportunities exist.</u>

124. Planning policies and decisions should promote an effective use of land in meeting the need for homes and other uses, while safeguarding and improving the environment and ensuring safe and healthy living conditions. <u>Strategic policies should set out a clear strategy for accommodating objectively assessed needs, in a way that makes as much use as possible of previously-developed or 'brownfield' land.</u>

125. Planning policies and decisions should:...

(c) <u>give substantial weight to the value of using suitable brownfield land within settlements for homes and other identified needs, proposals for which should be approved unless substantial harm would be caused,</u>

and support appropriate opportunities to remediate despoiled, degraded, derelict, contaminated or unstable land;

(d) promote and support the development of under-utilised land and buildings, especially if this would help to meet identified needs for housing where land supply is constrained and available sites could be used more effectively (for example converting space above shops, and building on or above service yards, car parks, lock-ups and railway infrastructure).

(2) The PPG

12.9. The PPG Chapter on Green Belt does not include any guidance on this aspect of the test.

12.10. The PPG Chapter on Brownfield land registers merely states:

"***What is previously developed (brownfield) land?***[65]

Previously developed land has the same meaning as land of that description in Annex 2 of the National Planning Policy Framework. Previously developed land is referred to as brownfield land."

(3) Interpretation

[1][b] Permanent Structure

12.11. The starting point for the first sub-definition is [1][b] the existence of a permanent structure on part of the site.

12.12. The term "structure" is not defined in either statute, policy or guidance, but is closely related to the definition of a building under s336 of the TCPA 1990: *"building" includes any structure or*

[65] PPG 59-003-20170728

erection, and any part of a building, as so defined, but does not include plant or machinery comprised in a building".

12.13. Given that the "structure" is referred to in the past tense "was occupied" and the width of [2] fixed surface infrastructure, it is likely that this component is not likely to cause frequent controversy, provided naturally that there is clear photographic or other documentary evidence of the former structure. The paradigm example would be a warehouse/shed or a petrol station canopy.

[1][c] Fixed Surface Infrastructure

12.14. The term "fixed surface infrastructure" is not defined in statute, although the Glossary definition in [2] makes clear that it may be satisfied by "large areas of hardstanding". The precise degree of "fixture" is not specified, but is controlled partly by the [1][a] "lawfully developed" element and partly by [3][d] the "blended into the landscape" restriction. In short, it must be lawful at the point of the decision and clearly visible.

[1][d] Curtilage

12.15. The NPPF recognises that PDL status should extend beyond the footprint of existing building to its curtilage. The NPPF is however clear that this is not an absolute limit: "*it should not be assumed that the whole of the curtilage should be developed*".

12.16. The term "curtilage" has been the subject of very extensive jurisprudence, albeit in many different legislative/common law situations (e.g. permitted development rights, heritage listing, and in various property contexts).

12.17. The leading case in the planning context remains *Methuen-Campbell v Walters* [1979] 2 QB 525, in which the Court of Appeal observed that the land must be:

"so intimately connected with [the building] as to lead to the conclusion that the former forms part and parcel of the latter."

12.18. The Court of Appeal considered the various authorities in *R(Hampshire CC) v Blackbushe Airport* [2021] EWCA Civ 398, [25]-[26] and confirmed that the test in *Methuen-Campbell* should be used today:

25.... The curtilage of a building is a single concept, and [Counsel] is right that it does not have different meanings in different statutory contexts. There is in truth only one test, and that is the test articulated by Buckley LJ in Methuen-Campbell, but that is not the same as BAL's "integral whole" test. The question whether the test is satisfied in any given case will depend on the facts and circumstances of that case.

26. The ambit (or physical extent) of the curtilage of a building in any given case will be a question of fact and degree. Various factors may be helpful in resolving that question, including, where relevant, a consideration of the statutory consequences of a finding that land (or a building or other structure or object on it) falls within or outside of the curtilage of a building. In certain contexts, the Court may be slightly more generous in its application of the relevant factors to reach a particular result, bearing in mind the purposes of the governing statute; for example, when determining whether an ancillary structure falls within the curtilage of a listed building. But that does not mean that the concept of curtilage is different in listed building cases.

12.19. In all cases, it will therefore be necessary to demonstrate that the land in question is physically proximate sufficient to be intimately connected (per the *Methuen-Campbell* definition). Additional factors may include single ownership, the absence of any dividing features (e.g. walls, hedges and other man-made and natural structures) and a history of direct connection (e.g. through pathways). Where the extent is disputed, reference may be made to the wide ambit of the Glossary Definition and the inclusion of the reference to "fixed surface infrastructure". This may be seen as the logical limit of the curtilage in many cases, subject to the specific nature of the building and its historic use.

[1][a] Lawfully Developed

12.20. Returning to the first-listed descriptor, the term "lawfully developed" envisages either (i) the structure/infrastructure itself was the subject of a planning permission for construction or change of use; or (ii) the elapse of time has meant that enforcement action is no longer available, by virtue of s171B TCPA 1990.

12.21. The prime example would be under section 171B (as amended by the Levelling-Up and Regeneration Act 2023 and subject to transitional provisions in respect of breaches prior to 25 April 2024):

(1) Where there has been a breach of planning control consisting in the carrying out without planning permission of building, engineering, mining or other operations in, on, over or under land, no enforcement action may be taken after the end of the period of—

(a) in the case of a breach of planning control in England, ten years beginning with the date on which the operations were substantially completed, and

12.22. The conventional route to demonstrating the lawfulness of the existing structure would be via a Certificate of Lawfulness of Existing Use/Development ("CLEUD") under section 191 TCPA.

12.23. The detailed jurisprudence and procedural aspects of the CLEUD and enforcement regimes falls outside the scope of this book. Ultimately, a critical issue for applicants will be the quality of their documentary evidence demonstrating the initiation of the works to construct a building or lay the hardstanding and the quality of the mapping of its footprint. In line with all Green Belt exceptions, decision-takers may adopt a strict approach to protect against overreach, noting the overall importance of the Green Belt under NPPF 142.

[2][a] Large areas of fixed surface infrastructure such as large areas of hardstanding

12.24. This has been addressed above. The objective here is to incorporate areas which have no building within them, for example car parks, or other similar expanses (airfields, depots) which would have previously been approached more restrictively in the past. In line with [3][d] the relevant infrastructure must not have blended into the landscape.

[2][b] Lawfully developed

12.25. The same controls apply as under [1], there must be clear evidence that the area of hardstanding was either subject to a planning permission or has otherwise become lawful through the operation of time.

Exclusion [3][a]: Land that is or was last occupied by agricultural or forestry buildings

12.26. The list of exclusions is quite wide, with each seeking to achieve a specific purpose/restriction.

12.27. The purpose of this control on PDL is to constrain the extent of construction in rural areas. This is important given the exception that is applied under NPPF 154(a) to allow the construction of agricultural/forestry buildings themselves.

12.28. It is important to note that the exclusion refers expressly to "buildings", rather than "infrastructure", i.e. the s336 TCPA definition. The paradigm example would be an agricultural barn.

12.29. The definition of agricultural is wide under s336 TCPA and therefore this exclusion will be construed broadly:

"agriculture" includes horticulture, fruit growing, seed growing, dairy farming, the breeding and keeping of livestock (including any creature kept for the production of food, wool, skins or fur, or for the purpose of its use in the farming of land), the use of land as grazing land, meadow land, osier land, market gardens and nursery grounds, and the use of land for woodlands where that use is ancillary to the farming of land for other agricultural purposes, and "agricultural" shall be construed accordingly;

12.30. The key difficulty is likely to arise in respect of the term "last occupied", where the building has been demolished. No specific timescale is given and therefore evidence of a previous structure may therefore disqualify the site.

12.31. In practice, such disputes may be rather narrow for three reasons. First, the agricultural nature of the use is likely to be construed broadly. It can be demonstrated by reference to the structure, its location and (as applicable) historic mapping. Second, abandonment of a pre-existing use (including agriculture) is a high threshold and will ordinarily require a significant elapse of time, potentially many years. Third, given the strong controls upon locational sustainability under Criterion C / NPPF 155(c), there will be clear limitations on the promotion of more isolated rural sites.

<u>Exclusion [3][b]: Land that has been developed for minerals extraction or waste disposal by landfill, where provision for restoration has been made through development management procedures</u>

12.32. The purpose of this exclusion is similar to that for agricultural buildings.

12.33. Minerals development is an express exception under NPPF 154(h)(i) and there is a clear wish to avoid such sites going immediately from minerals development into other uses.

12.34. There is also a clear objective to ensure that land (both minerals and waste) that has been expressly remediated remains so, in accordance with any restoration requirements, for example to recreational access. In practice, this exclusion is again likely to be relatively clear-cut, confirmed by the existence of prior minerals extraction or waste disposal.

Exclusion [3][c]: Land in built-up areas such as residential gardens, parks, recreation grounds and allotments

12.35. The term "built-up areas" is not defined in legislation or policy. The list is non-exhaustive, but still extensive.

12.36. It is important to note that this exclusion is directed primarily at avoiding development of sites inside settlement boundaries, to ensure that these do not benefit from the NPPF 124/125 conferral of substantial weight to brownfield land. In most larger settlements, such uses would fall outside the Green Belt anyway.

12.37. It is possible that a dispute may however arise on the edge of a "built-up area", e.g. the use of residential garden land or allotment sites. Some may argue that such land is not "in" i.e. within "the built-up area". However national policy has not adopted any major shift towards more intensive use of garden/allotment land, and such a change of use is therefore likely to be considered contrary to the overall objective of the PDL policy, with the express references to "permanent structures" and "fixed surface infrastructure".

Exclusion [3][d] "That was previously developed but where the remains of the permanent structure or fixed surface structure have blended into the landscape."

12.38. This exclusion is in two parts. It first requires positive identification of the relevant "permanent structure" and "fixed surface infrastructure" (and its curtilage) and the precise footprint of this area.

12.39. It then requires a judgement as to whether this has "blended into the landscape". This is primarily an aesthetic judgement, but would ordinarily need be supported by landscape evidence and some element of photography both aerial and at ground level. Ordinarily the "blending" will be evidenced by vegetation growth, some soil coverage and occasionally changes in the topography.[66]

12.40. The exception was traditionally targeted at preventing arguments that a site is previously developed if there was no visible impact on openness, or the site had in practice been left vacant for so long that the use has, in effect, been abandoned and therefore did not merit the term "previously developed".

(4) Checklist

12.41. Any case seeking to raise the PDL qualification should be accompanied by a separate relevant document or, for smaller sites, a bespoke section of the Planning Statement.

12.42. The indicative questions below can guide a clear conclusion:

Q1: Scope & Specificity

- What is the relevant portion of the site that is considered to be Previously Developed Land?
- Has this been precisely mapped on a plan, distinguishing the relevant structure and fixed surface infrastructure?

Q2) Permanent Structure

- What is the permanent structure relied upon? [plural as appropriate]

[66] 3354772 – Northaw (25 March 2025), DL17

- Precisely when was structure installed on the site?

- Was the structure lawfully developed (with planning permission or immune from enforcement action)?

- What is the fixed surface infrastructure associated with that structure?

- Does the fixed infrastructure fall within the curtilage of the structure?

Q3: Large Hardstanding

- Is the fixed infrastructure a large area of hardstanding ?

- Was that hardstanding lawfully developed (with planning permission or immune from enforcement action)?

Q4) Exclusions

- Is the Site occupied (or was it last occupied) by agricultural or forestry buildings?

- Has the land been developed for minerals extraction or waste disposal by landfill, where provision for restoration has been made through development management procedures?

- Is the land part of a residential garden, park, recreation ground or allotment, where the Site is within built-up area?

- If the Site was previously developed, have the remains of the permanent structure or fixed surface structure blended into the landscape?

CHAPTER THIRTEEN

"STRONG REASON FOR REFUSAL" POLICIES

(1) NPPF Text

13.1. The final component of the Glossary definition is formally separate from the Grey Belt-specific considerations:

> *'Grey belt' excludes land where the application of the policies relating to the areas or assets in footnote 7 (other than Green Belt) would provide a strong reason for refusing or restricting development.*
>
> *(7) The policies referred to are those in this Framework (rather than those in development plans) relating to:*
>
> **[Habitats and Ecology]**
>
> *habitats sites (and those sites listed in paragraph 194) and/or designated as Sites of Special Scientific Interest; … irreplaceable habitats;*
>
> **[Local Green Space]**
>
> *Local Green Space,*
>
> **[Protected Landscapes]**
>
> *a National Landscape, a National Park (or within the Broads Authority) or defined as Heritage Coast;*

[Heritage]

designated heritage assets (and other heritage assets of archaeological interest referred to in footnote 75); and

[Flooding]

areas at risk of flooding or coastal change.

(2) The PPG Text

13.2. The PPG explains that for the local plan-making assessment phase, the exercise may be conducted in a "provisional" manner "in advance of more detailed specific proposals":

> ***How should the application of footnote 7 be considered when identifying land as grey belt?***[67]
>
> *As defined in the NPPF, grey belt excludes land where the application of policies relating to the areas or assets in footnote 7 to the NPPF (other than Green Belt) would provide a strong reason for refusing or restricting development. In reaching this judgement, authorities should consider where areas of grey belt would be covered by or affect other designations in footnote 7. Where this is the case, it may only be possible to provisionally identify such land as grey belt in advance of more detailed specific proposals.*

13.3. The development management paragraph then states:

---

[67] Paragraph: 006 Reference ID: 64-006-20250225

How can Green Belt assessments be used in the development management process?[68]

An assessment of Green Belt will (alongside other considerations) inform the determination of applications which involve reaching a judgement as to whether proposals utilise grey belt land and whether development of the site would fundamentally undermine the purposes of the remaining Green Belt across the plan area.

Where grey belt sites are not identified in existing plans or Green Belt assessments, it is expected that authorities should consider evidence, in light of this guidance, on:

...

whether the application of policies to areas and assets of particular importance identified in footnote 7 to the NPPF (other than Green Belt) provide a strong reason to restrict development; ...

(3) Focus on the Development

13.4. The Glossary definition refers to the "land", i.e. the whole Site. However, the test is whether the policies "provide a strong reason to restrict development", which clearly denotes the development for which planning permission is being sought.

13.5. In effect, the purpose of the inclusion is to bring forward NPPF 11d(i) considerations as a kind of gateway assessment. This avoids any interpretational difficulty as to a perceived hierarchy of interests within NPPF 11d(i)/footnote 7, notably in respect of landscape/ecology. There had been extensive reference in the Manifesto and the Written Ministerial Statements to avoiding the

68 Paragraph: 009 Reference ID: 64-009-20250225

application of Grey Belt policy in protected landscapes. This form of words protects that objective.

(4) "Strong Reason" for Refusing/Restricting Development

13.6. The question of "strong" reason was clarified in the NPPF consultation response (Q6):[69]

A change has also been made to be clear that when assessing whether areas or assets of particular importance provide a reason for refusal, there should be a 'strong' basis for doing so when assessed against the policies in the National Planning Policy Framework (replacing the existing 'clear' reason). This reflects views that we heard about opportunities to strengthen the presumption's wording, in the context of the government's commitment to increasing the supply of homes, but still enables these key protections to be fully considered and enforced where it is appropriate to do so.

13.7. "Strong" is therefore intended to be a higher threshold than "clear", but the precise difference will inevitably be much-contested.

(5) The Footnote 7 Provisions

13.8. For present purposes, this Chapter shall list the key NPPF provisions and suggest some of the types of evidence that may be included within the application to confirm no conflict with this part of the Glossary Definition (as well as ultimately for NPPF 11d(i) purposes).

13.9. The detailed legislative, policy and evidential arrangements fall beyond the scope of this book. The essential point is that qualified professional evidence must be recruited in respect of each specialist topic and a relevant report provided to address each component,

[69] NPPF Consultation Response (12 December 2024)

wherever the relevant area or asset is in sufficient proximity to the site.

(6) Habitats and Ecology

[1] *habitats sites (and those sites listed in paragraph 194) and/or designated as Sites of Special Scientific Interest;*

Habitats Sites

13.10. Habitats Sites are defined in the NPPF Glossary, by express reference to Regulation 8 of the Conservation of Habitats and Species Regulations 2017 (as amended):

Habitats site

Any site which would be included within the definition at regulation 8 of the Conservation of Habitats and Species Regulations 2017 for the purpose of those regulations, including candidate Special Areas of Conservation, Sites of Community Importance, Special Areas of Conservation, Special Protection Areas and any relevant Marine Sites.

13.11. The footnote 7 definition therefore requires consideration of the array of protections under the Habitats Regulations 2017, notably the requirement for appropriate assessment under Regulation 63:

(1) A competent authority, before deciding to undertake, or give any consent, permission or other authorisation for, a plan or project which—

(a) is likely to have a significant effect on a European site or a European offshore marine site (either alone or in combination with other plans or projects), and

(b) is not directly connected with or necessary to the management of that site,

must make an appropriate assessment of the implications of the plan or project for that site in view of that site's conservation objectives.

(5) In the light of the conclusions of the assessment, and subject to regulation 64, the competent authority may agree to the plan or project only after having ascertained that it will not adversely affect the integrity of the European site or the European offshore marine site (as the case may be).

(6) In considering whether a plan or project will adversely affect the integrity of the site, the competent authority must have regard to the manner in which it is proposed to be carried out or to any conditions or restrictions subject to which it proposes that the consent, permission or other authorisation should be given.

Sites of Special Scientific Interest

13.12. Sites of Special Scientific Interest are designated under Section 28 of the Wildlife and Countryside Act 1981, and subject to a range of duties in respect of notification and consent (e.g. Sections 28E, 28G, 28H etc).

Sites in NPPF 189

13.13. The protection also extends to the wildlife aspects of the full list of sites referred to in NPPF 189: National Parks, the Broads, National Landscapes (formerly AONB):

Great weight should be given to conserving and enhancing landscape and scenic beauty in National Parks, the Broads and National Landscapes which have the highest status of protection in relation to these issues. The conservation and enhancement of wildlife and cultural heritage are also important considerations in these areas, and should be given great weight in National Parks and the Broads. The scale and extent of development within all these designated areas should be limited, while development within their setting should be sensitively located and designed to avoid or minimise adverse impacts on the designated areas.

13.14. The reference here to conservation and enhancement of wildlife stems from Section 59 of the Natural Environment and Rural Communities Act 2006 which amended the criteria for designation in section 5 of the National Parks and Access to the Countryside Act 1949 to include this objective.

Irreplaceable habitats

13.15. The term "irreplaceable habitats" is defined in the NPPF Glossary as:

> *Habitats which would be technically very difficult (or take a very significant time) to restore, recreate or replace once destroyed, taking into account their age, uniqueness, species diversity or rarity. They include ancient woodland, ancient and veteran trees, blanket bog, limestone pavement, sand dunes, salt marsh and lowland fen."*
>
> ...
>
> *Ancient or veteran tree: A tree which, because of its age, size and condition, is of exceptional biodiversity, cultural or heritage value. All ancient trees are veteran trees. Not all veteran trees are old enough to be ancient, but are old relative to other trees of the same species. Very few trees of any species reach the ancient life-stage.*
>
> *Ancient woodland: An area that has been wooded continuously since at least 1600 AD. It includes ancient semi-natural woodland and plantations on ancient woodland sites (PAWS).*

Strong Reason for Refusal on Habitats/Ecological Grounds

13.16. A "strong reason" for refusing development must be interpreted in accordance with the Habitats Regulations, and notably NPPF 193 and NPPF 195:

193. When determining planning applications, local planning authorities should apply the following principles:

a) if significant harm to biodiversity resulting from a development cannot be avoided (through locating on an alternative site with less harmful impacts), adequately mitigated, or, as a last resort, compensated for, then planning permission should be refused;

b) development on land within or outside a Site of Special Scientific Interest, and which is likely to have an adverse effect on it (either individually or in combination with other developments), should not normally be permitted. The only exception is where the benefits of the development in the location proposed clearly outweigh both its likely impact on the features of the site that make it of special scientific interest, and any broader impacts on the national network of Sites of Special Scientific Interest;

c) development resulting in the loss or deterioration of irreplaceable habitats (such as ancient woodland and ancient or veteran trees) should be refused, unless there are wholly exceptional reasons and a suitable compensation strategy exists; and

d) development whose primary objective is to conserve or enhance biodiversity should be supported; while opportunities to improve biodiversity in and around developments should be integrated as part of their design, especially where this can secure measurable net gains for biodiversity or enhance public access to nature where this is appropriate.

...

195. The presumption in favour of sustainable development does not apply where the plan or project is likely to have a significant effect on a habitats site (either alone or in combination with other plans or projects), unless an appropriate assessment has concluded that the plan or project will not adversely affect the integrity of the habitats site.

13.17. In short, if the Application development will give rise to a breach in relation to the specified areas of importance, then the Site will not qualify as Grey Belt. These include notably where there will be (1) significant effect on a habitats site (without appropriate assessment confirmation that there will be no adverse effect on integrity); (2) adverse effect on an SSSI (without the necessary exception) or (3) loss or deterioration of an irreplaceable habitat (without wholly exceptional reasons and a compensation strategy).

Habitats/Ecology Evidence

13.18. The Footnote 7 habitats and ecology protections are extensive. The precise kind of evidence that may be required will inevitably depend on the specific site location, the nature of the habitat/asset and the potential mitigation measures.

13.19. Ordinarily an application will need to be accompanied by Preliminary Ecological Appraisal / Assessment and (where applicable) a full Habitats Regulations Assessment sufficient to inform the Appropriate Assessment under the Conservation of Habitats and Species Regulations 2017 (as amended). Any impact on protected trees/ancient woodland would require a bespoke Arboricultural Assessment.[70]

(7) Land designated as Local Green Space

13.20. This exclusion protects land that has been designated as Local Green Space ("LGS") under NPPF 106-108:

> *106. The designation of land as Local Green Space through local and neighbourhood plans allows communities to identify and protect green areas of particular importance to them. Designating land as Local Green Space should be consistent with the local planning of sustainable development and complement investment in sufficient homes, jobs and*

[70] 3343193 and 3343194 – Felbridge (20 February 2025), DL17-L18

other essential services. Local Green Spaces should only be designated when a plan is prepared or updated, and be capable of enduring beyond the end of the plan period.

107. The Local Green Space designation should only be used where the green space is:

a) in reasonably close proximity to the community it serves;

b) demonstrably special to a local community and holds a particular local significance, for example because of its beauty, historic significance, recreational value (including as a playing field), tranquillity or richness of its wildlife; and

c) local in character and is not an extensive tract of land.

108. Policies and decisions for managing development within a Local Green Space should be consistent with national policy for Green Belts set out in chapter 13 of this Framework [45]

[Footnote 45] <u>Excluding provisions relating to grey belt and previously developed land set out in chapter 13.</u>

13.21. Footnote 45 makes clear that Grey Belt is effectively disapplied for LGS Sites and therefore any development would need to take a Very Special Circumstances route.

<u>(8) Protected Landscapes</u>

<u>National Landscape, a National Park (or within the Broads Authority) or defined as Heritage Coast</u>

13.22. The most relevant type of protected landscape is likely to be National Landscape (formerly Areas of Outstanding Natural Beauty (AONB) as most Grey Belt sites will generally be located at some distance from National Parks or Heritage Coasts.

13.23. National Landscapes, National Parks and the Broads benefit from bespoke statutory protection and the additional wording in NPPF 189-191:

189. Great weight should be given to conserving and enhancing landscape and scenic beauty in National Parks, the Broads and National Landscapes which have the highest status of protection in relation to these issues. The conservation and enhancement of wildlife and cultural heritage are also important considerations in these areas, and should be given great weight in National Parks and the Broads. The scale and extent of development within all these designated areas should be limited, while development within their setting should be sensitively located and designed to avoid or minimise adverse impacts on the designated areas

190. When considering applications for development within National Parks, the Broads and National Landscapes, permission should be refused for major development [67] other than in exceptional circumstances, and where it can be demonstrated that the development is in the public interest. Consideration of such applications should include an assessment of:

a) the need for the development, including in terms of any national considerations, and the impact of permitting it, or refusing it, upon the local economy;

b) the cost of, and scope for, developing outside the designated area, or meeting the need for it in some other way; and

c) any detrimental effect on the environment, the landscape and recreational opportunities, and the extent to which that could be moderated.

191. Within areas defined as Heritage Coast (and that do not already fall within one of the designated areas mentioned in paragraph 189), planning policies and decisions should be consistent with the special character of the area and the importance of its conservation. Major development within a Heritage Coast is unlikely to be appropriate, unless it is compatible with its special character.

[Footnote 67] For the purposes of paragraphs 190 and 191, whether a proposal is 'major development' is a matter for the decision maker, taking into account its nature, scale and setting, and whether it could have a significant adverse impact on the purposes for which the area has been designated or defined.

Strong Reason for Refusal on Protected Landscape Grounds

13.24. Where a development conflicts with the tests in NPPF 190, then there will be ordinarily be a strong reason for refusal ("*should be refused*").

13.25. In addition to the NPPF provisions, careful regard should now be had to the statutory duties in respect of National Landscapes/AONBs under s85(A1) of the Countryside and Rights of Way Act 2000:

85(A1) In exercising or performing any functions in relation to, or so as to affect, land in an area of outstanding natural beauty in England, a relevant authority … must seek to further the purpose of conserving and enhancing the natural beauty of the area of outstanding natural beauty.

13.26. The parallel duty for National Parks is set out within Sections 5(1) and 11A(1A) of the National Parks and Access to the Countryside Act 1949 (the latter as amended by Section 245 of the Levelling-up and Regeneration Act 2003):

5.— National Parks.

(1) The provisions of this Part of this Act shall have effect for the purpose—

(a) of conserving and enhancing the natural beauty, wildlife and cultural heritage of the areas specified in the next following subsection; and

(b) of promoting opportunities for the understanding and enjoyment of the special qualities of those areas by the public.

11A.— Duty of certain bodies and persons in relation to the purposes for which National Parks are designated.

...

(1A) In exercising or performing any functions in relation to, or so as to affect, land in any National Park in England, a relevant authority other than a devolved Welsh authority must seek to further the purposes specified in section 5(1) and if it appears that there is a conflict between those purposes, must attach greater weight to the purpose of conserving and enhancing the natural beauty, wildlife and cultural heritage of the area comprised in the National Park.

13.27. In *New Forest National Park Authority v SSHCLG* [2025] EWHC 726 (Admin), the High Court (Mould J) held at [86]-[87]:

"86. As things now stand, in my judgment, when determining an application for planning permission in relation to land within the area of a National Park, it is necessary for the decision maker to consider whether the proposed development will leave unharmed the natural beauty, wildlife and cultural heritage of the National Park in its existing state. If the decision maker is satisfied that the proposed development will leave the natural beauty, wildlife and cultural heritage of the National Park unharmed, he or she may grant planning permission on the basis that he or she has thereby discharged the duty under section 11A(1A) of the 1949 Act to seek to further the statutory purpose under section 5(1)(a) of that Act. In such a case, the decision maker will have properly sought to further the statutory purpose of conserving and enhancing the natural beauty, wildlife and cultural

heritage of the National Park, by satisfying themselves that to grant planning permission for the proposed development will leave the specified characteristics of the National Park unharmed.

87. The same analysis applies in relation to the second statutory purpose under section 5(1)(b) of the 1949 Act. Provided that the decision maker is satisfied that the proposed development will, if permitted, not diminish the opportunities for the understanding and enjoyment of the special qualities of the National Park by the public, he or she will have discharged the duty under section 11A(1A) of the 1949 Act."

13.28. Particular care will therefore be required with those sites that are not within the National Landscape or the National Park, but may be argued to fall within their setting. If the Site is at some distance from the relevant landscape, then a finding of "no harm" may be entirely justified, however, the statutory duty will still have to be referred to and the relevant NPPF tests applied. [71]

Protected Landscape Evidence

13.29. Any development that is within one of the protected landscape areas or within its setting would need to *at least* be accompanied by detailed landscape evidence, ordinarily in the form of a Landscape and Visual Impact Assessment.

13.30. However, the requisite evidence base for development within the protected landscape area boundaries would extend far wider to cover each of the components of NPPF 190(a)-(c). There may also be significant scrutiny of design matters, as presented in the Design and Access Statement.

---

71 3347410 – Wrotham, Sevenoaks (13 February 2025), DL15-16 and 41

(9) Heritage

Footnote 7[e]: Designated heritage assets (and other heritage assets of archaeological interest referred to in footnote 75)

13.31. Designated heritage assets are defined in the Glossary, and specifically distinguished from non-designated assets:

Designated heritage asset: A World Heritage Site, Scheduled Monument, Listed Building, Protected Wreck Site, Registered Park and Garden, Registered Battlefield or Conservation Area designated under the relevant legislation.

Heritage asset: A building, monument, site, place, area or landscape identified as having a degree of significance meriting consideration in planning decisions, because of its heritage interest. It includes designated heritage assets and assets identified by the local planning authority (including local listing).

13.32. Footnote 75 provides that:

Non-designated heritage assets of archaeological interest, which are demonstrably of equivalent significance to scheduled monuments, should be considered subject to the policies for designated heritage assets.

Strong Reason for Refusal on Heritage Grounds

13.33. A "strong reason for refusal" will be determined in accordance with the relevant statutory framework and NPPF Chapter 16, notably NPPF 213-215:

213. Any harm to, or loss of, the significance of a designated heritage asset (from its alteration or destruction, or from development within its setting), should require clear and convincing justification. Substantial harm to or loss of:

a) grade II listed buildings, or grade II registered parks or gardens, should be exceptional;

b) assets of the highest significance, notably scheduled monuments, protected wreck sites, registered battlefields, grade I and II listed buildings, grade I and II* registered parks and gardens, and World Heritage Sites, should be wholly exceptional.*

214. <u>Where a proposed development will lead to substantial harm to (or total loss of significance of) a designated heritage asset, local planning authorities should refuse consent</u>, unless it can be demonstrated that the substantial harm or total loss is necessary to achieve substantial public benefits that outweigh that harm or loss, or all of the following apply:

a) the nature of the heritage asset prevents all reasonable uses of the site; and

b) no viable use of the heritage asset itself can be found in the medium term through appropriate marketing that will enable its conservation; and

c) conservation by grant-funding or some form of not for profit, charitable or public ownership is demonstrably not possible; and

d) the harm or loss is outweighed by the benefit of bringing the site back into use.

215. <u>Where a development proposal will lead to less than substantial harm to the significance of a designated heritage asset, this harm should be weighed against the public benefits</u>

13.34. The most commonly encountered statutory duties are those in Sections 66(1) and 72(1) of the Planning (Listed Buildings and Conservation Areas) Act 1990 referring to listed buildings and conservation areas:

66(1) In considering whether to grant planning permission or permission in principle for development which affects a listed building or its setting, the local planning authority or, as the case may be, the Secretary of State shall have special regard to the desirability of preserving the building or its setting or any features of special architectural or historic interest which it possesses.

72(1) In the exercise, with respect to any buildings or other land in a conservation area, of any functions under or by virtue of any of the provisions mentioned in subsection (2), special attention shall be paid to the desirability of preserving or enhancing the character or appearance of that area.

13.35. The case law in respect of Section 66(1) in particular is extensive, and a detailed discussion falls beyond the scope of this book. The lead case remains *Barnwell Manor Wind Energy Limited v East Northamptonshire District Council* [2015] 1 WLR 45, [29], where the Court of Appeal held that *"...Parliament's intention in enacting section 66(1) was that decision-makers should give "considerable importance and weight" to the desirability of preserving the setting of listed buildings when carrying out the balancing exercise"*.

13.36. In *Jones v Mordue* [2015] EWCA Civ 1243, [28], the Court of Appeal further noted that a decision-maker that simply followed the NPPF provisions in the present NPPF 215 would be complying with the statutory duty:

Paragraph 134 of the NPPF appears as part of a fasciculus of paragraphs, set out above, which lay down an approach which corresponds with the duty in section 66(1) . Generally, a decision-maker who works through those paragraphs in accordance with their terms will have complied with the section 66(1) duty. When an expert planning inspector refers to a paragraph within that grouping of provisions (as the Inspector referred to paragraph 134 of the NPPF in the Decision Letter in this case) then – absent some positive contrary indication in other parts of the text of his reasons — the appropriate inference is that he has taken properly into account all those provisions, not that he has forgotten about all the other paragraphs apart from the specific one he has mentioned. Working through these paragraphs, a decision-maker who had properly directed himself by reference to them would indeed have arrived at the conclusion that the case fell within paragraph 134, as the Inspector did.

13.37. In summary, where an application development would give rise to less than substantial harm to a designated heritage asset, and that harm has been accorded considerable importance and weight, but is outweighed by the public benefits, then the Site will qualify as Grey Belt.[72]

Heritage Evidence

13.38. In any case where development is considered likely to fall within the setting of a listed building or a Conservation Area (or any of the designated heritage assets) a bespoke heritage assessment will be required.

(10) Flooding

Footnote 7[f] areas at risk of flooding or coastal change.

13.39. The Footnote 7[f] exclusion is to be interpreted in line with NPPF Chapter 14, most notably NPPF 170-182, especially NPPF 174-175 in respect of the sequential test:

174. Within this context the aim of the sequential test is to steer new development to areas with the lowest risk of flooding from any source. Development should not be allocated or permitted if there are reasonably available sites appropriate for the proposed development in

72 3346228 – Hadlow (21 February 2025), DL12-17

areas with a lower risk of flooding. The strategic flood risk assessment will provide the basis for applying this test.

175. The sequential test should be used in areas known to be at risk now or in the future from any form of flooding, except in situations where a site-specific flood risk assessment demonstrates that no built development within the site boundary, including access or escape routes, land raising or other potentially vulnerable elements, would be located on an area that would be at risk of flooding from any source, now and in the future (having regard to potential changes in flood risk).

177. Having applied the sequential test, if it is not possible for development to be located in areas with a lower risk of flooding (taking into account wider sustainable development objectives), the exception test may have to be applied. The need for the exception test will depend on the potential vulnerability of the site and of the development proposed, in line with the Flood Risk Vulnerability Classification set out in Annex 3.

178. The application of the exception test should be informed by a strategic or site-specific flood risk assessment, depending on whether it is being applied during plan production or at the application stage. To pass the exception test it should be demonstrated that:

a) the development would provide wider sustainability benefits to the community that outweigh the flood risk; and

b) the development will be safe for its lifetime taking account of the vulnerability of its users, without increasing flood risk elsewhere, and, where possible, will reduce flood risk overall.

179. Both elements of the exception test should be satisfied for development to be allocated or permitted

13.40. If it can be established through this exercise that no areas of development will give rise to anything greater than low risk of flooding, then the sequential test is not required to be met.

Strong Reason for Refusal on Flood Risk Grounds

13.41. A development that fails the sequential test or the exceptions test would not ordinarily qualify as Grey Belt, unless it was established in all the circumstances that there was not a "strong reason for refusal". This is presently an area of significant and dynamic change, especially in respect of the context of surface water flooding. Further PPG has been proposed in respect of the conduct of the sequential test.

Flood Risk Evidence

13.42. Where the site is subject to flood risk, then a Flook Risk Assessment and Drainage Strategy will be required to confirm compliance with the NPPF, and potentially Sequential Test and Exception Test assessment documents.

(11) Checklist

13.43. An abbreviated checklist to address the Footnote 7 criterion might include the following:

Q1) Habitats and Ecology:

- Is the site located within (or in a location that would give rise to any effects upon) a habitats site, SSSI, the wildlife aspects of a National Landscape/National Park or an irreplaceable habitat?
- Have all relevant reports/assessments been provided to show no conflict with the relevant statutory tests and NPPF 193 and 195 tests (including any appropriate assessment)?

- Have these conclusions been agreed/confirmed with Natural England and any relevant local nature statutory consultee?

- If not, have these responses been challenged and addressed in the application documentation?

Q2) Protected Landscapes

- Is the site located within or in the setting of a National Landscape, National Park or Heritage Coast?

- Have all relevant reports/assessments been provided to show no conflict with the relevant statutory tests and NPPF 189 and 190, including the duties under s85(1) of the Countryside and Rights of Way Act 1990 and s11A(1A) of the National Park Act and Access to the Countryside Act 1949

- Have these conclusions been agreed/confirmed with Natural England and any relevant local statutory consultee in respect of landscape?

- If not, have these responses been challenged and addressed in the application documentation?

Q3) Heritage

- Is the site located within or in the setting of any designated heritage assets?

- Have all relevant reports/assessments been provided to show no conflict with the relevant statutory tests (e.g. s66(1) of the Planning (Listed Buildings and Conservation Areas Act 1990) and NPPF 215?

- Have these conclusions been agreed/confirmed with Historic England and any relevant local statutory consultee in respect of heritage?

- If not, have these responses been challenged and addressed in the application documentation?

<u>Q4) Flood Risk</u>

- Is the site subject to a risk of flooding from any source?

- Have all relevant reports/assessments been provided to show that the risk of flooding is low in all cases?

- Alternatively, has a sequential test and exceptions test been carried out?

- Have these conclusions been agreed/confirmed with the Environment Agency, LLFA and the LPA itself?

- If not, have these responses been challenged and addressed in the application documentation?

CHAPTER FOURTEEN

ALL GREEN BELT PURPOSES ACROSS THE WHOLE PLAN AREA

(1) The NPPF Text

14.1. NPPF 155(a) contains a concluding provision, which controls for wider Green Belt harm:

155. The development of homes, commercial and other development in the Green Belt should also not be regarded as inappropriate where all the following apply:

a. The development would utilise grey belt land and ***would not fundamentally undermine the purposes (taken together) of the remaining Green Belt across the area of the plan****;*

[NPPF 143]

143. Green Belt serves 5 purposes:

(a) to check the unrestricted sprawl of large built-up areas;

(b) to prevent neighbouring towns merging into one another;

(c) to assist in safeguarding the countryside from encroachment;

(d) to preserve the setting and special character of historic towns; and

(e) to assist in urban regeneration, by encouraging the recycling of derelict and other urban land.

(2) The PPG Text

14.2. The PPG explains this test in several ways, first in the plan-making context:[73]

> ***How can the impact of releasing or development on the remaining Green Belt in the plan area be assessed?***
>
> *A Green Belt assessment should also consider the extent to which release or development of Green Belt land (including but not limited to grey belt land) would fundamentally undermine the purposes (taken together) of the remaining Green Belt across the plan area as whole.*
>
> *In reaching this judgement, authorities should consider whether, or the extent to which, the release or development of Green Belt Land would affect the ability of all the remaining Green Belt across the area of the plan from serving all five of the Green Belt purposes in a meaningful way.*

14.3. The term "meaningful way" is opaque, but evidently envisages a high threshold.

14.4. In the decision-taking context, it is further explained that:

> **How can Green Belt assessments be used in the development management process?**[74]
>
> *An assessment of Green Belt will (alongside other considerations) inform the determination of applications which involve reaching a judgement as to whether proposals utilise grey belt land and whether development of the site would fundamentally undermine the purposes of the remaining Green Belt across the plan area.*

---

[73] Paragraph: 008 Reference ID: 64-008-20250225

[74] Paragraph: 009 Reference ID: 64-009-20250225

Where grey belt sites are not identified in existing plans or Green Belt assessments, it is expected that authorities should consider evidence, in light of this guidance, on:

...

whether development of the site would <u>fundamentally undermine the purposes of the remaining Green Belt across the plan area</u>, as set out in national policy and this guidance.

14.5. The PPG does not provide any further guidance on how to interpret Purposes C (NPPF 143(c)) and E (NPPF 143(e)).

<u>(3) The Nature of the Test</u>

<u>The Nature of the Test</u>

14.6. This aspect of Criterion A is not a test that should regularly be breached for at least three reasons.

14.7. First, the unit of assessment is the <u>whole</u> remaining Green Belt across the plan area, which in the majority of cases would be a very large area.

14.8. Second, the threshold is a high one: "not fundamentally undermine".

14.9. Third, whilst the Glossary definition relates to the "land", this test bites only on the "development" itself. The extent to which the purposes are undermined can be mitigated by steps taken within the site itself.

14.10. Hypothetical situations in which the test could be triggered could include where the development is very large, and yet the site/land has somehow not passed the Glossary Definition in terms of strong contribution to purposes A, B and D. Another possible (but still rare) scenario could be where the LPA's Green Belt designated area is relatively small, for example where the authority boundary is located just overlapping the edge of a wider Green Belt. However, in this instance, there would be a strong argument for looking at how much of that neighbouring Green Belt was itself affected, as the portion of Green Belt would be serving the relevant purposes in a cross-boundary way.

14.11. Purposes A, B and D will have been considered in the earlier Glossary Definition assessment, albeit only in relation to the land itself. Accordingly, this Chapter focusses on Purposes C and E, before considering the Purposes as a whole.

(4) Green Belt Purpose C

Green Belt Purpose (c) To assist in safeguarding the countryside from encroachment

14.12. The third Green Belt purpose was not part of the three original 1955 Circular purposes, although paragraph 1 recorded an overarching objective of "*safeguarding surrounding countryside against further encroachment.*" This was echoed in Circular 14/84. Planning Policy Guidance 2 (PPG2) (1988) then crystallised the list as five policies.

14.13. An assessment under NPPF 155(a) would need to consider the terms "countryside", "encroachment" and the broader concept of "undermining the purpose".

Countryside

14.14. The countryside is not defined in legislation but is generally understood to include all land outside the built-up urban area. It will often be designated as such in the adopted development plan. Whilst it is possible to envisage situations where a site may be described as "peri-urban "or "rural fringe", caution should be applied in seeking to argue the purpose is not engaged at all if the site is located outside a settlement boundary and is otherwise open, without extensive structures upon it. Moreover the NPPF 155(a) test looks to the whole Green Belt area and thus the whole of the countryside that is protected by the designation.

Encroachment

14.15. "Encroachment" is another relatively low threshold term. All development that extends into the countryside will definitionally encroach upon it to some physical extent. Given the overarching objective to keep all Green Belt land permanently open, there will be few cases in which this purpose will not be engaged at all.

14.16. Historically, there has been much debate over the extent to which questions of perception and impact on the wider countryside are engaged. A development that builds up to a certain point on the ground may still be a visible presence across a wider area. Some caution needs to be applied to this approach in the NPPF 155(a) context, as the unit of assessment of the whole Green Belt area is much larger, and accordingly the extent of vantage points and wider countryside affected would ordinarily be extremely large. It is suggested that the better approach is to concentrate on physical encroachment, literally the development footprint itself.

Undermining Purpose C

14.17. The primary question is the extent of wider countryside that will remain across the whole plan area once the Site has been developed.

14.18. Ordinarily a simple comparison of the development's built up area with the wider countryside within the Green Belt will demonstrate that the Site forms only a very small portion of the area.

14.19. Borrowing from the PPG Table in respect of each of Purposes A, B and D, it will ordinarily be highly relevant to note the extent to which the site will be bounded by physical features (both man-made and natural) and the precise relationship with the existing built edge, such that the Site is already physically constrained, and thus the development cannot encroach beyond those limits.

14.20. In addition to this, it may be argued that that the scheme mitigates the extent of any wider harm by the placement of surrounding open space, such that there remains a clearly identifiable (and accessible) countryside area at the development edge. Significant planting at the development edge will also assist in arguing limited conflict with this purpose.

(5) Green Belt Purpose E

Green Belt Purpose (e) To assist in urban regeneration, by encouraging the recycling of derelict and other urban land

14.21. The fifth purpose is the one which is most commonly found not to be engaged. Again, it stems from Planning Policy Guidance 2 (PPG2) (1988).

Urban Regeneration: Encouraging the Recycling of Derelict and Other Urban Land

14.22. The purpose has been examined in a number of different ways in Green Belt Assessments over the years. Some Green Belt Assessments observe that the purpose promotes the use of all brownfield land (irrespective of the extent of derelict or other sites that are actually in need of regeneration). However, a more robust position is that the purpose is only engaged in locations where there is a demonstrable need for urban regeneration, because of an unusually high amount of derelict land (e.g. following industrial decline or historic under-investment).

14.23. This latter approach is more aligned with the policy intent in the Grey Belt context, i.e. the purpose will generally only be engaged where the LPA has extensive brownfield land and has identified areas requiring substantial regeneration, such that a cogent case can be demonstrated that the development of the Green Belt (or specifically a Site that has already met the Grey Belt Glossary definition) will impact that objective. Again, however, the unit of assessment is the Green Belt across the whole plan area.

Undermining Purpose E

14.24. It will ordinarily be complex to evidence the extent to which development of a single Green Belt site, normally a greenfield site with lower development costs, may draw investment and energy away from derelict brownfield sites. This will ordinarily require reference to a specific regeneration programme and actual analysis of the impact of diversion of investment. The degree of harm to the purpose will naturally depend upon the scale of the proposal and any clear evidence of impact.

(6) All Purposes

14.25. The NPPF 155(a) final exercise is a comprehensive and cumulative one. The Green Belt Assessment and the Planning Statement should contain a summary assessment of the scale of the developed area within the site, and the remaining Green Belt area, and then a systematic (albeit proportionate) summary of how each of the purposes will be impacted. Undermining one of the purposes (especially Purposes C and E) is not enough, the effect must be across all of them. The NPPF 155(a) final test is unlikely to prove a barrier to development if the Glossary Definition has already been met.

(7) Checklist

14.26. There are a number of different ways to assess NPPF 155(a), especially given the different purposes engaged. A possible structure might include the following:

Q1) Scale

- What is the developed area's size (in hectares)?

- What is the scale of the remaining Green Belt (in hectares)? [A rough estimate should be sufficient, there is no need to account for every recent planning permission, or emerging Plan allocations]

- What proportion of the Green Belt will therefore remain post-development?

Q2) Purposes A, B and D

- In the light of the findings that the site/land does not make a strong contribution to Purposes A, B and D, how far can it said that there is any other undermining of these purposes?

Q3) Purpose C

- Is the development site in the countryside?

- How far will the development encroach into that countryside?

- What extent of wider countryside will still be retained within the Green Belt across the whole Plan area?

- Will the Purpose across the whole plan area be "undermined" by the development ?

Q4) Purpose E

- How much derelict or other urban land in need of regeneration is there across the whole Plan area?

- Is the Green Belt performing an identifiable role in assisting in urban regeneration of that land? Has this been specifically evidenced?

- Given the development's specific size, would it harm urban regeneration across the whole Plan area?

Q5) All purposes

- Overall, would the development fundamentally undermine the purposes (taken together) of the remaining Green Belt across the area of the plan?

CHAPTER FIFTEEN

DEMONSTRABLE UNMET NEED

(1) The NPPF Text

15.1. NPPF 155(b) aka Criterion B provides a single test, alongside footnote 56:

> *b. There is a demonstrable unmet need for the type of development proposed* [FN56]*;*

> *(56) Which, in the case of applications involving the provision of housing, means the lack of a five year supply of deliverable housing sites, including the relevant buffer where applicable, or where the Housing Delivery Tests was below 75% of the housing requirement over the previous 3 years; and in the case of traveller sites means the lack of a 5 year supply of deliverable traveller sites assessed in line with Planning Policy for Traveller sites.*

(2) The PPG Text

15.2. The PPG contains no guidance on how the term "demonstrable unmet need" is to be calculated, although there is extensive guidance on land need & availability in the PPG Chapters on Housing and Economic Needs Assessment and Housing and Economic Land Availability Assessment.

(3) Housing Land Supply and the Housing Delivery Test

15.3. Footnote 56 ensures that the test is relatively simple and straightforward where there is an agreed shortfall in respect of housing land supply, or where the Housing Delivery Test has not been met to the requisite 75% over the past 3 years. Following the Government's alteration to the standard methodology for Local Housing Need (as set out in the PPG), many more LPAs have accepted in public statements that they do not have a 5YHLS.

15.4. The relevant tests and buffers are explained at NPPF 72, 78 and 79, alongside the Glossary definition of "Deliverable":

Identifying land for homes

72.Strategic policy-making authorities should have a clear understanding of the land available in their area through the preparation of a strategic housing land availability assessment. From this, planning policies should identify a sufficient supply and mix of sites, taking into account their availability, suitability and likely economic viability. Planning policies should identify a supply of:

a) specific, deliverable sites for five years following the intended date of adoption; and

b) specific, developable sites or broad locations for growth, for the subsequent years 6-10 and, where possible, for years 11-15 of the remaining plan period.

78.Strategic policies should include a trajectory illustrating the expected rate of housing delivery over the plan period, and all plans should consider whether it is appropriate to set out the anticipated rate of development for specific sites. Local planning authorities should identify and update annually a supply of specific deliverable sites sufficient to provide a minimum of five years' worth of housing against their housing requirement set out in adopted strategic policies, or against their local housing need where the strategic policies are more than five years old. The supply of specific deliverable sites should in addition include a buffer (moved forward from later in the plan period) of:

a) 5% to ensure choice and competition in the market for land; or

b) 20% where there has been significant under delivery of housing over the previous three years, to improve the prospect of achieving the planned supply; or

c) From 1 July 2026, for the purposes of decision-making only, 20% where a local planning authority has a housing requirement adopted in the last five years examined against a previous version of this Framework, and whose annual average housing requirement 42 is 80% or less of the most up to date local housing need figure calculated using the standard method set out in national planning practice guidance.

79. To maintain the supply of housing, local planning authorities should monitor progress in building out sites which have permission. <u>Where the Housing Delivery Test indicates that delivery has fallen below the local planning authority's housing requirement over the previous three years, the following policy consequences should apply:</u>

a) where delivery falls below 95% of the requirement over the previous three years, the authority should prepare an action plan to assess the causes of under-delivery and identify actions to increase delivery in future years;

b) where delivery falls below 85% of the requirement over the previous three years, the authority should include a buffer of 20% to their identified supply of specific deliverable sites as set out in paragraph 78 of this framework, in addition to the requirement for an action plan.

<u>c) where delivery falls below 75% of the requirement over the previous three years, the presumption in favour of sustainable development applies, as set out in footnote 8 of this Framework, in addition to the requirements for an action plan and 20% buffer.</u>

Deliverable

To be considered deliverable, sites for housing should be available now, offer a suitable location for development now, and be achievable with a realistic prospect that housing will be delivered on the site within 5 years. In particular:

a) sites which do not involve major development and have planning permission, and all sites with detailed planning permission should be considered deliverable until permission expires, unless there is clear evidence that homes will not be delivered within 5 years (for example because they are no longer viable, there is no longer a demand for the type of units or sites have long term phasing plans).

b) where a site has outline planning permission for major development, has been allocated in a development plan, has a grant of permission in principle, or is identified on a brownfield register, it should only be considered deliverable where there is clear evidence that housing completions will begin on site within 5 years.

15.5. Inevitably, where the housing land supply figure begins to approach 5 years, and even is alleged to exceed it, then questions of supply will become more contested with the LPA. All such applications would need to be accompanied by a detailed Housing Land Supply Assessment, identifying all sites where either deliverability or delivery rates are contested in line with the NPPF Glossary definition.

(4) Other Types of Unmet Housing Need

15.6. On one view, all housing cases must establish 5YHLS/HDT shortfalls to show "demonstrable unmet need", otherwise Criterion B cannot be met: "*Which, in the case of applications involving the provision of housing, means the lack of a five year supply of deliverable housing sites* [etc]"

15.7. However there is an arguable case that the footnote 56 definition is not the only route to passing NPPF 155(b) in housing cases, and that the term "means" should not be construed exhaustively.

15.8. The NPPF identifies elsewhere that housing need is not simply a question of pure numerical housing land supply, but of meeting the diversity of needs that now characterise modern society.

15.9. NPPF 61-63 emphasise the importance of meeting housing needs in full, especially for identified groups:

> *61. To support the Government's objective of significantly boosting the supply of homes, it is important that a sufficient amount and variety of land can come forward where it is needed, <u>that the needs of groups with specific housing requirements are addressed and that land with permission is developed without unnecessary delay</u>. The overall aim should be to meet an area's identified housing need, including with an appropriate mix of housing types for the local community.*
>
> *62.. To determine the minimum number of homes needed, strategic policies should be informed by a local housing need assessment, conducted using the standard method in national planning practice guidance. In addition to the local housing need figure, any needs that cannot be met within neighbouring areas should also be taken into account in establishing the amount of housing to be planned for.*
>
> *63. Within this context of establishing need, the size, type and tenure of housing needed for different groups in the community should be assessed and reflected in planning policies. <u>These groups should include (but are not limited to) those who require affordable housing (including Social Rent); families with children; looked after children ;older people (including those who require retirement housing, housing-with-care and care homes); students; people with disabilities; service families; travellers ; people who rent their homes and people wishing to commission or build their own homes.</u>*

15.10. In the context of specialised forms of housing, most notably housing for older people, the wording of NPPF 155(a) would appear flexible enough to argue that even if there is a 5YHLS, then there will still be a broader demonstrable unmet need for that type of development, i.e. as a specialist type of housing. Another example could be custom and self-build schemes where the LPA expressly has an unmet "demand" figure, applying the calculation in Section 2A of the Self-Build and Custom Housebuilding Act 2015.

15.11. The counter-argument that footnote 56 defines the test exclusively, such that the test will no longer apply at all once the LPA recovers a 5YHLS, would seem out of step with the wider intentions of policy to deliver a diverse range of different types of housing to reflect the different types of need. However, if this is the position, then the case may pivot to a VSC reserve position, citing the extent of the need for that specialist type of housing.

(5) Commercial and Employment Development

15.12. For commercial/employment development, more bespoke assessment will be required, either through Employment Land Assessment or an additional argument made by close reference to NPPF Chapter 6 which contains an expanded NPPF 86(c) which emphasises a wide range of types of new development, many of which have tended to be promoted on Green Belt land (including on what would now be considered Grey Belt), alongside NPPF 87:

86(c) pay particular regard to facilitating development to meet the needs of a modern economy, including by identifying suitable locations for uses such as laboratories, gigafactories, data centres, digital infrastructure, freight and logistics;

87. Planning policies and decisions should recognise and address the specific locational requirements of different sectors. This includes making provision for:

a) clusters or networks of knowledge and data-driven, creative or high technology industries; and for new, expanded or upgraded facilities and infrastructure that are needed to support the growth of these industries (including data centres and grid connections);

b) storage and distribution operations at a variety of scales and in suitably accessible locations that allow for the efficient and reliable handling of goods, especially where this is needed to support the supply chain, transport innovation and decarbonisation; and

c) the expansion or modernisation of other industries of local, regional or national importance to support economic growth and resilience.

15.13. There is no formal limit to the kinds of "unmet need" that may arise, and creative, but well-researched and documented cases on evidence will ordinarily have strong prospects of satisfying this test.

15.14. The term "demonstrable" is not synonymous with either "significant" or "substantial", simply that the need has literally been demonstrated, proven with a clear evidence base.

<u>(6) Energy Development</u>

15.15. In the case of renewable energy, e.g. battery storage and solar farms, the case for demonstrable unmet need will ordinarily be agreed, given the strong national policy support and general acceptance that the need for such development is far greater than is currently being supplied.[75]

[75] 3354822 – Land at Wild Fowl Farm (17 February 2025), DL20-21

(7) Transport Development

15.16. A demonstrable need for transport development has also been readily accepted in the early cases, where there is both national policy support and local data identifying need.[76]

(8) Checklist

15.17. The following questions may assist in structuring the case (in shorthand):

Q1) Housing Development

- Does the LPA have a five year housing land supply?
- Was the LPA's Housing Delivery Test score below 75% of the housing requirement over the previous 3 years
- Notwithstanding 5YHLS/HDT, is there a demonstrable need for the specific type of housing across the LPA area?

Q2) Other Development (especially Commercial and Energy)

- Does the adopted development plan recognise a local need for the type of development?
- Does monitoring or other land availability assessment record that need as unmet locally?
- Does the emerging development plan recognise a local need for the type of development?

[76] 3347410 – Wrotham, Sevenoaks (13 February 2025), DL48-60: 24-hour truck stop facility for up to 200 HGVs; 3345318 – Tatton Services (5 March 2025), DL13-16 and DL35

- Has the emerging plan evidence base identified that the need is unmet locally (e.g. through a call for sites, or other interim report)?

- Does national policy recognise a need for the type of development?

- Does any other form of Central Government or regional assessment recognise a need for the type of development?

- Do national or regional documents record that need as unmet?

CHAPTER SIXTEEN

SUSTAINABLE LOCATION

(1) The NPPF Text

16.1. Criterion C / NPP155(c) is another single-sentence test, with cross references to the wider NPPF:

> *c. The development would be in a sustainable location, with particular reference to paragraphs 110 and 115 of this Framework; and*

16.2. NPPF paragraphs 110 and 115 provide:

> *110.* [1] *The planning system should actively manage patterns of growth in support of these objectives.* [2] *Significant development should be focused on locations which are or can be made sustainable, through limiting the need to travel and offering a genuine choice of transport modes.* [3] *This can help to reduce congestion and emissions, and improve air quality and public health.* [4] *However, opportunities to maximise sustainable transport solutions will vary between urban and rural areas, and this should be taken into account in both plan-making and decision-making.*
>
> ...
>
> *115. In assessing sites that may be allocated for development in plans, or specific applications for development, it should be ensured that:*
>
> *(a) sustainable transport modes are prioritised taking account of the <u>vision</u> for the site, the type of development and its location;*
>
> *(b) safe and suitable access to the site can be achieved for all users;*

(c) the design of streets, parking areas, other transport elements and the content of associated standards reflects current national guidance, including the National Design Guide and the National Model Design Code; and

(d) any significant impacts from the development on the transport network (in terms of capacity and congestion), or on highway safety, can be cost effectively mitigated to an acceptable degree through a vision-led approach.

16.3. NPPF 118 requires the production of a transport statement/assessment in the following circumstances:

118. All developments that will generate significant amounts of movement should be required to provide a travel plan, and the application should be supported by a vision-led transport statement or transport assessment so that the likely impacts of the proposal can be assessed.

16.4. The terms "sustainable transport modes" and "vision-led" are defined in the NPPF Glossary:

Sustainable transport modes: Any efficient, safe and accessible means of transport with overall low impact on the environment, including walking and cycling, ultra low and zero emission vehicles, car sharing and public transport.

Vision-led approach: an approach to transport planning based on setting outcomes for a development based on achieving well-designed, sustainable and popular places, and providing the transport solutions to deliver those outcomes as opposed to predicting future demand to provide capacity (often referred to as 'predict and provide').

(2) The PPG Text

16.5. The PPG provides no express guidance on the interpretation of NPPF 155(c) or NPPF 110 and 115.

(3) NPPF 110

16.6. The two paragraphs should be approached systematically, sentence by sentence. They are formally separate, but are still closely inter-related.

Active Management of Patterns of Growth

16.7. The overarching requirement for active management of patterns of growth is a general objective, and is best considered as an introduction to the wider provision rather than a free-standing test.

Significant Development

16.8. The term "significant" envisages a size threshold, i.e. number of units, or scale, giving rise to a commensurately large number of traffic movements. The second and third sentences should be read together: the objective is to prevent a level of development that would give rise to either congestion or emissions (both in respect of air quality and climate change). It is therefore arguable that this test only catches larger forms of development, indeed arguably somewhat larger than the major development threshold (10 dwellings).

Urban v Rural

16.9. The final sentence recognises that opportunities to "*maximise sustainable transport solutions*" may differ between urban and rural areas. That is at least supportive of the proposition that a more positive approach should be taken to rural sites, recognising that they cannot provide every aspect of sustainable transport.

16.10. All of this provides important context for how NPPF 115 should be interpreted.

<u>(4) NPPF 115</u>

16.11. NPPF 115 sets out a four-stage test which should be addressed systematically, ideally by detailed cross-reference to the Transport Statement.

<u>NPPF 115(a): Sustainable Transport Modes</u>

16.12. The Transport Statement should identify which of the sustainable transport modes listed can be used to access the site, in line with the vision-led approach.

16.13. This will ordinarily require a detailed record of walking, cycling and public transport distances, including any relevant improvements or financial contributions that will aid their delivery.

<u>NPPF 115(b): Safe and Suitable Access to the Site</u>

16.14. The second test relates to access <u>to</u> the site, not within the Site itself. The reference to all "users" envisages primarily residents of the site, but also visitors (e.g. family, friends, visitors, deliveries).

16.15. The primary consideration is safety/suitability of the access, i.e. highways safety. However, this must be read consistently alongside NPPF 116, which sets a high threshold:

> *116. Development should only be prevented or refused on highways grounds if there would be an unacceptable impact on highway safety, or the residual cumulative impacts on the road network, following mitigation, would be <u>severe</u>, taking into account all reasonable future scenarios.*

16.16. The next consideration will then be pedestrian access, including by those using wheelchairs, prams/pushchairs or with other constraints on movement. This will often involve an examination of the pavements, their widths and overall condition and any relevant crossing points.

16.17. In line with NPPF 110's fourth sentence, careful regard should be had to the urban-rural split, and the inevitable differences in quality between urban locations and more rural ones. The test does not state that there must be a pavement or walkway in all circumstances. The test turns on "suitability". There must be recognition that rural sites may either involve some element of walking within the road, or may be accessed only by vehicles.

NPPF 115(c): Design

16.18. The third test relates to the highways design of the site itself and is therefore more loosely connected to locational sustainability. Street design, the level and design of the parking may all be relevant to how the site is accessed, but are unlikely to be centre-stage considerations within the NPPPF 155(c) analysis.

NPPF 115(d): Transport Network and Highway Safety

16.19. In a similar fashion to sub-paragraph 115(b), this test falls to be assessed in the wider context set by NPPF 116.

(5) NPPF 11d(ii) and the Presumption in Favour of Sustainable Development

16.20. NPPF 110 and 115 considerations return under the NPPF 11d presumption, such that whether a site that is locationally sustainable will be scrutinised at that stage too.

(6) Transport Evidence

16.21. For many Grey Belt sites which are adjacent to the built-up area, and located closer to existing services, this Criterion may be agreed and is unlikely to be a disqualifying factor. However, the Criterion will generally always benefit from a clear case being presented through a Transport Statement/Assessment as to the extent to which the Site is either already sustainable, or can be made so with additional provision, e.g. new footpaths, investment in public transport or other measures.[77] Where the development is for energy development, e.g. battery storage, regard will be had to the low number of movements required in the operational phase.[78]

(7) Checklist

16.22. The Planning Statement and Transport Statement should include detailed reference to NPPF 155(c), plus NPPF 110 and 115 as follows:

Q1) Development Type?

- What is the development type?

- Will it give rise to regular vehicular movements during its operational phase?

[77] 3339699 – Dormansland (22 January 2025), DL12; Godalming (27 January 2025), DL20; 3342701 – Colney Heath (3 February 2025), DL22-24; 3346228 – Hadlow (21 February 2025), DL30; 3345053 – Fobbing (24 February 2025), DL14; 3346415 – Poole (3 March 2025), DL47; 3352222 –

[78] 3347424 – Great Barr, Walsall (14 February 2025), DL31; 3354822 – Land at Wild Fowl Farm (17 February 2025), DL22

Q2) Development Plan

- What level of the settlement hierarchy is the Site located in?

- Does the development plan recognise that such settlements can make provision for even limited growth?

- Is there any emerging development plan evidence examining the settlement hierarchy and the opportunities for growth across a wider range of settlements?

Q3) Sustainable Transport Modes

- What are the principal local facilities/services and how far are they accessible by road/footpaths?

- What is the walking time to these locations?

- What is the cycling time to these locations?

- What local bus services are available, to which destinations and with what regularity?

- What local train services are available, to which destinations and with what regularity?

Q4) NPPF 110 and Significant Development

- Is the proposal for "significant development", having regard to its scale, type and overall transport movements?

- What are the opportunities to maximise sustainable transport?

- Is the development in an urban location, or a rural location where opportunities to maximise sustainable transport are more limited?

Q5) NPPF 115 and Transport Assessment

- What sustainable transport modes have been prioritised taking account of the vision for the site, the type of development and its location?

- Can safe and suitable access to the site be achieved for all users?

- Does the design of streets, parking areas, other transport elements and the content of associated standards reflects current national guidance, including the National Design Guide and the National Model Design Code?

- Are there any significant impacts from the development on the transport network (in terms of capacity and congestion), or on highway safety, which can be cost effectively mitigated to an acceptable degree through a vision-led approach?

CHAPTER SEVENTEEN

GOLDEN RULE (1): AFFORDABLE HOUSING

(1) The NPPF Text

17.1. NPPF 155(d) and NPPF 156 render the Golden Rules a mandatory requirement for all major housing development in the Grey Belt.

17.2. Importantly, NPPF 156 extends the Golden Rules to non-Grey Belt applications as well:

155. The development of homes, commercial and other development in the Green Belt should also not be regarded as inappropriate where all the following apply:

d. Where applicable the development proposed meets the 'Golden Rules' requirements set out in paragraphs 156-157 below.

156. Where major development involving the provision of housing is proposed on land released from the Green Belt through plan preparation or review, <u>or on sites in the Green Belt subject to a planning application</u>, the following contributions ('Golden Rules') should be made:...

<u>Major development</u> [91]

<u>For housing, development where 10 or more homes will be provided, or the site has an area of 0.5 hectares or more</u>. For non-residential development it means additional floorspace of 1,000m2 or more, or a site of 1 hectare or more, or as otherwise provided in the Town and

Country Planning (Development Management Procedure) (England) Order 2015.

[Footnote 91] Other than for the specific purposes of paragraphs 190 and 191 in this Framework [Note: Applications for development within National Parks, the Broads and National Landscapes and Heritage Coast]

17.3. The major development threshold is controversial as it is out of step with the Town and Country Planning (Development Management Procedure) (England) Order 2015 definition in Article 2:

"major development" means development involving any one or more of the following—

...

(c) the provision of dwellinghouses where—

(i) the number of dwellinghouses to be provided is 10 or more; or

(ii) <u>the development is to be carried out on a site having an area of 0.5 hectares or more and it is not known whether the development falls within sub-paragraph (c)(i)</u>;

(d) the provision of a building or buildings where the floor space to be created by the development is 1,000 square metres or more; or

(e) <u>development carried out on a site having an area of 1 hectare or more</u>;

17.4. The provision is also potentially at odds with NPPF 65 which exempts development below the major threshold:

65. <u>Provision of affordable housing should not be sought for residential developments that are not major developments</u>, other than in *designated rural areas (where policies may set out a lower threshold of 5 units or fewer). ….*

17.5. Nevertheless the definition is strict, as indicated by footnote 91. All housing development on sites above 0.5 hectares must make the contributions requested, and if they do not, they will fall outside the Grey Belt definition.

(2) NPPF 156(a), 157 and 67-68

17.6. Affordable housing is arguably the single most important component of the Government's reforms in respect of the residential sector. Government wishes to see far higher levels of affordable housing delivered, albeit not necessarily at all costs, in a manner that would constrain delivery.

17.7. Golden Rule (1) seeks to set a clear percentage, whilst reducing the scope for dispute as to viability. It is instructive to consider NPPF 156, then 157 and finally NPPF 67-68, alongside the PPG Chapter on Viability.

17.8. Whilst NPPF 156 merely uses the open term "reflects", NPPF 157 is framed in mandatory terms with a very fixed figure.

> *156a. affordable housing which reflects either: (i) development plan policies produced in accordance with paragraphs 67-68 of this Framework; or (ii) until such policies are in place, the policy set out in paragraph 157 below;*
>
> *157.* [1] *Before development plan policies for affordable housing are updated in line with paragraphs 67-68 of this Framework, the affordable housing contribution required to satisfy the Golden Rules is 15 percentage points above the highest existing affordable housing requirement which would otherwise apply to the development, subject to a cap of 50%.* [2] *In the absence of a pre-existing requirement for affordable housing, a 50% affordable housing contribution should*

apply by default. [3] *The use of site-specific viability assessment for land within or released from the Green Belt should be subject to the approach set out in national planning practice guidance on viability.*

[Footnote 60] The 50% cap does not apply to rural exception sites or community-led development exception sites, or if the local planning authority has a relevant existing policy which would apply to the development which is above 50%.

17.9. The 15% additional target is mandatory. Where the 15% increase results in a percentage which does not reflect a full dwelling, it may be possible to agree an additional financial contribution to off-site provision to make up the difference.

17.10. NPPF 67-68 set out a target for new plans, which will only apply once the provisions are fully in force:

67. As part of the 'Golden Rules' for Green Belt development set out in paragraphs 156-157 of this Framework, a specific affordable housing requirement (or requirements) should be set for major development involving the provision of housing, either on land which is proposed to be released from the Green Belt or which may be permitted on land within the Green Belt. This requirement should:

a) be set at a higher level than that which would otherwise apply to land which is not within or proposed to be released from the Green Belt; and

b) require at least 50% of the housing to be affordable, unless this would make the development of these sites unviable (when tested in accordance with national planning practice guidance on viability).

68. The affordable housing requirement for land within or released from the Green Belt may be set as a single rate or be set at differential rates, subject to the criteria above.

(3) The PPG Text

17.11. The PPG Green Belt Chapter directs expressly to the PPG Viability Chapter. The relevant PPG provisions are then framed in very strict terms:

Golden Rules for Green Belt development[79]

Where development takes place on land situated in, or released from, the Green Belt and is subject to the 'Golden Rules' set out in paragraph 156 of the National Planning Policy Framework, site specific viability assessment should not be undertaken or taken into account for the purpose of reducing developer contributions, including affordable housing. The government intends to review this Viability Guidance and will be considering whether there are circumstances in which site-specific viability assessment may be taken into account, for example, on large sites and Previously Developed Land.

Prior to development plan policies for affordable housing being updated in accordance with paragraph 67 in the National Planning Policy Framework, the amount of affordable housing contributions required are subject to an overall cap of 50% (see paragraph 157 of the NPPF). This 50% cap does not prevent a developer from agreeing to provide affordable housing contributions which exceed the 50% cap, in any particular case.

In paragraph 157, the highest existing affordable housing requirement that would otherwise apply means the highest requirement that the local planning authority could seek in line with its existing policy. For example, (a) if a policy is framed as "up to 30%" then the uplift is applied to 30%; and (b) if a policy is framed as "30% subject to viability" then the uplift should be applied to 30% regardless of

79 Paragraph: 029 Reference ID: 10-029-20241212

viability. The percentage uplift should be applied to the proportion of affordable housing that would otherwise be delivered on site.

17.12. Where a zero affordable housing requirement applies, whilst one early decision found the appropriate figure to be 15%,[80] a later decision has confirmed that the default 50% should apply, in the absence of a "clear policy".[81]

17.13. The PPG will have to be updated in due course to provide any different option below NPPF 67(b)'s 50% standard. No target date has been set for the publication of the revised PPG guidance for large sites and PDL. The implication is that Government wishes to see the 15% uplift become established for greenfield sites, without qualification, until new DPDs/Local Plans are adopted.

17.14. The earlier consultation versions exploring "at least 50%" across all sites and the national guidance in Annex 4 evidently were not considered to strike the appropriate balance and would have led to major viability assessment disputes across many sites.

(4) Checklist

17.15. As the Golden Rules are mandatory and relatively strict in their structure, the central requirement for any planning application is an agreement as to the quantum and type of affordable housing that will be provided.

17.16. Where an Application is proceeding to an appeal, then the draft Section 106 Agreement (or Unilateral Undertaking) will need to be prepared in draft in accordance with the Planning Inspectorate's

---

80 3348677 – Land at Wilton Park, Beaconsfield (14 February 2025), DL19-24

81 3354772 – Northaw (25 March 2025), DL31-32

Good Practice Guide [82] and submitted in line with the Inspectorate's Procedural Guide deadlines.[83]

82 https://www.gov.uk/government/publications/planning-obligations-good-practice-advice/planning-obligations-good-practice-advice

83 https://www.gov.uk/government/publications/planning-appeals-procedural-guide/procedural-guide-planning-appeals-england#planning-obligations Section 18.2

CHAPTER EIGHTEEN

GOLDEN RULE (2): NECESSARY INFRASTRUCTURE

(1) The NPPF Text

18.1. NPPF 156(b) is brief and not intended to be complex in application:

156. the following contributions ('Golden Rules') should be made:

...

b. necessary improvements to local or national infrastructure;

(2) The PPG Text

18.2. There is no relevant PPG guidance on the application of the test.

(3) NPPF 58 and Regulation 122 of the Community Infrastructure Levy Regulations 2010

18.3. NPPF 156(b) appears to have a very specific purpose. It ensures that the developer makes full contributions to infrastructure, notwithstanding the higher affordable housing contribution. In other words, there should be no trade-off or transfer of the dispute as to viability to these other components.

18.4. The reference to "necessary" is to NPPF 58 and Regulation 122(a) of the Community Infrastructure Levy Regulations 2010

58. Planning obligations must only be sought where they meet all of the following tests [FN 25]

(a) necessary to make the development acceptable in planning terms;

(b) directly related to the development; and

(c) fairly and reasonably related in scale and kind to the development.

(25) Set out in regulation 122(2) of the Community Infrastructure Levy Regulations 2010.

18.5. Regulation 122 provides:

(2) … a planning obligation may only constitute a reason for granting planning permission for the development if the obligation is—

(a) necessary to make the development acceptable in planning terms;

(b) directly related to the development; and

(c) fairly and reasonably related in scale and kind to the development.

18.6. Such controls are further strictly controlled by the significant case law in respect of materiality and financial contributions (*R(Wright) v Resilient Energy Severndale Ltd* [2019] UKSC 53, citing *Tesco Stores Ltd v Secretary of State for the Environment* [1995] 1 WLR 759).

(4) Evidence and Checklist

18.7. The Planning Statement and any relevant Heads of Terms should expressly refer to the contributions which are being made and the extent of agreement on the improvements to infrastructure.

CHAPTER NINETEEN

GOLDEN RULE (3): PUBLICLY ACCESSIBLE GREEN SPACE

(1) The NPPF Text

19.1. NPPF 156(c) and NPPF 159 are to be read together:

> *c. the provision of new, or improvements to existing, green spaces that are accessible to the public. New residents should be able to access good quality green spaces within a short walk of their home, whether through onsite provision or through access to offsite spaces.*
>
> *159.* [1] *The improvements to green spaces required as part of the Golden Rules should contribute positively to the landscape setting of the development, support nature recovery and meet local standards for green space provision where these exist in the development plan.* [2] *Where no locally specific standards exist, development proposals should meet national standards relevant to the development (these include Natural England standards on accessible green space and urban greening factor and Green Flag criteria).* [3] *Where land has been identified as having particular potential for habitat creation or nature recovery within Local Nature Recovery Strategies, proposals should contribute towards these outcomes.*

(2) The PPG Text

19.2. The PPG further explains:

How can major housing development on land which is released from the Green Belt through plan making, or on sites in the Green Belt, contribute to accessible green space?[84]

The following contributions to accessible green space should be considered:

- [1] *New residents and the wider public should be able to access good quality green spaces which are safe; visually stimulating and attractive; well-designed; sustainably managed and maintained; and seek to meet the needs of the communities which they serve.*

- [2] *Accessible green spaces are areas of vegetation set within a landscape or townscape, often including blue space, which are available for public use free of charge and with limited time restrictions.*

- [3] *Where possible access to green spaces should include safe active travel routes and should be served by public transport, which also means providing the necessary infrastructure (such as footpaths and bridleways).*

- [4] *Proposals should consider how the creation or enhancement of existing green spaces can contribute to the priorities for nature recovery set out within the relevant Local Nature Recovery Strategies, providing greater benefit to nature and contributing to the delivery of wider environmental outcomes.*

- [5] *Where appropriate, authorities should consider the use of conditions or planning obligations. The Community Infrastructure Levy can also be used to fund improvements to existing greenspaces or the provision of new ones. Local authorities*

[84] Paragraph: 012 Reference ID: 64-012-20250225

should consider arrangements for the long-term maintenance of green spaces.

(3) Requirements

Local Standards and the Natural England Guidelines

19.3. The primary requirement in NPPF 159[1] is that local standards (in the adopted plan) should be met.

19.4. Where the LPA has no locally specific standards for the purposes of NPPF 159[2], the Natural England guidelines are to be applied, currently from January 2023.[85]

19.5. The PPG provides limited assistance on how to interpret these. However, the pivotal provision here is the NPPF's term: "short walk of their home" and using this guide, it is possible to interpret the Natural England guidance accordingly.

19.6. The Natural England guidance Foreword sets the following objective:

"*So, the Green Infrastructure Standards aim to support planners in addressing these inequalities through recommending a target for:*

• *everyone to have access to and benefit from good quality green and blue spaces within 15 minutes' walk from home.*"

19.7. Paragraph 2.8 distinguishes standards and targets:

Standard: Everyone has access to good quality parks, green and blue spaces close to home for health and wellbeing, to meet the Accessible

[85] Green Infrastructure Standards for England – Summary – Green Infrastructure Framework – Principles and Standards for England https://designatedsites.naturalengland.org.uk/GreenInfrastructure/Home.aspx

Greenspace Standards, with an initial focus on access to green and blue spaces within 15 minutes' walk from home.

Target: The local authority will aim for x% of people to have access to good quality parks, green and blue spaces close to home for health and wellbeing, to meet the Accessible Greenspace Standards, with an initial focus on access to green and blue spaces within 15 minutes' walk from home by 2030, and y% by 2040 and 100% by date z.

19.8. Chapter 6 explains the Headline Green Infrastructure standards and Chapter 7 explains the "Access to Greenspace Close of Home Target". This is then defined at paragraph 7.1:

7.1 Local Authorities are encouraged to adopt a local Greenspace Close to Home Access target:

Everyone has access to a variety of good quality green and blue spaces within fifteen minutes' walk of their home by date x (local authorities to set date).

7.2 This could be defined in terms of the Accessible Greenspace Standards (Appendix 2):

EITHER a Doorstep OR Local Accessible Greenspace:

• A Doorstep Accessible Greenspace of at least 0.5ha within 200 metres (under 5 mins walk),

• A Local Accessible Natural Greenspace of at least 2ha within 300 metres (5 mins walk from home)

AND a Neighbourhood Accessible Natural Greenspace

• A medium sized Neighbourhood Accessible Natural Greenspace (10ha) within 1km (15 minutes' walk from home).

7.3 <u>As a minimum, there should be an ambition for everyone to have access to a variety of greenspace within 15 minutes' walk from home</u>. This could be a stepping stone to achieving a fuller range of size-proximity Accessible Greenspace Standards.

7.3 Natural England has done initial baseline analysis of the 15 minute target in its Mapping Database, but further work is needed to refine this. It will be available in 2023.

19.9. These are then further explored in Appendix 2 – Accessible Greenspace Standards, specifically:

Size Proximity Criteria

<u>Within 15 minutes' walk:</u>

<u>EITHER a Doorstep OR Local Accessible Greenspace</u>

<u>• A doorstep greenspace of at least 0.5ha within 200 metres, or</u>

<u>• A local natural greenspace of at least 2ha within 300 metres walk from home.</u>

<u>AND</u>

<u>• A medium sized neighbourhood natural greenspace (10ha) within 1km.</u>

19.10. There is considerable further tabulation within the Appendix notably at Table 1.

19.11. Taking all of these elements together, to qualify under the Golden Rules, a development must meet the 15 minute walk size proximity criteria, either by providing this space on site or making a contribution to an off-site location within the required distances.

19.12. The requirement is likely to be interpreted relatively strictly. If residents cannot access a good quality (i.e. qualifying) green space within 15 minutes, then the site will not have met the Golden Rules.

Qualitative Considerations

19.13. The PPG introduces a range of further qualitative considerations, including that the spaces must be "*good quality…safe; visually stimulating and attractive; well-designed; sustainably managed and maintained; and seek to meet the needs of the communities which they serve.*"

19.14. Applicants should therefore be ambitious and positive in the design work that is carried out, so that they can argue strongly for the quality of what is provided. However, the PPG is not intended to complicate the application of the test. Provided that the relevant local standard or Natural England standard is met, there should not be an exhaustive discussion of whether the green space is sufficiently "attractive" or "well-designed".

Access

19.15. "Accessibility" is defined by the PPG as "*available for public use free of charge and with limited time restrictions*". This may be guaranteed by condition, but is often more fully addressed through a Section 106 Agreement, with the establishment of a Management Company which is required to provide access at all times (save for short exceptions, e.g. maintenance).

Safe Active Travel Routes

19.16. The requirement for "safe active travel routes" and "public transport" (and facilitating necessary infrastructure) would appear to relate to off-site green spaces and is only to apply "where possible".

Nature Recovery

19.17. The requirement to "consider" nature recovery, by reference to Local Nature Recovery Strategies should also be fully explained in the Planning Statement or any parallel reports.

Conditions, Planning Obligations and CIL

19.18. The PPG's final advisory note is to consider the range of powers to promote access, fund improvement and ensure their long-term maintenance. Again, this emphasises the importance of early production of a detailed Section 106 Agreement, providing the necessary management and funding (where applicable)

(4) Checklist

19.19. The Planning Statement should reference each of the NPPF and PPG sentences/sub-paragraphs noting carefully the distinction between those elements that are mandatory and those which are merely advisory:

Q1) On-Site Provision

- Is the relevant green space to be provided on site?

- Can the new residents access the green spaces within a short walk of their home?

- Does the green space area meet local standards (where in force)?

- If not, does the green space area meet Natural England standards as set out in the latest guidance?

- Is the green space of good quality (e.g. vegetation/planting, layout, pathways, seating)?

- Will the green space be visually stimulating and attractive?

- Is the green space overall well-designed?

Q2) On-Site Controls

- How will the green space be managed and maintained?

- Has funding been provided through the Section 106 Agreement, or through future arrangements (e.g. service charges)?

- Will there be a management company?

- Is public access to the green space controlled by condition or by the Section 106 Agreement?

Q3) Off-Site Provision

- Is the relevant green space requirement to be met by off-site provision?

- Is this a new green space or an existing green space (e.g. a public park)?

- What is the current quality of that off-site green space?

- Can the new residents access that green spaces within a short walk of their home, applying local standards (where in force) or the Natural England standards?

- Are there safe active travel routes or public transport available to the off-site green space provision?

Q4) Off-Site Controls

- Is that space currently publicly accessible and how is this guaranteed?

- How will the off-site green space be managed and maintained?

- Has funding been allowed for through the Section 106 Agreement?

- Does the LPA allocate CIL payments to the green space's upkeep?

CHAPTER TWENTY

VERY SPECIAL CIRCUMSTANCES AS A RESERVE POSITION

(1) Introduction

20.1. An application or appeal proposal may fail to meet one or more of the Grey Belt Glossary definition requirements and the relevant Criteria, in a number of different ways, for example:

(1) The Site may be found to make a strong contribution to one (or more) of Purposes A, B or D;

(2) There may not be a demonstrable unmet need for a housing development, e.g. on a narrow interpretation of paragraph 56: that the authority can demonstrate a 5 year supply of housing;

(3) The Golden Rules may apply to the development, but the requisite affordable housing contribution is not viable, and therefore cannot be provided.

20.2. This is not an exhaustive list. It includes situations where there may still be a range of powerful positive considerations in favour of development, and relatively limited harms (beyond the Green Belt harms that must be considered for inappropriate development).

20.3. In such circumstances, it is advisable that the Planning Statement and associated supporting documentation set out a reserve position that the development should still be granted permission on the basis of Very Special Circumstances.

20.4. This Chapter sets out a structured approach to such a case. It is merely a summary of the key issues, and cannot be exhaustive. In particular, it does not seek to explain all of the ways in which a VSC case should avoid undermining the earlier Grey Belt submissions. The Planning Statement should not present the VSC case on the basis of "counterfactual"-type arguments: i.e. "if the LPA was to conclude that the Site does make a Strong contribution to Purpose A". This may undermine the central Grey Belt case and be treated as an implied concession. Instead a single consistent line should be taken on all issues.

(2) NPPF 153 and the Structure of a VSC Case

20.5. NPPF 153 sets out the Very Special Circumstances test in full:

153. When considering any planning application, local planning authorities should ensure that substantial weight is given to any harm to the Green Belt, including harm to its openness [55]. Inappropriate development is, by definition, harmful to the Green Belt and should not be approved except in very special circumstances. 'Very special circumstances' will not exist unless the potential harm to the Green Belt by reason of inappropriateness, and any other harm resulting from the proposal, is clearly outweighed by other considerations.

(55) Other than in the case of development on previously developed land or grey belt land, where development is not inappropriate.

20.6. The NPPF defines inappropriate development in a manner largely consistent with the original Circular 42/55, and with earlier versions of PPG2. Put simply, all development is to be regarded as inappropriate save that within the exceptions for 155 (Grey Belt) and 154(a)-(h) (Other Exceptions).

Stage 1: Identify Green Belt Harms

20.7. The fundamental starting point for any Green Belt case reliant on VSC is to begin with a full assessment of Green Belt harms, noting NPPF 153's emphasis that decision-takers: "*should ensure that substantial weight is given to any harm to the Green Belt.*"

20.8. This is the highest weighting in the NPPF, with the only comparable adjective provided in (a) the statutory context of heritage protection (NPPF 212-215) and (b) the supportive context of development of brownfield land (NPPF 125(c)).

20.9. All application/appeal documents should consider the three types of Green Belt harm: (1) definitional harm; (2) harm to openness and (3) harm to Green Belt purposes.

Stage 2: Other Harms

20.10. National policy then requires "other harms" to be added to the Green Belt harm in the balance. This reflects a position first established in PPG2 (1988).

Stage 3: Other Considerations

20.11. The concept of "other considerations" is arguably the most important and yet the most enigmatic in Green Belt and the wider NPPF.

20.12. The term is conventionally understood primarily to cover the benefits of delivering planning permission, which are capable of outweighing the harms (to which substantial weight must attach).

20.13. However, "other considerations" is expressly an unlimited category. It is capable of covering (a) the status of the current and emerging development plan; (b) an absence of alternatives, (c) fallback, (d) personal circumstances and indeed many other matters.

20.14. It is important to note that that the "Golden Rules" under NPPF 156(a)-(c) will apply to all major housing under the Very Special Circumstances test, and they are formally an "other consideration" in their own right. Therefore any limitation in this respect will need to be explained thoroughly.

Stage 4: Clearly Outweighed

20.15. Finally, NPPF 153 requires that the "*other considerations*" must "*clearly outweigh the potential harm to the Green Belt by reason of inappropriateness, and any other harm resulting from the proposal*". This wording is long-standing, reflecting the PPG2 paragraph [3.2] wording. This final requirement imposes an unusually high bar constraint on both applicants/appellants and decision-makers in their reasoning.

(3) The Challenge of the Very Special Circumstances Test

20.16. The Very Special Circumstances test is challenging to apply for at least three reasons, requiring a considerable degree of rigour in the drafting of planning documents.

The Threshold

20.17. First, the test is expressly worded as a very high threshold: the circumstances must be not merely "special" or even "exceptional", but "very special". The intended purpose is to prevent development save in a very limited range of circumstances. All cases must therefore begin from a recognition that they are seeking to achieve a result that is intentionally hard to satisfy. There are no shortcuts. The case must genuinely stand out.

Broad Discretion

20.18. Second, the test is entirely discretionary. There are no internal qualifications or sub-tests (save in respect of renewable energy under NPPF 160, and for Golden Rules compliant major housing development under NPPF 158). There is also very limited additional guidance, for example through the Planning Practice Guidance. Successive Governments have therefore preserved for decision-takers (including the Secretary of State and Ministers on recovered appeals/call-in decisions) a substantial room for manoeuvre and discretion. Identifying precisely what will pass the threshold, especially at scale, is no easy task, and requires a very careful consideration of the proposal and what it can offer.

Political Controversy

20.19. Third, the Green Belt became ever more controversial as a popular and political topic over the decades, particularly in the 2000s and 2010s. The extent to which this has abated under the present Government is still being worked out at application and at appeal.

20.20. The term "Green Belt" continues to receive extensive newspaper and other media coverage, undoubtedly due to partial confusion with the distinct concepts of "greenfield" and "landscape". Many applications therefore generate extensive public interest and high levels of objection.

20.21. A significant majority of decisions int this field will therefore continue to be taken by Planning Committees, until delegation arrangements are altered by the Planning and Infrastructure Bill. The Secretary of State (and in London, the Mayor) also take a strong interest in Green Belt and larger schemes have an increased likelihood of being either recovered (following refusal at first instance) or called-in. In short, the overall "profile" of Green Belt cases is always high.

(4) Stage 1: Green Belt Harms

The Three Types of Harm

20.22. The first of the four key stages for the Very Special Circumstances test is the identification of the three distinct types of Green Belt harm that a proposal may give rise to:

1) Definitional Harm (aka Harm by reason of being "Inappropriate Development")

2) Harm to Openness

3) Harm to the Green Belt Purposes

20.23. The first type of harm "Definitional harm" arises from the single phrase: "*Inappropriate development is, by definition, harmful to the Green Belt*". The second and third types of harm are formally "*other harms resulting from the proposal*", as confirmed by the Court of Appeal in *Redhill Aerodrome v SSCLG* [2014] EWCA Civ 1386, following the earlier decision in *R (River Club) v Secretary of State for Communities and Local Government* [2009] EWHC 2674 (Admin). The High Court held in that case, by reference to the earlier similar text in PPG 2, paragraph 3.2:

"'*Any other harm' must therefore refer to some other harm than that which is caused through the development being inappropriate. It can refer to harm in the Green Belt context, therefore, but need not necessarily do so. Accordingly, I hold that 'any other harm' in para 3.2 is to be given its plain and ordinary meaning and refers to harm which is identified and which is additional to harm caused through the development being inappropriate.*"

20.24. National policy under NPPF 153 requires any harm to the Green Belt to be accorded substantial weight: "*When considering any* *planning application, local planning authorities should ensure that substantial weight is given to **any harm** to the Green Belt.*"

20.25. It is therefore critical that all planning documentation, including Planning Statements, Design & Access Statements, Green Belt Assessments and Proofs of Evidence at appeal grapple with each element individually and provide a clear assessment of the degree of harm that will arise.

20.26. There is no hierarchy between the harms, and little to be gained from omitting a clear judgement on each. A failure squarely to address such an aspect of harm will not assist the planning officer, or on appeal, an Inspector.

20.27. It is essential to bear in mind the built-in imbalance in the VSC test. VSC cases succeed because the other considerations (ordinarily the benefits) clearly outweigh Green Belt harm to which substantial weight must be attached in any event. Applicants who seek to downplay an aspect of harm may also face difficulties defending that position through all stages of determination (e.g. at appeal). Proper acceptance of the level of harm may also provide critical insight into how the package of benefits and mitigation measures that needs to be assembled to outweigh harm.

20.28. As the court observed in the case of *Sefton MBC v SSHCLG* [2021] EWHC 1082 (Admin), the concept of substantial weight is essentially a "metaphor" and therefore early acceptance and recognition of this level will ultimately strengthen the overall case:

33. The Claimant's argument is also flawed by taking metaphorical language unduly literally. The reference to "substantial weight" being given to harm is ultimately a metaphor as is the reference to the harm being "clearly outweighed" by other considerations. The exercise to be undertaken is not one of balancing weights on scales nor even one of saying that harm to the Green Belt is equivalent to a particular weight (say 10 stone) while a different circumstance such as an applicant's family circumstances can never be rated as equivalent to more than a different weight (say 5 stone). Rather the language of weight and weighing is being used to emphasise the importance of the Green Belt. It is used to make it clear to decision makers that they cannot approve inappropriate development in the Green Belt unless the considerations in favour of the development are such as truly constitute very special circumstances so that the development can be permitted notwithstanding the importance given to the Green Belt. …

20.29. In this Chapter, we shall address each of the harms in turn and common methods of addressing these aspects.

(1) Definitional Harm

20.30. The term "Definitional harm" is the simplest type of harm to describe and weigh although it has a more conceptual than physical character.

20.31. The term "inappropriate development" is effectively a label which arises from the later line: "*A local planning authority should regard the construction of new buildings as inappropriate in the Green Belt.*" There is no such thing as "appropriate" development, simply development that is "not inappropriate" because covered by a relevant exception.

20.32. Definitional harm is therefore common to all VSC cases, but is still a matter to be accorded substantial weight.

20.33. In *Doncaster Metropolitan Borough Council v Secretary of State for the Environment, Transport and the Regions* [2002] EWHC 808 (Admin), [68] the High Court observed the importance of not overlooking this part of the test:

"*68. … it is very important that full weight is given to the proposition that inappropriate development is by definition harmful to the Green Belt. That policy is a reflection of the fact that there may be many applications in the Green Belt where the proposal would be relatively inconspicuous or have a limited effect on the openness of the Green Belt, but if such arguments were to be repeated the cumulative effect of many permissions would destroy the very qualities which underlie Green Belt designation. Hence the importance of recognising at all times that inappropriate development is by definition harmful, and then going on to consider whether there will be additional harm by reason of such matters as loss of openness and impact on the function of the Green Belt.*"

(2) Harm to Openness

20.34. The next step is then to determine the degree to which the development will harm the openness of the Green Belt – in the context where preservation of openness of Green Belt land is a fundamental aim:

"*the fundamental aim of Green Belt policy is to prevent urban sprawl by keeping land permanently open; the essential characteristics of Green Belts are their openness and their permanence*"

20.35. Openness has been explored briefly above in Chapter 4. The PPG provides:

What factors can be taken into account when considering the potential impact of development on the openness of the Green Belt?[86]

Assessing the impact of a proposal on the openness of the Green Belt, where it is relevant to do so, requires a judgement based on the circumstances of the case. By way of example, the courts have identified a number of matters which may need to be taken into account in making this assessment. These include, but are not limited to:

[86] Paragraph: 013 Reference ID: 64-013-20250225

- *openness is capable of having both spatial and visual aspects – in other words, the visual impact of the proposal may be relevant, as could its volume*

- *the duration of the development, and its remediability – taking into account any provisions to return land to its original state or to an equivalent (or improved) state of openness*

- *the degree of activity likely to be generated, such as traffic generation*

20.36. The "spatial" and "visual" aspects were confirmed by the Supreme Court in *R (Samuel Smith Old Brewery (Tadcaster) and others) v North Yorkshire County Council* [2020] UKSC 3, endorsing the earlier judgment of the Court of Appeal in *Turner v SSCLG & East Dorset Council* [2016] EWCA Civ 466 and disagreeing with certain aspects of the Court of Appeal's judgment in *Timmins v Gedling Borough Council* [2014] EWHC 654 (Admin), [78] that it was: "*wrong in principle to arrive at a specific conclusion as to openness by reference to visual impact.*"

"*22. The concept of "openness" in para 90 of the NPPF seems to me a good example of such a broad policy concept. It is naturally read as referring back to the underlying aim of Green Belt policy, stated at the beginning of this section: "to prevent urban sprawl by keeping land permanently open ...". Openness is the counterpart of urban sprawl and is also linked to the purposes to be served by the Green Belt. As PPG2 made clear, it is not necessarily a statement about the visual qualities of the land, though in some cases this may be an aspect of the planning judgement involved in applying this broad policy concept. Nor does it imply freedom from any form of development. Paragraph 90 shows that some forms of development, including mineral extraction, may in principle be appropriate, and compatible with the concept of openness. A large quarry may not be visually attractive while it lasts, but the minerals can only be extracted where they are found, and the impact is temporary and subject to restoration. Further, as a barrier to urban sprawl a quarry may be regarded in Green Belt policy terms as no less effective than a stretch of agricultural land....*

25. Turner [14] *"The concept of 'openness of the Green Belt' is not narrowly limited to the volumetric approach suggested by [counsel]. The word 'openness' is open-textured and a number of factors are capable of being relevant when it comes to applying it to the particular facts of a specific case. Prominent among these will be factors relevant to how built up the Green Belt is now and how built up it would be if redevelopment occurs ... and factors relevant to the visual impact on the aspect of openness which the Green Belt presents." (para 14)*

...

Before us there was no challenge to the correctness of this statement of approach. However, it tells one nothing about how visual effects may or may not be taken into account in other circumstances. That is a matter not of legal principle, but of planning judgement for the planning authority or the inspector."

[39] "*As explained in my discussion of the authorities, the matters relevant to openness in any particular case are a matter of planning judgement, not law*."

20.37. Although the *Samuel Smith* judgement upheld an Officer's report that contained relatively limited consideration of visual impacts expressly under openness, the effect in respect of inappropriate development is that all decision-takers should clearly identify their consideration of both spatial and visual impacts. We shall address these twin aspects now.

Spatial Aspect of Openness

20.38. The PPG defines the "spatial" impact of development as equating to its "volume".

20.39. It is often helpful to consider first the 2-dimensional extent of the development (i.e. its footprint) and then the 3-dimensional volumetric aspects (i.e. height/scale, bulk and mass).

20.40. Applicants may consider the spatial impact (1) at the site level and (2) in respect of the wider Green Belt. This needs to be approached with some caution to avoid downplaying the former by reference to the latter.

20.41. Much will depend upon the number of dwellings or other type of buildings (e.g. warehouses) which are proposed for the site. Most major development (e.g. 10+ dwellings) will have a spatial impact upon openness of the Site that needs to be properly graded. A submission that this amounts to very "limited" harm to openness at the site level is unlikely to be accepted by decision-takers. It is therefore always best for an applicant to grapple with the extent of the loss of openness in this context and not seek to downplay it.

20.42. Some ways to argue that there will be a reduced spatial impact may include the inclusion of open space within the development (at both site level and in respect of the wider Green Belt) or the inclusion of a clear landscaping barrier at the development's edge.

Visual Aspect of Openness

20.43. The visual aspect of openness is closely related to spatial matters, but nonetheless formally distinct.

20.44. The visual effect of a proposal is closely aligned with the landscape assessment concept of "visual effects". It will ordinarily be necessary to commission a Landscape and Visual Impact Appraisal or Landscape Visual Appraisal applying the Guidelines on Landscape and Visual Impact Assessment, 3rd edition ("GLVIA")).

20.45. "Visual effects" require consideration of the experience of receptors (i.e. those observing the site from private and public vantage points). It may therefore be relevant to consider the immediate context to the site, for example the extent to which it is surrounded by built form and the nature/scale of that built form. It may also be of some relevance to consider whether the Site is obscured or shielded from public vantage points with consequent reduction in the visual effects from such vantage points.

20.46. Ultimately, it is again important to ensure that all relevant visual effects are recorded and a clear finding reached on the degree of harm arising.

Duration of Development and Reversibility

20.47. Applications for inappropriate development that will be time-limited (for example, renewable energy development) may refer to the lack of permanent loss of openness.

Level of Activity

20.48. Vehicular movements and parking are the most common example of level of activity cited as giving rise to impacts on openness. In the domestic setting, reference is also often made to domestic activities such as play equipment or garden furniture.

20.49. It may also be necessary to refer to storage or other industrial activities within employment sites.

Overall Impacts

20.50. Following *Samuel Smith*, it is permissible to conclude with an overall finding on harm to openness, provided the findings in respect of both spatial and visual aspects are clearly set out and graded.

20.51. In the context of determining whether the sports facilities exceptions was met ("provided they preserve its openness") the High Court noted in *R (Amanda Boot) v Elmbridge BC* [2017]

EWHC 12 (Admin), [27]-[40] that openness could not be "preserved" if there was any adverse impact, agreeing with submissions to this effect ([27(i)]:

> "*The ordinary meaning of the word 'preserve' is defined in the OED as meaning, ' to keep safe from injury, harm or destruction ' In South Lakeland DC v Secretary of State for the Environment [1992] 2 AC 141 , at 150 Lord Bridge approved the passage from the judgment of Mann LJ in the Court of Appeal that concluded:*
>
> *"The statutorily desirable object of preserving the character or appearance of an area is achieved either by a positive contribution to preservation or by development which leaves character or appearance unharmed, that is to say, preserved."*

20.52. In a similar way, it is important fully to acknowledge impact. A "limited" impact on any aspect of openness is not a matter to be downplayed to "no harm" or even "negligible harm". It is a specific finding of harm that needs to accorded substantial weight in any event.

<u>3) Harm to Green Belt Purposes</u>

20.53. The Green Belt purposes have been addressed extensively above in Chapters 9, 10, 11 and 14. The key assessment here is the harm that the development will create, although the extent to which the Site contributes to the purpose may be considered en route to that overall finding.

20.54. In the VSC context, outside the Glossary definition, there is no hierarchy or sub-division and therefore each must be assessed in its own right, with clear conclusions reached on the extent of the harm.

20.55. The assessment should be carried out for Purposes A, B and D against the PPG Table,[87] applying the same Strong, Moderate, Weak, None, gradated approach.

20.56. It may be possible to exclude purposes altogether. As observed in earlier Chapters, Purposes A and B are limited to settlements of specific scale (large built-up areas and towns) and Purposes D and E are limited to particular kinds of settlement (historic towns and settlements with urban regeneration). The PPG therefore now provides a clearer basis for identifying no harm. However, almost all cases will involve some harm to Green Belt Purpose C (encroachment of the countryside), and harm to this purpose alone is still sufficient to amount to a relevant harm that must be accorded substantial weight. There is, as yet, no express basis in the PPG or elsewhere for treating Purpose C as a less weighty consideration in the balance, notwithstanding its omission from the Grey Belt purposes.

Conclusions on Harm

20.57. Any harm to the Green Belt must always be expressly conferred substantial weight in the planning balance, and there is no hierarchy of harms (or within the harms). Definitional harm will arise on account of the inappropriate nature of the development and therefore will not be determinative. Harm to openness must be examined in both spatial and visual aspects, and where applicable by reference to duration and activity.

20.58. It is important to clearly set out each of the individual findings in respect of both spatial and visual impacts, even if an overall verdict on openness is reached. The assessment of harm to the purposes requires a careful assessment of the wording of each purpose and the specific geographical locations protected.

[87] Paragraph: 005 Reference ID: 64-005-20250225

20.59. In summary, Green Belt harm requires precision and a realistic approach. Given the structure of the test, the extent of harm will rarely be as determinative to the overall outcome as "other considerations", notably the benefits case.

(5) Stage 2: "Any Other Harm Resulting from the Proposal"

20.60. The second key stage under national policy requires that "any other [non-Green Belt] harm resulting from the proposal" be added to the Green Belt harm prior to the consideration of the "other considerations".

20.61. This is a relatively straightforward position to apply and was confirmed by the Court of Appeal in *Redhill Aerodrome v SSCLG* [2014] EWCA Civ 1386 (reversing the judgment of the High Court below).

20.62. In that case, the Claimant had argued that the wording "any other harm" referred to "any other harm to the Green Belt". The Court upheld the Secretary of State's submissions that this was in fact "any other harm that is relevant for planning purposes, such as harm to landscape character, adverse visual impact, noise disturbance or adverse traffic impact, as submitted by the defendants" (see paragraph 3).

20.63. The judgment is notable today for its consideration of the earlier policy wording under PPG2, paragraph 3.2 which also used the term "any other harm". In an earlier case, *R (River Club) v Secretary of State for Communities and Local Government* [2009] EWHC 2674 (Admin), the High Court had found that this was additional:

"*'Any other harm' must therefore refer to some other harm than that which is caused through the development being inappropriate. It can refer to harm in the Green Belt context, therefore, but need not necessarily do so. Accordingly, I hold that 'any other harm' in para 3.2 is to be given its plain and ordinary meaning and refers to harm which is identified and which is additional to harm caused through the development being inappropriate.*"

20.64. The Court of Appeal upheld the same approach for the new NPPF wording. The judgment merits consideration today, as it makes a number of observations that are of significant importance in understanding both this issue and how to address transitional situations in national policy.

20.65. The earlier PPG2 paragraph 3.2 wording had provided (in full):

"*3.2 Inappropriate development is, by definition, harmful to the Green Belt. It is for the applicant to show why permission should be granted. Very special circumstances to justify inappropriate development will not exist unless the harm by reason of inappropriateness, and any other harm, is clearly outweighed by other considerations. In view of the presumption against inappropriate development, the Secretary of State will attach substantial weight to the harm to the Green Belt when considering any planning application or appeal concerning such development.*"

20.66. The Court of Appeal found that such a change (excluding non-Green Belt harm) would be significant, making the case for development less difficult:

"*15. It is common ground that excluding non-Green Belt harm from "any other harm" in the second sentence of para 88 of the Framework would make it less difficult for applicants and appellants to obtain planning permission for inappropriate development in the Green Belt because the task of establishing "very special circumstances", while never easy, would be made less difficult. All of the considerations in favour of granting permission would now be weighed against only some, rather than all of the planning harm that would be caused by an inappropriate development.*"

20.67. The Court of Appeal then pointed to all the contrary indications for a change to Green Belt policy of this kind. This aspect of the judgment is of considerable contemporary importance in demonstrating how to interpret distinctions between older and newer policy wording when the text of the policy is changed:

"*16. If it had been the Government's intention to make such a significant change to Green Belt policy in the Framework one would have expected that there would have been a clear statement to that effect. Mr Katkowski accepts that there is no such statement. In my judgment, all of the indications are to the contrary:*

(1) While there have been some detailed changes to Green Belt policy in the Framework, protecting the Green Belt remains one of the core planning principles, the fundamental aim of Green Belt policy to prevent urban sprawl by keeping land open, the essential characteristics of Green Belts, and the five purposes that they serve, all remain unchanged. By contrast with para 86 of the Framework, which does change the policy approach to the inclusion of villages within the Green Belt, para 87 emphasises the continuation of previous Green Belt policy (in PPG2) in respect of inappropriate development: "As with previous Green Belt policy …"

(2) The impact assessment in respect of the Framework published by the Department for Communities and Local Government in July 2012 said that "The Government strongly supports the Green Belt and does not intend to change the central policy that inappropriate development in the Green Belt should not be allowed". Under the sub-heading "Policy changes" the impact assessment said that "Core Green Belt protection will remain in place." It then identified four proposed "minor changes to the detail of current policy" which would resolve technical issues, but not harm the key purpose of the Green Belt, "as in all cases the test to preserve the openness and purposes of including land in the Green Belt will be maintained." On the face of it, paras 87 and 88 of the Framework would appear to constitute the "central policy" which the Government did not intend to change.

(3) That there was no intention to change this aspect of Green Belt policy is confirmed by the inspector's statement in para 19 of her decision: that the River Club approach to "any other harm" in the balancing exercise is reflected in decisions by the Secretary of State since the publication of the Framework. <u>We were not referred to any decision in which a different approach has been taken to "any other harm" since the publication of the Framework.</u>

*17. I readily accept that these indications are not conclusive. The Framework means what it says, and not what the Secretary of State would like it to mean: see the authorities cited by the judge in paras 18 and 19 of her judgment. <u>However, if the Framework has effected this change in Green Belt policy it is clear that it has done so unintentionally</u>. Mr Katkowski did not submit that there was any material difference between paras 3.1–3.2 of PPG2 and paras 87–88 of the Framework. He was right not to do so. The text of the policy has been reorganised (see paras 2 and 7 above), but all of its essential characteristics—"inappropriate development is, by definition, harmful to the Green Belt", so that it "should not be approved except in very special circumstances", which "will not exist unless the harm by reason of inappropriateness, and any other harm, is clearly outweighed by other considerations", and the "substantial weight" which must be given to "harm to the Green Belt"—remain the same. Mr Katkowski submitted that the change in policy was to be inferred, not from the wording of paras 87–88, but from the other policies in the Framework which "wrapped around" Green Belt policy, and which were, he submitted, very different in some respects from previous policies in the *282 earlier policy documents which were replaced by the Framework. At an early stage in his submissions he said that at the heart of his case was "Context, context, context".*

<u>Para 88</u>

18. There is no dispute that the words in para 88 should not be construed in isolation, and must be construed in the context of the Framework as a whole, but Mr James Maurici QC and Mr Stephen

Whale for the defendants rightly submit that the starting point must be the words of the policy in para 88. Not only are the words "any other harm" in the second sentence of that paragraph unqualified, they are contained within a paragraph that expressly refers, twice, to "harm to the Green Belt." When the policy wishes to restrict the type of harm to harm to the Green Belt it is careful to say so in terms.

19. The defendants also submit that the judge's approach to "any other harm" would lead to an imbalance in the weighing exercise that is at the heart of para 88. In para 51 of her judgment, having rejected the second and third defendants' submission that the effect on landscape character and the visual impact of the proposed development were harms to the Green Belt, Patterson J continued, at para 51:

"The effect on the landscape character and the visual impact of a development proposal are clearly material considerations but are different from a consideration of harm to a Green Belt. If a development proposal contributed to the enhancement of the landscape, visual amenity and biodiversity within the Green Belt those could well be factors in its favour as part of a very special circumstances balancing exercise."

20. It is common ground that all "other considerations", which will by definition be non-Green Belt factors, such as the employment and economic advantages referred to by the inspector in her decision in this case, must be included in the weighing exercise. On the judge's approach, if an inappropriate development in the Green Belt is beneficial in terms of the appearance of the landscape, visual amenity, biodiversity or, presumably any other matter relevant for planning purposes such as the setting of a listed building, or transportation arrangements, it must be weighed in the balance when deciding whether "very special circumstances" exist; but if the inappropriate development is harmful to any of those non-Green Belt considerations, that harm must not be weighed in the balance when deciding whether "very special circumstances" exist. I accept the defendants' submission that this imbalance is illogical. If all of the "other considerations" in favour of granting permission, which will, by definition, be non-Green Belt factors, must go into the weighing exercise, there is no sensible reason why "any other harm", whether it is Green Belt or non-Green Belt harm, should not also go into the weighing exercise."

20.68. The central point is therefore a straightforward one. "Other harm" includes non-Green Belt harm to create a more straightforward singular balance. A situation that placed such harm outside this equation would evidently be more complex to apply.

20.69. The factors singled out by the court for confirming the lack of any express change are notable, and may prove of assistance in Grey Belt situations as well:

1) Express reference to earlier Green Belt policy within the core national policy text

2) The accompanying impact assessment and any relevant consultation material;

3) The lack of any other comparable Secretary of State or Inspector-level decision;

4) The lack of any expressed intention to alter the policy

5) The immediate context of the words

6) The comparison with "other considerations"

Types of Other Harm

20.70. Non-Green Belt "other harm" is an extremely wide, potentially inexhaustible category. A typical example of non-Green Belt harm on larger schemes is harm in landscape terms or to the character and appearance of the area. However it is important to note that well-contained sites or sites with substantial landscaping proposed may give rise to no significant harm at all, to the extent of giving rise to no conflict with the development plan in this respect.

20.71. Depending on the location of the Site, harms may also arise in respect of many other technical and environmental areas. Other common areas include heritage, ecology/biodiversity, loss of agricultural land, highways and harm to living conditions.

20.72. As noted earlier in Chapter 11, it is very important to apply s66(1) and s72(1) of the Planning (Listed Buildings and Conservation Areas) Act 1990 and the parallel NPPF provisions, and accord the requisite weight to even "less than substantial harm". Heritage harm that is found to be outweighed separately by the benefits is still qualifying harm and weighed in the balance. It should not be recorded as "no harm".

Itemisation and Classification

20.73. It vital that any harm is individually itemised and classified within the supporting planning documentation in a manner that assists the decision-taker. The degree of such harm will therefore need to set out clearly, with a clear scale of weighting. There is no fixed set of standards/descriptors in planning policy. However, an increasingly common approach is the use of multiple adjectives and descriptors in a manner that approximates closely to a gradated scale:

- Very Substantial

- Substantial

- Very Significant

- Significant

- Moderate

- Limited

- Very Limited

- Negligible/No Harm

20.74. Other simpler scales may also be used, noting the observation in *Sefton* as to the metaphorical nature of the concept of "weight".

20.75. If no harm is identified for a given element, then this should not be weighed in the balance, and will be in effect a "neutral" factor.

Removing Harms/Policy Conflicts Ahead of Final Determination

20.76. VSC cases are complex and have an increased likelihood of going to appeal. There is therefore considerable benefit in removing as many harms/policy conflicts as possible well ahead of the issue of any first instance decision (and thereafter at appeal), through the submission of more detailed information or through other negotiation with the LPA. The task of persuasion will be all the harder if the decision-taker has to contend with multiple non-Green Belt factors.

Conclusion on Green Belt Harms

20.77. The topic of "Other Harms" requires a similar rigour and structured approach to that for Green Belt harms. This harm should be carefully itemised and described. Such harms are rarely decisive in their own right, but should not be allowed to become a complicating factor. Because Green Belt cases are complex enough already, it is advisable to remove all policy conflicts as much possible. Wherever possible, look for opportunities to turn initial weaknesses into strengths, by explaining how the development has been carefully designed to mitigate harms.

(6) Stage 3: Other Considerations

20.78. The third stage of the VSC test is to identify and assess the "other considerations" which are capable of clearly outweighing (when assessed as a whole) the Green Belt harm and non-Green Belt harm.

20.79. The term "other considerations" is best considered in two parts:

(a) The Benefits case: The positive results / advantages that will directly result from the development; and

(b) Additional "other considerations": Other circumstances which support the grant of permission

20.80. This section will begin by setting out some of the core principles governing the "other considerations":

- The unlimited nature of other considerations
- Their non-Green Belt nature
- Absence of harm is not an "other consideration"
- The importance of rigour and structure

20.81. It will then address the Benefits case in four parts:

- Development Purpose
- Economic Benefits
- Social Benefits
- Environmental Benefits (including access and visual enhancement)

20.82. The four main other common types of "other consideration" falling outside the category of benefits, but often closely related are:

- Timing (including Local Plan Delays)

- Alternatives

- Fallback

- Personal Circumstances

20.83. The Golden Rules are technically also "other considerations". Permission can still be granted in situations of non-compliance relying on the overall VSC test. For example, NPPF 156(a) involves a very strict approach to viability, and it is arguable that NPPF 156(b) and (c) may operate in similar ways as well – i.e. where infrastructure or recreational benefits cannot be delivered.

The Unlimited Nature of Other Considerations

20.84. It is well-established that the category of "other considerations" is effectively unlimited, and cannot be constrained by jurisprudence from the courts.

20.85. This was emphasised by the High Court in *Brentwood BC v SSE* [1996] 72 P&CR 61 at [67]-[68] in respect of the old PPG2 paragraph 3.2 wording:

> *67. There is thus a balancing exercise between, on the one hand, the harm, whether that is harm by virtue of inappropriate development in the green belt by itself or further actual harm to the green belt—the existence and the degree of the actual harm will weigh in the balance—and, on the other hand, the factors by way of benefit or advantage which may in any particular case outweigh the harm. I do not seek in any way to limit the scope of very special circumstances, which should be for the decision maker. For example, there is, as here, that category*

of cases which are special, the fall back category, where, since the applicant can implement a development causing similar or greater harm, the question of benefits need not arise. Those cases aside, it is clear from PPG2 and the authorities of the Court of Appeal giving guidance in relation to PPG2, that the decision maker is required to look for factors having the character or quality that they lie in the balance against harm .

68. Those factors can vary widely. They can be green belt factors as such; for example, that the development may preserve or increase openness or contribute to green belt functions. They can be other planning factors, such as, perhaps, a building of exceptional architectural quality. They can be factors derived from national or other economic needs. They can be factors relating to personal circumstances. The list is endless and it would not be for the court to restrict it. But, in my judgment, they share the common feature referred to above, that they outweigh harm. In my judgment, this Inspector has misunderstood the nature of the balancing exercise prescribed by PPG2 as that exercise has been explained by the Court of Appeal.

20.86. The Court of Appeal made a similar observation in *Wychavon DC v SSCLG* [2008] EWCA Civ 692, Carnwath LJ observing at [23] that the Secretary of State had made an express decision not to circumscribe the factors that might amount to "other considerations":

"23. At the general level, a judgment must be made as to whether, or in what circumstances, the societal value attached to the protection of the homes of gypsies as individuals can in principle be treated as sufficiently important to outweigh the public value represented by the protection of the Green Belt. That might have been thought to be a matter properly to be addressed by the Secretary of State by way of national guidance. It would perhaps have been more helpful if the PPG or the 2006 guidance had addressed this issue in terms. As it is, the guidance neither excludes nor restricts the consideration of any potentially relevant factors (including personal circumstances). The

PPG limits itself to indicating that the balance of such factors must be such as "clearly" to outweigh Green Belt considerations. It is thus left to each inspector to make his own judgement as to how to strike that balance in a particular case."

20.87. In *R (Basildon District Council) v First Secretary of State and Temple* [2004] EWHC (Admin) 2759 Sullivan J observed at [17] that there was no need for every factor relied upon to be special in its own right:

> *"... in planning, as in ordinary life, a number of ordinary factors may when combined together result in something very special. Whether any particular combination amounts to very special circumstances for the purposes of PPG2 will be a matter for the planning judgment of the decision-taker."*

20.88. These three cases remain important authorities and should be cited within Planning Statements, Proofs of Evidence and other submissions as applicable.

Non-Green Belt Nature

20.89. The Court of Appeal confirmed in *Redhill Aerodrome* that the "other considerations" must be of a non-Green Belt nature:

> *"20. It is common ground that all "other considerations", which will by definition be non-Green Belt factors, such as the employment and economic advantages referred to by the inspector in her decision in this case, must be included in the weighing exercise. On the judge's approach, if an inappropriate development in the Green Belt is beneficial in terms of the appearance of the landscape, visual amenity, biodiversity or, presumably any other matter relevant for planning purposes such as the setting of a listed building, or transportation arrangements, it must be weighed in the balance when deciding whether "very special circumstances" exist; but if the inappropriate development is harmful to any of those non-Green Belt considerations,*

that harm must not be weighed in the balance when deciding whether "very special circumstances" exist. I accept the defendants' submission that this imbalance is illogical. If all of the "other considerations" in favour of granting permission, which will, by definition, be non-Green Belt factors, must go into the weighing exercise, there is no sensible reason why "any other harm", whether it is Green Belt or non-Green Belt harm, should not also go into the weighing exercise."

20.90. There is a potential conflict within the earlier case law on this point, as the earlier judgment of Brentwood specified: "*68. Those factors can vary widely. They can be green belt factors as such; for example, that the development may preserve or increase openness or contribute to green belt functions.*"

20.91. It is submitted that the correct approach to current policy is that the extent to which a development "preserves or increases openness" or "contributes to green belt functions" should be limited to the first stage of analysis – i.e. the extent of the relevant Green Belt harm (as explored above).

20.92. A distinct question is that of beneficial use of the Green Belt and the improvement of access. This is wholly distinct from openness and Green Belt purposes factors.

Absence of Harm

20.93. An absence of harm or a reduced level of harm is not a positive consideration in support of the scheme and therefore cannot amount to an "other consideration". This is an important point that is often overlooked in application submissions.

20.94. As the Court held in *R (Lee Valley Regional Park Authority) v Broxbourne BC* [2015] EWHC 185 (Admin), [47]:

47. … If these are very special circumstances, they all ignore the harm done by reason of the very inappropriateness of this development in the

Green Belt. It is also difficult to see how the absence of some more severe harm to the Green Belt could be a very special circumstance permitting harm by reason of inappropriateness, unless perhaps the development must take place in the Green Belt and the question is which is the least harmful location for it, which was not the issue here. The lower quality of an area of Green Belt land does not reduce the harm done by inappropriate development, and though it may or may not affect any particular specific harm, the way in which the lesser quality of the surface area of the Green Belt might reduce harm to openness would require careful explanation. It may also be right that the development would not result in the actual merging of urban areas; were it in fact to do so, that would be a very strong form of harm. But the absence of such a form of severe harm cannot reduce the harm by reason of inappropriateness or the harm actually done to the openness of the Green Belt. The assertion that the urban area would not "extend excessively into the open countryside" or "unacceptably into high quality Green Belt" in reality is an unrecognised but real assertion of harm by inappropriateness, and of specific but not great harm to openness. That cannot be a very special circumstance at all. Those passages merely set out as positive points a degree of the harm, not very special circumstances clearly outweighing it.

20.95. The list of "other considerations" should therefore be scrupulous in avoiding any reference to a reduced level (or even absence) of harm.

Rigour and Structure

20.96. In the case of *Pertemps Investment Ltd v SSCLG* [2015] EWHC 2308 (Admin), the High Court observed the importance of rigour in the assessment of the other considerations and the overall very special circumstances:

"*25. The meaning and proper application of national policy for development in the Green Belt has been considered by the courts on a number of occasions (see, in particular, Pehrsson v Secretary of State for the Environment [1990] W.L. 753177 , Doncaster Metropolitan Borough Council v Secretary of State for the Environment, Transport and the Regions [2002] EWHC 808 (Admin) , R. (on the application of Basildon District Council v First Secretary of State [2004] EWHC 2759 (Admin) , Wychavon District Council v Secretary of State for Communities and Local Government [2008] EWCA Civ 692 , and more recently Europa Oil and Gas Ltd. v Secretary of State for Communities and Local Government [2014] EWCA Civ 825 , and Redhill Aerodrome Ltd. v Secretary of State for Communities and Local Government [2014] EWCA Civ 1386). I need not explore that case law here. It is not controversial. As the parties in this case accept, the court has consistently recognized both the decision-maker's primary task of ascertaining whether or not the proposal in hand is "inappropriate" development in the Green Belt and the rigour required in considering whether the applicant for planning permission has demonstrated "very special circumstances" to justify the approval of development that is inappropriate."*

20.97. Rigour can be considered as synonymous with structure, or what might be described as "structured argument".

20.98. All application and appeal documentation should apply a "decision-taker-centred" approach (as described at the outset of Chapter 5) that guides the decision-taker as to how they might articulate the planning balance.

20.99. The best Planning Statements, Statements of Case and Proofs of Evidence text on "other considerations" often tend to involve a smaller number of key "other considerations" and are very clearly structured, with each other consideration clearly numbered and explained in its own right. Such submissions identify the core benefits, closely tie them to the respective national policy tests and provide robust and realistic assessments of weight (in tabular form).

20.100. Structured argument is of course always key to the success of any planning application. However VSC cases place particular demands upon applicants, to an extent arguably unmatched in any other field.

20.101. An allied concept to structure is that of specificity. Applications must specify to a significant degree their respective harms and benefits. Whilst some "other considerations" may be ordinary or commonplace, the overall case should not have a generic or general nature. This will be of particular importance when we consider benefits (considered below).

20.102. Finally, it is important to separate out each "other consideration" and not to term it a very special circumstance in its own right. This is both to correctly follow the national policy wording (VSC being the endpoint) and also to reflect the position in *Basildon* (cited above), that each consideration need not be "very special" in its own right.

Benefits Generally

20.103. A planning benefit is a positive outcome or advantage that arises directly from the grant of permission.

20.104. The category of planning benefits is effectively unlimited, however there are general conventions that apply in both Officer's Reports and Inspector's appeal decisions, reflecting the structure of national policy and benefits are normally organised into five key headings:

- The Development Type and Purpose (including meeting need)

- Economic Benefits (aligned with the first pillar of sustainable development)

- Social Benefits (as above for the second pillar)

- Environmental Benefits (as above for the third pillar)

- The Golden Rules (NPPF 158)

20.105. Each of these categories can be broken down further into sub-categories of benefit. However, three rules should be observed, consistent with the importance of structure in the presentation.

20.106. First, the list of individual benefits should not be too long. Some applicants equate "very special" with "numerous", perhaps relying on the *Basildon* formula that "*a number of ordinary factors may when combined together result in something very special*". Overly long lists of benefits risk confusing the decision-maker, or diminishing the impact of the key points. Often, they will include both large and small factors that may appear to be mismatched, potentially diluting the power and impact of the larger factor.

20.107. Second, the benefits list should not "double-count". This is of particular importance when it comes to the development purpose. Occasionally applicants seek to present the benefits of providing housing described in multiple different ways under the three pillars, for example, as a benefit in their own right (development purpose), a social benefit ("providing much-needed housing"), an economic benefit and an environmental benefit ("providing housing in a sustainable location"). The better approach would be a more granular and specific approach.

20.108. Third, particular care applies to benefits that are a legal obligation of the development. The potential factors include (a) s106 contributions towards public services (education, libraries, open space, NHS and police); (b) Community Infrastructure Levy Payments; (c) Council Tax payable by residents. Such payments would be made in any event, and if they are ever considered material benefits, only capable of attracting relatively limited weight.

Development Purpose

20.109. The benefits that will arise directly from the development's principal purpose should anchor the benefits case and be expressed as a specific benefit. This will often be equivalent to meeting a specific type of need, for example:

- The extent to which a residential development provides a specific number of houses/dwellings capable of meeting housing need, as measured in housing needs assessment documents (e.g. Strategic Housing Market Assessments or equivalent)

- The extent to which a commercial / employment development provides jobs or meets local need for employment space, as measured in Employment Land Assessments), or sustaining or expanding an existing business)

- Meeting a need for a rural worker's dwelling or tourist accommodation

- Meeting a need for renewable energy devleopment or other infrastructure

20.110. Expressing the development purpose as the principal or initial benefit reflects how a decision-maker is likely to write up the decision. It also avoids the complexity of double-counting and resultant dilution observed above. It is therefore important not to merge these core aspects of the development purpose with the later three pillars.

Economic Benefits

20.111. The NPPF describes the "economic" pillar of sustainable development as follows:

"An economic objective – to help build a strong, responsive and competitive economy, by ensuring that sufficient land of the right types is available in the right places and at the right time to support growth, innovation and improved productivity; and by identifying and coordinating the provision of infrastructure"

20.112. The analysis of economic benefits should have close regard to the respective chapters of economic policy in national policy, within NPPF Chapter 6. Reference should also be made to other Government documents, including for example, the Milestones for Mission-Led Government (November 2024).

20.113. For a housing development, this will generally include (i) the creation of construction jobs; (ii) training and skills for those in the construction industry; (iii) local expenditure by residents.

20.114. Where a development is expressly for commercial/employment purposes, care should be taken to separate and identify the additional economic benefits that will arise over and above job creation on site, for example training and skills, or the wider economic benefits that may arise from job creation (e.g. increased expenditure in the local community).

Social Benefits

20.115. The NPPF describes the social pillar:

"a social objective – to support strong, vibrant and healthy communities, by ensuring that a sufficient number and range of homes can be provided to meet the needs of present and future generations; and by fostering well-designed beautiful and safe places, with accessible services and open spaces that reflect current and future needs and support communities' health, social and cultural well-being;"

20.116. For housing proposals, the social pillar is closely connected with the delivery of housing, but as observed above, it is best not to separate out pure housing benefits from broader socio-economic ones. Key examples can include health benefits from recreation and access to open space, and the promotion of community interaction in such spaces. A particularly important aspect is the enhancement of the beneficial use of the Green Belt, for example by improving access, providing opportunities for outdoor sport and recreation.

20.117. For commercial/employment proposals, the social benefits may include the health benefits that arise from job creation and increased income.

20.118. Whilst reference is made to good design under this heading, this should be regarded as distinct from aesthetic aspects of good design that should be included under environmental benefits.

Environmental Benefits

20.119. The NPPF describes the environmental pillar:

"*an environmental objective – to protect and enhance our natural, built and historic environment; including making effective use of land, improving biodiversity, using natural resources prudently, minimising waste and pollution, and mitigating and adapting to climate change, including moving to a low carbon economy.*"

20.120. The environmental benefits are generally to be equated with natural/ecological improvements which directly impact the site, e.g. high quality landscaping and biodiversity improvements.

20.121. However, they may also extend to visual or environmental improvements by changing the appearance of a site that already has some built form, for example, the removal of existing buildings, thereby increasing openness.

20.122. Mitigating climate change is a complex area. It will often be argued by local planning authorities that the most common ways to address this, e.g. the installation of electric charging points or contributions towards a bus service are simply policy compliant measures and would arise in any event. It is therefore advisable to identify specific additional measures, for example design features which go beyond Building Standards to improve energy efficiency or water use within the Site.

The Golden Rules (NPPF 156-158)

20.123. The Golden Rules have been explored extensively above in Chapters 17, 18 and 19.

20.124. NPPF 158 provides: *158. A development which complies with the Golden Rules should be given significant weight in favour of the grant of permission.*

20.125. This should not however be seen as a limitation or ceiling on the weight to be accorded the benefits. It is in effect a separate benefit, taking into account the combination of all three types of benefit: affordable housing, infrastructure and accessible green space. Those matters can still be accorded weight in their own right.

20.126. A key question is how to consider the Golden Rules where a qualifying development does not meet them. As explored in Chapter 17, this may occur for example where a scheme does not make provision for sufficient affordable housing either because it is too small (e.g. below 5 units) or because it is of a type that cannot viably provide affordable units or a contribution (e.g. older persons housing). Within the specific context of VSC, this argument will need to be weighed in the whole balance with a comprehensive description of why the relevant Golden Rule has not been complied with, and is otherwise not applicable. The VSC test is not stated to be subject to full compliance with all Golden Rules.

Weighing the Benefits

20.127. It is essential that a Planning Statement or Appeal Proof of Evidence then expressly sets out the weight to be attributed to each identified benefit. It is common to draw these up in a tabular form, which is clear for the decision-taker and will allow cross-comparison between the respective parties' case at appeal.

20.128. As identified above it is common to use the following gradated scale:

- Very Substantial
- Substantial
- Very Significant
- Significant
- Moderate
- Limited
- Very Limited
- Negligible/No Harm

20.129. Considerable care should be taken in respect of how to weigh the development purpose and the individual economic, social and environmental aspects. Reliance on the *Basildon* approach of simply combining a list of benefits together is unlikely to prove successful.

20.130. Given that substantial weight is attached to any Green Belt harm, there should be at least one benefit on the other side accorded "substantial" and ideally "very substantial" weight.

20.131. However the assessment must be realistic. There is little point in exaggerating "moderate" benefits as "significant" ones, without a clear national policy hook or detailed evidence demonstrating how the proposal genuinely stands out.

Timing and Local Plan Delays

20.132. Under the previous NPPF era (2012-2024) the primary "other consideration" for major schemes would ordinarily be the extent of the need for housing and employment land, coupled with the delays to the local plan. This has not necessarily changed under the current Government, but the timescales have been reset (to a limited extent) by the new NPPF, and Annex 1.

20.133. All VSC cases will engage questions of timing: why grant permission now? Why not await the progress of the local plan and the use of the exceptional circumstances test, especially given its far greater width under the new NPPF?

20.134. The answer will generally be found in Government's overarching policy, as expressed in the Written Ministerial Statements and other policy announcements: i.e. to address housing needs or to drive economic growth. However, each case will benefit from an individual justification which brings out the personal/commercial or local factors. Applicants will need to explain the rationale for seeking an early decision without undue delay.

20.135. The evidence base should record the full history of development plan progress during the past 1-5 years, as applicable, especially where there have been express decisions to delay plan-making prior to 2024.

Alternatives

20.136. There is no requirement in national policy to explain why a Green Belt site is being developed over another site as part of a planning application. Whilst a sequential approach is used for Local Plans and exceptional circumstances (NPPF 148), there is no parallel provision for decision-taking. Indeed national policy uses such approaches relatively sparingly (for example in retail development, flood risk and the National Landscape context).

20.137. Nevertheless, applicants for larger schemes often explore whether an alternative site assessment can add to the VSC case, and this can be an "other consideration".

20.138. The general principles on alternatives were summarised in *R (Save Stonehenge) v Secretary of State for Transport* [2021] EWHC 2161 (Admin), [268]-[275]:

> *268. The principles on whether alternative sites or options may permissibly be taken into account or whether, going further, they are an "obviously material consideration" which must be taken into account, are well-established and need only be summarised here.*
>
> *269. The analysis by Simon Brown J (as he then was) in Trusthouse Forte v Secretary of State for the Environment (1987) 53 P & CR 293 at 299-300 has subsequently been endorsed in several authorities. First, land may be developed in any way which is acceptable for planning purposes. The fact that other land exists upon which the development proposed would be yet more acceptable for such purposes would not justify the refusal of planning permission for that proposal. But, secondly, where there are clear planning objections to development upon a particular site then "it may well be relevant and indeed necessary" to consider where there is a more appropriate site elsewhere. "This is particularly so where the development is bound to have significant adverse effects and where the major argument advanced in support of the application is that the need for the development outweighs the planning disadvantages inherent in it." Examples of this second situation may include infrastructure projects of national importance. The judge added that even in some cases which have these characteristics, it may not be necessary to consider alternatives if the*

environmental impact is relatively slight and the objections not especially strong.

270. The Court of Appeal approved a similar set of principles in R (Mount Cook Land Limited) v Westminster City Council [2017] PTSR 116 at [30] . Thus, in the absence of conflict with planning policy and/or other planning harm, the relative advantages of alternative uses on the application site or of the same use on alternative sites are normally irrelevant. In those "exceptional circumstances" where alternatives might be relevant, vague or inchoate schemes, or which have no real possibility of coming about, are either irrelevant, or where relevant, should be given little or no weight.

271. Essentially the same approach was set out by the Court of Appeal in R (Jones) v North Warwickshire Borough Council [2001] PLCR 31 at [22] to [30] . At [30] Laws LJ stated:-

".... it seems to me that all these materials broadly point to a general proposition, which is that consideration of alternative sites would only be relevant to a planning application in exceptional circumstances. Generally speaking—and I lay down no fixed rule, any more than did Oliver L.J. or Simon Brown J.— such circumstances will particularly arise where the proposed development, though desirable in itself, involves on the site proposed such conspicuous adverse effects that the possibility of an alternative site lacking such drawbacks necessarily itself becomes, in the mind of a reasonable local authority, a relevant planning consideration upon the application in question."

272. In Derbyshire Dales District Council v Secretary of State for Communities and Local Government [2010] 1 P&CR 19 Carnwath LJ emphasised the need to draw a distinction between two categories of legal error: first, where it is said that the decision-maker erred by taking alternatives into account and second, where it is said that he had erred by failing to take them into account ([17] and [35]). In the second category an error of law cannot arise unless there was a legal or policy requirement to take alternatives into account, or such alternatives were an "obviously material" consideration in the case so that it was irrational not to take them into account ([16] to [28]).

273. In R (Langley Park School for Girls Governing Body) v Bromley London Borough Council [2009] EWCA Civ 734 the Court of Appeal was concerned with alternative options within the same area of land as the application site, rather than alternative sites for the same development. In that case it was necessary for the decision-maker to consider whether the openness and visual amenity of Metropolitan Open Land ("MOL") would be harmed by a proposal to erect new school buildings. MOL policy is very similar to that applied within a Green Belt. The local planning authority did not take into account the claimant's contention that the proposed buildings could be located in a less open part of the application site resulting in less harm to the MOL. Sullivan LJ referred to the second principle in Trusthouse Forte and said that it must apply with equal, if not greater, force where the alternative suggested relates to different siting within the same application site rather than a different site altogether ([45 to 46]). He added that no "exceptional circumstances" had to be shown in such a case ([40]).

274. At [52-53] Sullivan LJ stated:-

"52. It does not follow that in every case the "mere" possibility that an alternative scheme might do less harm must be given no weight. In the Trusthouse Forte case the Secretary of State was entitled to conclude that the normal forces of supply and demand would operate to meet the need for hotel accommodation on another site in the Bristol area even though no specific alternative site had been identified. There is no "one size fits all" rule. The starting point must be the extent of the harm in planning terms (conflict with policy etc.) that would be caused by the application. If little or no harm would be caused by granting permission there would be no need to consider whether the harm (or the lack of it) might be avoided. The less the harm the more likely it would be (all other things being equal) that the local planning authority would need to be thoroughly persuaded of the merits of

avoiding or reducing it by adopting an alternative scheme. At the other end of the spectrum, if a local planning authority considered that a proposed development would do really serious harm it would be entitled to refuse planning permission if it had not been persuaded by the applicant that there was no possibility, whether by adopting an alternative scheme, or otherwise, of avoiding or reducing that harm.

53. Where any particular application falls within this spectrum; whether there is a need to consider the possibility of avoiding or reducing the planning harm that would be caused by a particular proposal; and if so, how far evidence in support of that possibility, or the lack of it, should have been worked up in detail by the objectors or the applicant for permission; are all matters of planning judgment for the local planning authority. In the present case the members were not asked to make that judgment. They were effectively told at the onset that they could ignore Point (b), and did so simply because the application for planning permission did not include the alternative siting for which the objectors were contending, and the members were considering the merits of that application."

275. The decision cited by Mr Taylor QC in First Secretary of State v Sainsbury's Supermarkets Limited [*[2007] EWCA Civ 1083*] *is entirely consistent with the principles set out above. In that case, the Secretary of State did in fact take the alternative scheme promoted by Sainsbury's into account. He did not treat it as irrelevant. He decided that it should be given little weight, which was a matter of judgment and not irrational ([30 and 32]). Accordingly, that was not a case, like the present one* 3 *, where the error of law under consideration fell within the second of the two categories identified by Carnwath LJ in Derbyshire Dales District Council (see [272] above).*

276. The wider issue which the Court of Appeal went on to address at [33] to [38] of the Sainsbury's case does not arise in our case, namely must planning permission be refused for a proposal which is judged to be "acceptable" because there is an alternative scheme which is considered to be more acceptable. True enough, the decision on acceptability in that case was a balanced judgment which had regard to harm to heritage assets, but that was undoubtedly an example of the first principle stated in *Trusthouse Forte* *(see [269] above). The court did not have to consider the second principle, which is concerned with whether a decision-maker may be obliged to take an alternative into account. Indeed, in the present case, there is no issue about whether alternatives for the western cutting should have been taken into account. …*

20.139. It is important to distinguish three scenarios: (1) Alternative Sites Outside the Green Belt; (2) Alternative Sites Within the Green Belt and (3) Alternative Configurations within the Site.

(1) Alternative Sites Outside the Green Belt

20.140. There is no national policy requirement to conduct a search for sites outside the Green Belt, by contrast with National Landscapes/Areas of Outstanding Natural Beauty. Such an exercise can therefore only ever be voluntary. It is likely only necessary for developments of a major scale, for example very significant commercial schemes.

20.141. In conducting the alternatives assessment exercise, it will be necessary to begin by setting out the size of site required, and then determining how far to allow a tolerance/expansion or reduction either side (e.g. +/- 10/20%). One should then identify the appropriate geographical "area of search", using a methodology based on travel distances or on administrative boundaries (e.g. LPA or adjacent LPAs). It is common for LPAs to request disaggregation of the development; however, this may not always be practical given the development nature and considerations of viability.

20.142. Fundamentally, there is no legal constraint on how this exercise should be conducted. The important thing is to ensure that there is clarity in the methodology applied and in the documentation / tabulation of the decisions as to why other sites are not suitable.

(2) Alternative Sites Within the Green Belt

20.143. There is equally no requirement in policy or practice to conduct a site search for alternative sites within the Green Belt where the development will give rise to a lesser degree of Green Belt harm. This includes any search for Grey Belt sites with lesser impact. NPPF 148 in respect of Local Plans envisages a significant degree of flexibility in the application of this approach in the plan-making context. Such an approach should therefore be avoided as it is likely to be impractical and contrary to the current Government's policy intentions in respect of rapid determination of applications without delay.

(3) Alternative Configurations within the Site.

20.144. For smaller to medium size schemes, it may occasionally be helpful to demonstrate the decisions that have been taken to minimise the impact on openness of the building, for example, at the reduction in height, or placement of development in a location where the impact on openness will be reduced.

20.145. The question of alternative configuration within the site was a key issue in *R (Langley Park School for Girls Governing Body) v Bromley London Borough Council* [2009] EWCA Civ 734 which remains one of the few High Court judgements expressly addressing the question of Green Belt alternatives. The Court of Appeal held that where a project is harmful, applying Government and/or local policy, then it would normally be refused. If it is acceptable taking policy into account then the fact that there is another scheme that might be better is not material. However, if the scheme is judged to be harmful, having applied policy, but nevertheless desirable, the question of whether there is an alternative site may become material.

Alternatives Generally

20.146. In summary, the general lack of a suitable site for the development outside the Green Belt and that the proposal needs to be located in the Green Belt is capable of amounting to an "other consideration", but the exercise is not mandatory and should only be embarked upon cognisant of the resource that will be required and the extensive time that this could take (mapping, site visits, measurement, tabulation and report-writing).

Fallback

20.147. The existence of a fallback position (e.g. an extant planning permission) is also capable of being an "other consideration".

20.148. There have been many cases in respect of the fallback, but the best summary of the applicable principles remains that in *Gambone v Secretary of State for Communities and Local Government* [2014] EWHC 952 (Admin):

> *25. The fallback argument is in truth no more or less than an approach to material considerations in circumstances where there are, or may be, the opportunity to use land in a particular way, the effects of which will need to be taken into account by the decision-maker. That involves a two-stage approach. The first stage of that approach is to decide whether or not the way in which the land may be developed is a matter which amounts to a material consideration. It will amount to a material consideration on the authorities, in my view, where there is a greater than theoretical possibility that that development might take place. It could be development for which there is already planning permission, or it could be development that is already in situ. It can also be development which by virtue of the operation of legal entitlements, such as the General Permitted Development Order , could take place.*

26. Once the question of whether or not it is material to the decision has been concluded, applying that threshold of theoretical possibility, the question which then arises for the decision-maker is as to what weight should be attached to it. The weight which might be attached to it will vary materially from case to case and will be particularly fact sensitive. Issues that the decision-maker will wish no doubt to bear in mind are as set out in the authorities I have alluded to above such as the extent of the prospect that that use will occur. Allied to that will be a consideration of the scale of the harm which would arise. Those factors will all then form part of the overall judgment as to whether or not permission should be granted. It may be the case that development that has less harm than that which is being contemplated by the application is material applying the first threshold, and then needs to be taken into account and weight given to it.

27. However, the question of whether or not there is more or less harm applies at the second stage of the assessment and not at the first stage when deciding whether or not such existing land use entitlements, as may exist in the case, should be regarded as material. In short, there is nothing magical about a fallback argument, it is simply the application of sensible legal principles to a consideration of what may amount to a material consideration, and then the application of weight to that in context in order to arrive at the appropriate weight to be afforded to it as an ingredient in the planning balance.

20.149. In *R(Mansell) v Tonbridge and Malling BC* [2017] EWCA Civ 1314, the Court of Appeal expanded on this slightly:

27. The status of a fallback development as a material consideration in a planning decision is not a novel concept. It is very familiar. Three things can be said about it:

(1) Here, as in other aspects of the law of planning, the court must resist a prescriptive or formulaic approach, and must keep in mind the scope for a lawful exercise of planning judgment by a decision-maker.

(2) The relevant law as to a "real prospect" of a fallback development being implemented was applied by this court in Samuel Smith Old Brewery (see, in particular, paragraphs 17 to 30 of Sullivan L.J.'s judgment, with which the Master of the Rolls and Toulson L.J. agreed; and the judgment of Supperstone J. in R. (on the application of Kverndal) v London Borough of Hounslow Council [2015] EWHC 3084 (Admin), at paragraphs 17 and 42 to 53). As Sullivan L.J. said in his judgment in Samuel Smith Old Brewery, in this context a "real" prospect is the antithesis of one that is "merely theoretical" (paragraph 20). The basic principle is that "... for a prospect to be a real prospect, it does not have to be probable or likely: a possibility will suffice" (paragraph 21). Previous decisions at first instance, including Ahern and Brentwood Borough Council v Secretary of State for the Environment [1996] 72 P. & C.R. 61 must be read with care in the light of that statement of the law, and bearing in mind, as Sullivan L.J. emphasized, "... "fall back" cases tend to be very fact-specific" (ibid.). The role of planning judgment is vital. And "[it] is important ... not to constrain what is, or should be, in each case the exercise of a broad planning discretion, based on the individual circumstances of that case, by seeking to constrain appeal decisions within judicial formulations that are not enactments of general application but are themselves simply the judge's response to the facts of the case before the court" (paragraph 22).

(3) <u>Therefore, when the court is considering whether a decision-maker has properly identified a "real prospect" of a fallback development being carried out should planning permission for the proposed development be refused, there is no rule of law that, in every case, the "real prospect" will depend, for example, on the site having been allocated for the alternative development in the development plan or planning permission having been granted for that development, or on there being a firm design for the alternative scheme, or on the landowner or developer having said precisely how he would make use of any permitted development rights available to him under the GPDO</u>. In some cases that degree of clarity and commitment may be necessary; in

others, not. This will always be a matter for the decision-maker's planning judgment in the particular circumstances of the case in hand.

20.150. In the specific context of Green Belt, *David and Edith Lloyd v SSCLG & Dacorum Borough Council* [2013] EWHC 3076 (Admin), [17] the High Court held:

17. I accept Ms Leventhal's submission that the Inspector dealt with these issues in the right order by considering first the effect of the development itself and second whether any benefits achieved by implementation of that development (by reason of avoidance of the fallback position) amounted to "very special circumstances" outweighing that harm. She referred me to Brentwood DC v SSE and Gray (1996) 72 P&CR 61 in which the Deputy Judge held that an Inspector must approach the matter in this way and not by considering the harm caused by the development as a matter of comparison between it and the fallback position. One might question whether the difference of approach would be likely to affect the outcome in many cases; ultimately the Inspector has to make a planning judgment balancing the harm against the benefit of the proposal, and whether he takes a favourable point as reducing harm or increasing benefit should not in principle change the overall balance. But that is a point for another day; in relation to the present case the Inspector was not wrong to approach the matter as he did.

20.151. Fallback arguments are particularly common in respect of small-scale development or within part-brownfield sites. A successful fallback argument will require careful measurement and mapping of the existing development (where extant), the additional development permitted and the proposed development.

20.152. To pass the first stage, it is necessary to make sure that there is no evidence before the LPA questioning viability or identifying any other significant/insuperable obstacles to delivery. However, this is a low threshold ("more than merely theoretical") and ordinarily not difficult to surmount.

20.153. The second stage is critical, but it should not be overplayed. Ordinarily the lesser degree of harm from the proposal should be Green Belt harm (i.e. a reduction in height or bulk), but merely modest changes are unlikely to be persuasive. A good example of an effective approach can be the collection of the volume of built development in a focal point/single building, rather than dispersed across the site.

Personal Circumstances

20.154. Personal circumstances may include a need for a specific form of accommodation, health, education, family life. This justification has most frequently been pursued in gypsy and traveller cases often involving the placement of a mobile home within the Green Belt.

20.155. The validity of personal circumstances as a free-standing "other consideration" was confirmed in *Wychavon DC v SSCLG* [2008] EWCA Civ 692, [23]-[24]:

> *23. At the general level, a judgment must be made as to whether, or in what circumstances, the societal value attached to the protection of the homes of gypsies as individuals can in principle be treated as sufficiently important to outweigh the public value represented by the protection of the Green Belt. That might have been thought to be a matter properly to be addressed by the Secretary of State by way of national guidance. It would perhaps have been more helpful if the PPG or the 2006 guidance had addressed this issue in terms. As it is, the guidance neither excludes nor restricts the consideration of any potentially relevant factors (including personal circumstances). The PPG limits itself to indicating that the balance of such factors must be such as "clearly" to outweigh Green Belt considerations. It is thus left to each inspector to make his own judgement as to how to strike that balance in a particular case.*
>
> *24 At the particular level there has to be a judgment how if at all the balance is affected by factors in the individual case: for example, on the*

one hand, public or private need, or personal circumstances, such as compelling health or education requirements; on the other, particular factors increasing or diminishing the environmental impact of the proposals in the locality, or (as in this case) limiting its effect in time. This judgment must necessarily be one to be made by the planning inspector, on the basis of the evidence before him and his view of the site."

Conclusion

20.156. In summary, the case on "other considerations" should be (a) focussed, (b) positive, (c) diverse (in the range of benefits), (d) thoroughly evidenced and (e) carefully articulated.

20.157. The courts have expressly defined the nature of "other considerations" capable of amounting to VSC as not akin to "rare". However a decision-taker will scrutinise the extent to which the application genuinely stands out – put simply, how easily this scheme and the relevant benefits/considerations could be replicated on similar sites within the Green Belt. Applicants therefore need to consider hard how the benefits or specific features of the application genuinely stand out.

(7) Stage 4: Overall Decision

20.158. The fourth and final stage is to reach a decision on whether there are "very special circumstances" specifically that: "*the potential harm to the Green Belt by reason of inappropriateness, and any other harm resulting from the proposal, is clearly outweighed by other considerations.*"

"Clearly Outweighs"

20.159. The test is "clearly outweighed". It is not sufficient for the "other considerations" simply to "tip the balance". Whilst there is no specific case law on this point, an applicant will need to emphasise that there is no "flat" balance or equivalence, but a clear exceedance.

Qualitative Nature

20.160. The Courts have emphasised many times that the test is a qualitative one and not a quantitative one. For many years, the leading case was *Wychavon DC v SSCLG* [2008] EWCA Civ 692, where the Court of Appeal held:

> "*the word 'special` in PPG 2 connotes not a quantitative test but a qualitative judgment as to the weight to be given to the particular factor for planning purposes*".

20.161. The principles have most clearly been set out in the modern NPPF era in *Sefton MBC v SSHCLG* [2021] EWHC 1082 (Admin), a very important judgment assessing the historic case law and earlier policy, underscoring the absence of a precise metric for "very special", and the importance of an overall verdict. This judgment is an important guide to decision-takers about the broad nature of their discretion and thus may be particularly helpful in persuading them to grant permission without concern that there is a particular quantum/metric that should be calculated.

20.162. The High Court began by emphasising the *Bloor Homes / St Modwen* principles (explored in Chapter 8) confirming the wide ambit of judgement in respect of matters of weight:

> *27. It is an error of law for a decision maker to fail to apply the NPPF correctly (see Bloor Homes Ltd v SSCLG [2014] EWHC 754 (Admin), [2017] PTSR 319 at [19 (4)]). The NPPF is to be interpreted objectively with its proper construction being a matter of law for the court but the NPPF and other policy statements are to be read as such and not as statutes and their construction by the court is to have regard to their nature as policy statements (see again Bloor Homes Ltd at [19(4)], Tesco Stores Ltd v Dundee City Council [2012]*

UKSC 13, [2012] PTSR 303 at [19] , and Hopkins Homes Ltd v SSCLG [2017] UKSC 37, [2017] 1 WLR 1865 at [22] – [26] and [72] – [75]). The decisions of the Secretary of State and of inspectors appointed by him must set out the reasons for the conclusion reached and must do so adequately and intelligibly but they are to be construed "in a reasonably flexible way" having regard to their nature and audience (Bloor Homes Ltd at [19(1) and (2)]). The court must remember always that matters of planning judgement are matters for the decision maker and not the court (Bloor Homes Ltd at [19(3)]).

28. In Bloor Homes Ltd Lindblom J said, at [19(3)], that the weight to be attached to any material consideration is a matter for the decision maker and not the court. In context Lindblom J was making two points. The first was that matters of planning judgement are for the decision maker and not for the court. The second was that provided relevant matters are considered the weight to be given to any particular relevant matter is, subject to Wednesbury irrationality, a question for the decision maker. It was, rightly, not suggested that this principle precluded Mr. Riley-Smith's argument as to the proper application of paragraph 144 of the NPPF. That argument was that as a matter of law the proper application of the NPPF required a particular degree of weight to be given and for the balancing exercise to be performed in a particular way.

20.163. The Court then addressed an argument by the claimant that there should be a specific weight attached to individual harms:

31. In my judgement the Claimant's interpretation of paragraph 144 fails to take proper account of the nature and purpose of the NPPF and of paragraph 144 in particular. The NPPF is not a statute and is not to be construed as such, rather it is guidance to decision makers and paragraph 144 is giving guidance as to how a particular exercise of planning judgement should be approached. Those making planning decisions must apply the NPPF and must interpret it correctly but the nature of the decision-making process is in turn relevant as to how the policy is to be interpreted. That is because the interpretation is to have regard to the persons by whom and in what setting the policy is to be applied. In that regard it is important to remember the way in which Lindblom LJ in East Staffordshire BC v SSCLG [2017] EWCA Civ 893, [2018] PTSR 88 at [50] characterised the decision making and his consequent warning to the court saying:

"I would, however, stress the need for the court to adopt, if it can, a simple approach in cases such as this. Excessive legalism has no place in the planning system, or in proceedings before the Planning Court, or in subsequent appeals to this court. The court should always resist over complication of concepts that are basically simple. Planning decision-making is far from being a mechanical, or quasi-mathematical activity. It is essentially a flexible process, not rigid or formulaic. It involves, largely, an exercise of planning judgment, in which the decision-maker must understand relevant national and local policy correctly and apply it lawfully to the particular facts and circumstances of the case in hand, in accordance with the requirements of the statutory scheme. The duties imposed by section 70(2) of the 1990 Act and section 38(6) of the 2004 Act leave with the decision-maker a wide discretion. The making of a planning decision is, therefore, quite different from the adjudication by a court on an issue of law..."

32. <u>The Claimant's approach to the interpretation of paragraph 144 is vitiated by an excessively forensic analysis and by a failure to read that paragraph in the light of paragraph 143</u>. It is paragraph 143 which sets out the proposition that inappropriate development is by definition harmful to the Green Belt and it is paragraph 143 which sets out the requirement that such development should not be approved unless there are very special circumstances. The second sentence of paragraph 144 is in terms setting out the only situation in which it will be appropriate to find that there are very special circumstances. It is clearly intended as an elucidation and development of paragraph 143. The first sentence of paragraph 144 is to be read in the light of the paragraph which precedes it and the sentence in the same paragraph which follows it. That first sentence is not setting out a new requirement separate from paragraph 143 but is part and parcel of the *elucidation of paragraph 143 which paragraph 144 is intended to provide.*

33. The Claimant's argument is also flawed by taking metaphorical language unduly literally. The reference to "substantial weight" being given to harm is ultimately a metaphor as is the reference to the harm being "clearly outweighed" by other considerations. The exercise to be undertaken is not one of balancing weights on scales nor even one of saying that harm to the Green Belt is equivalent to a particular weight (say 10 stone) while a different circumstance such as an applicant's family circumstances can never be rated as equivalent to more than a different weight (say 5 stone). Rather the language of weight and weighing is being used to emphasise the importance of the Green Belt. It is used to make it clear to decision makers that they cannot approve inappropriate development in the Green Belt unless the considerations in favour of the development are such as truly constitute very special circumstances so that the development can be permitted notwithstanding the importance given to the Green Belt. The realisation that the reference to weight is ultimately a metaphor highlights a practical difficulty in the approach for which Mr. Riley-Smith presses. How is the decision maker to decide what is equivalent to "substantial + substantial"? The Claimant envisages the balancing exercise being quasi-mathematical but if that is the appropriate exercise then paragraph 144 fails to provide the decision maker with guidance as to the values to be placed in the necessary mathematical calculations.

34. When paragraphs 143 and 144 are read together they can be seen as explaining that very special circumstances are needed before inappropriate development in the Green Belt can be permitted. In setting out that explanation they emphasise the seriousness of harm to the Green Belt in order to ensure that the decision maker understands and has in mind the nature of the very special circumstances requirement. They require the decision maker to have real regard to the importance of the Green Belt and the seriousness of any harm to it. They do not, however, require a particular mathematical exercise nor do they require substantial weight to be allocated to each element of harm as a mathematical exercise with each tranche of substantial weight then to be added to a balance. The exercise of planning judgement is not to be an artificially sequenced two-stage process but a single exercise of judgement to assess whether there are very special circumstances which justify the grant of permission notwithstanding the particular importance of the Green Belt.

20.164. The High Court confirmed this interpretation through a detailed analysis of the policy wording prior to the NPPF under PPG2, notably *Doncaster MBC v SSETR*, [67]-[71], *Wychavon DC v SSCLG [2008] EWCA Civ 692*, [21]-[23], distinguishing *R(Chelmsford BC) First Secretary of State [2003] EWHC 2978 (Admin), [2004] 2 P & C R 677*, all older authorities that had found the same approach applied to PPG2.

20.165. The court then considered *Atkins v Tandridge City Council* [2015] EWHC 1947 (Admin) [35]-[36] and *Redhill Aerodrome Ltd v SSCLG* [2014] EWCA Civ 1386, noting that both had found "*no material change between the effect of paragraph 3.2 of PPG2 and paragraphs 87 and 88 of the NPPF.*

20.166. The court concluded:

49. In my judgement it is highly material to note that paragraphs 143 and 144 are in almost identical language to the former paragraphs 87 and 88. The opening words of paragraph 87 "as with previous Green Belt policy" have not been carried over. However, that is not surprising because there is no need in the current guidance to explain whether it was or was not consistent with previous guidance. However, those opening words of paragraph 87 are revealing as indicating that the new wording was seen as a continuation of the previous policy. The continuation into paragraphs 143 and 144 of the wording of paragraphs 87 and 88 is also noteworthy. In my judgement the "cardinal test" (to adopt Dove J's description) and the "essential characteristics" of the policy (adopting the words of Sullivan LJ) have remained the same through the changing iterations of PPG2, the former paragraphs 87 and 88, and the current paragraphs 143 and 144. The wording has been rearranged but the nature of the guidance and consequently the nature of the exercise to be undertaken by the decision maker have not altered.

...

59. It follows that I have concluded that the approach applicable under PPG2 paragraph 3.2 and paragraphs 87 and 88 of the former version of the NPPF remains applicable in respect of paragraphs 143 and 144 of the current version of the NPPF. It is not necessary for substantial weight to be allocated to each Green Belt harm at the first stage of a two-stage process with each allocated weight being applied at the second stage. Instead the approach enunciated by Sullivan J in the Doncaster case, my understanding of which I have explained at [34] above, remains good law.

20.167. In summary, the Court discouraged a "forensic" or "mathematical" approach to VSC, emphasising the importance of an overall single judgement.

(8) Key Judgments

20.168. The Planning Statement will need to provide a very detailed summary of the case under each of the Stages. The targeted deployment of the relevant case law in a Planning Statement or Proof of Evidence will ensure the necessary focus on the more legal (i.e. policy interpretation) aspects of the test:

1) Openness / Green Belt Harm

- *R (Samuel Smith Old Brewery) v Yorkshire CC* [2020] UKSC 3

- *Turner v SSCLG* [2016] EWCA Civ 46

2) Other Harm

- *SSCLG & Others v Redhill Aerodrome Ltd* [2014] EWCA Civ 1386

3) Other Considerations

- *Brentwood BC v SSE* [1996] 72 P&CR 61
- *Basildon v First Secretary of State and Temple* [2004] EWHC 2759 (Admin);
- *Wychavon DC v SSCLG* [2008] EWCA Civ 692

4) Very Special Circumstances

- *Sefton Metropolitan Borough Council v SSHCLG & Jerry Doherty* [2021] EWHC 1082 (Admin)

(9) Checklist

20.169. A potential VSC checklist cannot be exhaustive. There are myriad different scenarios. Reduced to its simplest:

Q1) Stage 1: Green Belt Harms

- Definitional harm (this is standard)
- What is the harm to openness in spatial terms and visual terms?
- Which Green Belt purposes are affected, and to what degree?
- Has each element of Green Belt harm been identified and individually and collectively been accorded substantial weight?

Q2) Stage 2: Other Non-Green Belt Harms

- What other non-Green Belt harms have been identified?
- What is the weight accorded to those harms individually?

Q3) Stage 3: Other Considerations

- What benefits will arise from the development?
- What weight should be accorded these benefits individually?
- What other considerations weigh in favour of the grant of permission?
- If major housing, does the development comply with all of the Golden Rules?
- When will the emerging development plan be adopted?
- Is there a relevant fallback?
- Are the relevant personal circumstances?

Q4) Stage 4: Clearly Outweigh

- Do the benefits and totality of other considerations clearly outweigh the Green Belt and non-Green Belt harms?
- Are there therefore Very Special Circumstances for a grant of planning permission?

CHAPTER TWENTY-ONE

PRESUMPTION IN FAVOUR OF SUSTAINABLE DEVELOPMENT

(1) Introduction

21.1. A successful Grey Belt case will definitionally have passed NPPF 11d(i), because the Glossary Definition excludes land where Footnote 7 provides a strong reason for refusal.

21.2. The assessment will then pass onto NPPF 11d(ii):

For decision-taking this means:

c) approving development proposals that accord with an up-to-date development plan without delay; or

d) where there are no relevant development plan policies, or the policies which are most important for determining the application are out-of-date [FN 8], granting permission unless:

...

ii. any adverse impacts of doing so would significantly and demonstrably outweigh the benefits, when assessed against the policies in this Framework taken as a whole, having particular regard to key policies for directing development to sustainable locations, making effective use of land, securing well-designed places and providing affordable homes, individually or in combination [9].

...

Footnote 8: This includes, for applications involving the provision of housing, situations where: the local planning authority cannot demonstrate a five year supply of deliverable housing sites (with the appropriate buffer as set out in paragraph 78; or where the Housing Delivery Test indicates that the delivery of housing was substantially below (less than 75% of) the housing requirement over the previous three years. See also paragraph 232.

Footnote 9: The policies referred to are those in paragraphs 66 and 84 of chapter 5; 91 of chapter 7; 110 and 115 of chapter 9; 129 of chapter 11; and 135 and 139 of chapter 12.

21.3. NPPF 232 further provides:

232. <u>However, existing policies should not be considered out-of-date simply because they were adopted or made prior to the publication of this Framework. Due weight should be given to them, according to their degree of consistency with this Framework (the closer the policies in the plan to the policies in the Framework, the greater the weight that may be given)</u>. Where a local planning authority can demonstrate a five year supply of deliverable housing sites (with the appropriate buffer as set out in paragraph 78 and where the Housing Delivery Test indicates that the delivery of housing is more than 75% of the housing requirement over the previous three years, policies should not be regarded as out-of-date on the basis that the most up to date local housing need figure (calculated using the standard method set out in planning practice guidance) is greater than the housing requirement set out in adopted strategic policies, for a period of five years from the date of the plan's adoption.

21.4. This chapter covers some of the issues that will arise in applying the presumption, which has been the subject of much litigation over the years.

(2) Most Important Policies Out of Date

21.5. In the housing context, a housing land supply shortfall below 5 years (or a Housing Delivery Test score of less than 75%) will automatically trigger NPPF 11d(ii) by the operation of footnote 8.

21.6. However, the most important policies can still be "out of date" even if there is a 5YHLS, and certainly in non-housing cases where the footnote does not apply.

21.7. The starting point is *Bloor Homes East Midlands Limited v SSCLG* [2014] EWHC 754 (Admin); [2017] PTSR 1283. The Court considered the older NPPF (2012) paragraph 14 wording and noted:

> *44. In the context of decision-taking paragraph 14 identifies three possible shortcomings in the development plan, any one of which would require the authority to grant planning permission unless it is clear in the light of the policies of the NPPF that the benefits of doing so would be "significantly and demonstrably" outweighed by "any adverse impacts", or there are specific policies in the NPPF indicating that "development should be restricted". The three possible shortcomings are the absence of the plan, its silence, and its relevant policies having become out of date.*
>
> *45. These are three distinct concepts. A development plan will be "absent" if none has been adopted for the relevant area and the relevant period. If there is such a plan, it may be "silent" because it lacks policy relevant to the project under consideration.* ***And if the plan does have relevant policies these may have been overtaken by things that have happened since it was adopted, either on the ground or in some change in national policy, or for some other reason, so that they are now "out-of-date".*** *Absence will be a matter of fact. Silence will be either a matter of fact or a matter of construction, or both. And the question of whether relevant policies are no longer up to date will be either a matter of fact or perhaps a matter of both fact and judgment.*

21.8. In *Suffolk Coastal District Council v Hopkins Homes Ltd* [2017] UKSC 37, the Supreme Court considered the older NPPF (2012) 49 wording: "policies for the supply of housing" and noted:

"I would have regarded the meaning of paragraph 49 itself, taken in context, as reasonably clear, and not susceptible to much legal analysis. It comes within a group of paragraphs dealing with delivery of housing. The context is given by paragraph 47 which sets the objective of boosting the supply of housing. In that context the words "policies for the supply of housing" appear to do no more than indicate the category of policies with which we are concerned, in other words "housing supply policies"."

58. In so far as the paragraph 47 objectives are not met by the housing supply policies as they stand, it is quite natural to describe those policies as "out-of-date" to that extent.

21.9. The NPPF (2012) 49 approach was however abandoned in the NPPF (2018) 11d wording in favour of the "most important policies" trigger.

21.10. The key case on the test is therefore *Wavendon Properties Ltd v SSHCLG* [2019] EWHC 1524 (Admin); [2019] PTSR 2077:

55. [Counsel for the Defendant Secretary of State] *submitted that the correct interpretation is that the exercise required by paragraph 11(d) in relation to the assessment of the question as to whether or not the policies which were of most importance for determining the application were out-of-date is as follows. Akin with* [Counsel for the Claimant], *he contended that* ***the first step was to identify which were the policies which were most important for determining the application. Having done so, it is then necessary for the decision-taker to examine each of those policies, applying the Framework and the approach in the Bloor case, to see whether they are out-of-date. Having done so, the next step required by paragraph 11(d) is an assessment of all the basket of policies most important to the***

decision in the round to reach a conclusion as to whether, taken overall, they could be concluded to be out-of- date or not for the purposes of the decision. If they were out-of-date then the presumption would be triggered.

56. [Counsel for the Defendant] *contended that there was no warrant for the interpretation that once one of the most important policies for determining the application had been found out-of- date the tilted balance would apply. He observed that the policy specifically does not say that the tilted balance would apply when "one of" or "any of" the important policies for determining the application has been found to be out-of-date. To answer the question posed by paragraph 11(d) it is necessary, having identified those policies which are most important for the determination of the application, to examine them individually and then consider whether taken in the round, bearing in mind some may be consistent and some in-consistent with the Framework, and some may have been overtaken by events and others not, whether the overall assessment is that the basket of policies is rightly to be considered out-of-date. That will, of course, be a planning judgment dependent upon the evaluation of the policies for consistency with the Framework (see paragraph 212 and 213) taken together with the relevant facts of the particular decision at the time it is being examined.*

57. [Counsel for the Defendant] *submitted that the First Defendant's decision was consistent with that approach. He drew attention to the fact that the policies referred to in paragraph 10 of the decision letter by reference to the Inspector's report ranged wider than simply policy S10 and WS5. Bearing in mind a larger basket of policies was involved in considering the application of paragraph 11(d) there was nothing in the First Defendant's decision to suggest that paragraph 11(d) had been overlooked or misinterpreted. The First Defendant could be taken to be familiar with the provisions of his own policy, and the fact that he did not apply the tilted balance to the decision in the present case carries the clear inference that his evaluation of all of the policies that were of most importance in determining the application when examined individually and then taken as a whole and in the round were not properly to be considered to be out-of-date.*

58. I am satisfied that [the Defendant Secretary of State's] *interpretation of the Framework in this connection is correct. It needs to be remembered, in accordance with the principles of interpretation set out above, that this is a policy designed to shape and direct the exercise of planning judgment. It is neither a rule nor a tick box instruction. The language does not warrant the conclusion that it requires every one of the most important policies to be up-of-date before the tilted balance is not to be engaged. In my view the plain words of the policy clearly require that having established which are the policies most important for determining the application, and having examined each of them in relation to the question of whether or not they are out of date applying the current Framework and the approach set out in the Bloor case, an overall judgment must be formed as to whether or not taken as a whole these policies are to regarded as out-of- date for the purpose of the decision. This approach is also consistent with the Framework's emphasis (consonant with the statutory framework) that the decision- taking process should be plan-led, and the question of consistency with the development plan is to be determined against the policies of the development plan taken as a whole. A similar holistic approach to the consideration of whether the most important policies in relation to the decision are out-of-date is consistent with the purpose of the policy to put up-to-date plans and plan-led decision-taking at the heart of the development control process. The application of the tilted balance in cases where only one policy of several of those most important for the decision was out-of- date and, several others were up-to-date and did not support the grant of consent, would be inconsistent with that purpose.*

21.11. The "*Wavendon* basket" approach should be applied under the NPPF (2024), in housing cases where there is a 5YHLS or where there is another type of datedness or deficiency in the plan, for example because there has been insufficient provision of employment land or a specialist form of housing, or because the relevant policies are out of step with the current NPPF (see NPPF 232).

21.12. The first stage is that all of the most important policies should be gathered – normally (but not exclusively) those where a relevant conflict has been identified. At the appeal stage, this will be denoted by the Decision Notice's Reasons for Refusal.

21.13. The second stage is to assess each policy for datedness, including any lack of accordance with the NPPF.

21.14. The third stage is then to consider as a whole whether the most important policies are out of date.

21.15. Careful regard will be required to NPPF 232 and the provisions of the NPPF. Often the quickest route will be to argue that the demonstrable unmet need for the type of development has been caused by an out-of-date spatial strategy and inflexible settlement boundaries.

21.16. A development plan Green Belt policy that does not include a Grey Belt test (i.e. all development plans until the first contemporary-era Local Plan is adopted post-2024) will plainly not match the NPPF's Chapter 13 provisions. Although it may be argued that if the policy allows for inappropriate development, then the proposal is in accordance with such a policy for the purposes of s38(6) PCPA.

(3) The Tilted Balance

21.17. The tilted balance requires that permission be granted where the benefits are not significantly and demonstrably outweighed by the harms.

21.18. The NPPF 158 requirement to accord "significant weight" to compliance with the Golden Rules is a key consideration at this stage, but does not act as any kind of ceiling as to the weight to be accorded the benefits of the housing or any other more specific benefits.

21.19. It should be noted that in this exercise the harms to the Green Belt in terms of openness and the Green Belt purposes are effectively to be excluded, because the scheme is definitionally "not inappropriate". This is confirmed by the PPG:

> ***How should harm to the Green Belt including harm to its openness be considered if a development is not inappropriate development?***[88]
>
> *Footnote 55 to the NPPF sets out that if development is considered to be not inappropriate development on previously developed land or grey belt, then this is excluded from the policy requirement to give substantial weight to any harm to the Green Belt, including to its openness.*
>
> *This is consistent with rulings from the courts on these matters that, where development (of any kind, now including development on grey belt or previously developed land) is not considered to be inappropriate in the Green Belt, it follows that the test of impacts to openness or to Green Belt purposes are addressed and that therefore a proposal does not have to be justified by "very special circumstances".*

(4) The Footnote 9 Policies

21.20. The Footnote 9 policies list is extensive, and rendered slightly opaque by the cross-referencing of the numbers. However, its application in most Grey Belt cases is assisted by the fact that several of the tests will already have been assessed. For completeness, these are addressed here.

[88] Paragraph: 014 Reference ID: 64-014-20250225

Directing Development to Sustainable Locations (NPPF 84, 110 and 115

21.21. A Grey Belt development will already have assessed this component under Criterion B (NPPF 155(b)), applying an express assessment against NPPF 110 and 115.

21.22. The additional paragraph in NPPF 84 is therefore unlikely to apply to the majority of Grey Belt schemes (although there may be certain exceptions, relying on the broader approach to both NPPF 110 and 115(a) for urban vs rural locations):

84. Planning policies and decisions should avoid the development of isolated homes in the countryside unless one or more of the following circumstances apply:

a) there is an essential need for a rural worker, including those taking majority control of a farm business, to live permanently at or near their place of work in the countryside;

b) the development would represent the optimal viable use of a heritage asset or would be appropriate enabling development to secure the future of heritage assets;

c) the development would re-use redundant or disused buildings and enhance its immediate setting;

d) the development would involve the subdivision of an existing residential building; or

e) the design is of exceptional quality, in that it:

i. is truly outstanding, reflecting the highest standards in architecture, and would help to raise standards of design more generally in rural areas; and ii. would significantly enhance its immediate setting, and be sensitive to the defining characteristics of the local area.

21.23. The same is true for NPPF 91 and the retail sequential test:

91. Local planning authorities should apply a sequential test to planning applications for main town centre uses which are neither in an existing centre nor in accordance with an up-to-date plan. Main town centre uses should be located in town centres, then in edge of centre locations; and only if suitable sites are not available (or expected to become available within a reasonable period) should out of centre sites be considered.

<u>Making Effective Use of Land (NPPF 129)</u>

21.24. NPPF 129 provides for the efficient use of land, through the following considerations:

129. Planning policies and decisions should support development that makes efficient use of land, taking into account:

(a) the identified need for different types of housing and other forms of development, and the availability of land suitable for accommodating it;

(b) local market conditions and viability;

(c) the availability and capacity of infrastructure and services – both existing and proposed – as well as their potential for further improvement and the scope to promote sustainable travel modes that limit future car use;

(d) the desirability of maintaining an area's prevailing character and setting (including residential gardens), or of promoting regeneration and change; and

(d) the importance of securing well-designed, attractive and healthy places.

21.25. There is nothing here which is bespoke to Grey Belt cases, save perhaps Golden Rule (3) and accessible green space.

Securing Well-Designed Places (NPPF 135 and 139)

21.26. NPPF 135 and 139 provide:

135. Planning policies and decisions should ensure that developments:

(a) will function well and add to the overall quality of the area, not just for the short term but over the lifetime of the development;

(b) are visually attractive as a result of good architecture, layout and appropriate and effective landscaping;

(c) are sympathetic to local character and history, including the surrounding built environment and landscape setting, while not preventing or discouraging appropriate innovation or change (such as increased densities);

(d) establish or maintain a strong sense of place, using the arrangement of streets, spaces, building types and materials to create attractive, welcoming and distinctive places to live, work and visit;

(e) optimise the potential of the site to accommodate and sustain an appropriate amount and mix of development (including green and other public space) and support local facilities and transport networks; and

(f) create places that are safe, inclusive and accessible and which promote health and well-being, with a high standard of amenity for existing and future users; and where crime and disorder, and the fear of crime, do not undermine the quality of life or community cohesion and resilience.

139. Development that is not well designed should be refused, especially where it fails to reflect local design policies and government guidance on design, taking into account any local design guidance and supplementary planning documents which use visual tools such as design guides and codes. Conversely, significant weight should be given to:

(a) development which reflects local design policies and government guidance on design, taking into account any local design guidance and supplementary planning documents which use visual tools such as design guides and codes; and/or

(b) outstanding or innovative designs which promote high levels of sustainability, or help raise the standard of design more generally in an area, so long as they fit in with the overall form and layout of their surroundings.

21.27. Again, whilst Grey Belt does not guarantee any specific level or type of design, the combination of a detailed Planning Statement, a well-illustrated Design and Access Statement and a clearly presented case are the hallmarks of all successful Grey Belt cases – and accordingly a strong argument can usually be made for the quality of the design.

Providing Affordable Housing (NPPF 66)

21.28. Paragraph 66 provides:

66. Where major development involving the provision of housing is proposed, planning policies and decisions should expect that the mix of affordable housing required meets identified local needs, across Social Rent, other affordable housing for rent and affordable home ownership tenures.

21.29. A Grey Belt proposal should ordinarily have complied with (and indeed exceeded) this element by Golden Rule (1) under NPPF

156(a) and 157, such that there will be no conflict with this element.

(5) Checklist

21.30. All Grey Belt cases should end with a clear description of whether the proposal is in accordance with the plan overall for the purposes of Section 38(6) PCPA, and if there is any conflict whether the presumption is engaged and how the tilted balance applies as a material consideration:

Q1) Footnote 8

- Are the most important policies automatically deemed to be out of date by virtue of a 5YHLS shortfall or the HDT score?

Q2) Most Important Policies and the Wavendon Basket Approach

- What is the full list of most important policies?

- Which of those policies are up-to-date (in accordance with the NPPF)?

- Which of those policies are out of date (not in accordance with the NPPF, or otherwise overtaken by events on the ground on in national policy?)

- Overall, are the most important policies up-to-date or out-of-date?

Q3) Tilted Balance

- What are the benefits of granting permission?

- What weight should be accorded to those benefits individually?

- What are the adverse effects of granting permission?

- What weight should be accorded to those adverse effects individually?

- Do the adverse effect of granting permission significantly and demonstrably outweigh the benefits?

Q4) Section 38(6)

- Is the development in accordance with the development plan, considered as a whole?

- If not, do material considerations, including the presumption in favour of sustainable development indicate that permission should be granted notwithstanding that conflict?

CHAPTER TWENTY-TWO

CONCLUSIONS AND FURTHER REFORMS

A 21st Century Green Belt Policy

22.1. In concluding this book, it is worth reflecting back on the Deputy Prime Minister/Secretary of State's July 2024 words: "*A Green Belt designed for England in the middle of the twentieth century now must be updated for an England in the middle of the twenty first.*"[89]

22.2. The Grey Belt exception to inappropriate development is clearly a 21st century policy. It has already gone a considerable way towards unlocking the major obstacles that characterised Green Belt release in the early 2020s. The policy is now driving the release of a much larger category of sites, whilst delivering important uplifts in the benefits provided – and much more quickly than ever before.

22.3. In due course, Grey Belt will be incorporated into National Development Management Policies and continue to perform a powerful role in ensuring targeted release of the Green Belt where there remains demonstrable need and all other requirements are met. The Minister observed before the House of Lords Select Committee, that the effect of Grey Belt will therefore be "*a modest amount of land that will make a difference*", but also "*impactful*". Significant expanses of Green Belt will remain, but a considerable amount of housing and other development will still be delivered.

[89] Rt Hon Angela Rayner MP, the Deputy Prime Minister and Secretary of State for Housing, Communities and Local Government, Written Ministerial Statement: "Building the homes We need" (30 July 2024)

A Limited Lifespan?

22.4. With the surge in grants of permission and accelerated plan-making activity, it is possible to foresee the bespoke decision-taking provisions in NPPF 155 relating to applications becoming temporarily redundant where either (1) the authority adopts a plan allocating sufficient land to meet housing land supply or (2) grants permissions to exceed the 5 year housing supply figure. Much will however depend upon the speed of plan preparation, examination and adoption in the middle years of the Government's 5-year term.

22.5. Ultimately, the Grey Belt NPPF 155 provisions look set to be relevant for some time to come. First, the increase in the buffer under NPPF 78(c) looks set to ensure a significant portion of LPAs will not have a 5YHLS for a considerable period. Second, if Local Plans are adopted without a sufficiently robust deliverable supply, then further 5YHLS shortfalls may emerge. In this way, NPPF 155 will be a constant and valuable presence in the development management context.

A Blueprint for Other Policies

22.6. Grey Belt may have an even more far-reaching character: as a template for wider policy reform. Whilst decision-making can never be algorithmic, Grey Belt allows for greater precision in the evidential exercise.

22.7. Grey Belt therefore represents a forerunner of prospective future policy reforms, and a general shift towards planning policy that is much more focussed on delivery and more straightforward to operate. Grey Belt policy therefore looks decisively towards 2050. It is a key policy reform on the journey to a planning system that is faster, fully digitised, more data-driven and transparent, and far more effective in meeting housing and economic needs..

MORE BOOKS BY LAW BRIEF PUBLISHING

A selection of our other titles available now:-

'A Practical Guide to Probation Breaches and Other Applications' by Mark Thomas
'A Practical Guide to Remarriage and Divorce' by Cordelia Williams & Claire Howard
'A Practical Guide to Privacy, Transparency, Reporting Restrictions and Closed Proceedings in the Court of Protection' by Laura Mannering
'Beaumont on Barristers – A Guide to Defending Disciplinary Proceedings (Second Edition)' by Marc Beaumont
'A Practical Guide to Payments for Environmental Services' by Ben Sharples
'A Practical Guide to the Law of Pregnancy and Maternity at Work' by Rebecca Thomas
'A Practical Guide to Redundancy – Second Edition' by Philip Hyland & Collette Moore
'A Practical Guide to International Issues for Scottish Family Lawyers' by Susie Mountain, Donna McKay, Ken MacDonald
'A Practical Guide to the Law on Deprivation of Liberty' by Ben Troke
'A Practical Guide to Rights over Airspace and Subsoil – Second Edition' by Daniel Gatty
'A Practical Guide to the Law in Relation to Inquests' by Ramya Nagesh
'A Practical Guide to the Construction and Rectification of Wills and Trust Instruments (Second Edition)' by Edward Hewitt
'A Practical Guide to Data Protection in Social Housing' by Clare Paterson
'A Practical Guide to Spousal Maintenance – Second Edition' by Liz Cowell
'A Practical Guide to International Parental Child Abduction Law (England and Wales)' by Dr Onyója Momoh
'A Practical Guide to Deprivation of British Citizenship' by Sean Ell
'A Practical Guide to Commercial Property Service Charges' by Rachel Garton
'A Practical Guide to Clinical Negligence – Third Edition' by Geoffrey Simpson-Scott (Geoff)
'A Practical Guide to the Rights of Grandparents in Children Proceedings – Second Edition' by Stuart Barlow

'The Electronic Communications Code: A Practical Guide – Second Edition' by Kerry Bretherton KC, James Castle, Mark Loveday

'A Practical Guide to the Independent School Standards – September 2023 Edition' by Sarah McKimm

'A Practical Guide to Estate Administration and Crypto Assets' by Richard Marshall

'A Practical Guide to Parental Alienation in Private and Public Law Children Cases' by Sam King QC & Frankie Shama

'Contested Heritage – Removing Art from Land and Historic Buildings' by Richard Harwood QC, Catherine Dobson, David Sawtell

'The Limits of Separate Legal Personality: When Those Running a Company Can Be Held Personally Liable for Losses Caused to Third Parties Outside of the Company' by Dr Mike Wilkinson

'A Practical Guide to Transgender Law' by Robin Moira White & Nicola Newbegin

'A Practical Guide to 'Stranded Spouses' in Family Law' by Mani Singh Basi

'A Practical Guide to Residential Freehold Conveyancing' by Lorraine Richardson

'A Practical Guide to Pensions on Divorce for Lawyers' by Bryan Scant

'A Practical Guide to Challenging Sham Marriage Allegations in Immigration Law' by Priya Solanki

'A Practical Guide to Digital Communications Evidence in Criminal Law' by Sam Willis

'A Practical Guide to Legal Rights in Scotland' by Sarah-Jane Macdonald

'A Practical Guide to New Build Conveyancing' by Paul Sams & Rebecca East

'A Practical Guide to Inherited Wealth on Divorce' by Hayley Trim

'A Practical Guide to Practice Direction 12J and Domestic Abuse in Private Law Children Proceedings' by Rebecca Cross & Malvika Jaganmohan

'A Practical Guide to Confiscation and Restraint' by Narita Bahra QC, John Carl Townsend, David Winch

'A Practical Guide to the Law of Forests in Scotland' by Philip Buchan

'A Practical Guide to Health and Medical Cases in Immigration Law' by Rebecca Chapman & Miranda Butler

'A Practical Guide to Bad Character Evidence for Criminal Practitioners by Aparna Rao

'A Practical Guide to Extradition Law post-Brexit' by Myles Grandison et al

'A Practical Guide to Hoarding and Mental Health for Housing Lawyers' by Rachel Coyle

'Stephens on Contractual Indemnities' by Richard Stephens
'A Practical Guide to the EU Succession Regulation' by Richard Frimston
'A Practical Guide to Solicitor and Client Costs – Second Edition' by Robin Dunne
'Constructive Dismissal – Practice Pointers and Principles' by Benjimin Burgher
'A Practical Guide to Religion and Belief Discrimination Claims in the Workplace' by Kashif Ali
'A Practical Guide to the Law of Medical Treatment Decisions' by Ben Troke
'Fundamental Dishonesty and QOCS in Personal Injury Proceedings: Law and Practice' by Jake Rowley
'A Practical Guide to the Law in Relation to School Exclusions' by Charlotte Hadfield & Alice de Coverley
'A Practical Guide to Divorce for the Silver Separators' by Karin Walker
'The Right to be Forgotten – The Law and Practical Issues' by Melissa Stock
'A Practical Guide to Planning Law and Rights of Way in National Parks, the Broads and AONBs' by James Maurici QC, James Neill et al
'A Practical Guide to Election Law' by Tom Tabori
'A Practical Guide to the Law in Relation to Surrogacy' by Andrew Powell
'A Practical Guide to Claims Arising from Fatal Accidents – Second Edition' by James Patience
'A Practical Guide to Asbestos Claims' by Jonathan Owen & Gareth McAloon
'A Practical Guide to Stamp Duty Land Tax in England and Northern Ireland' by Suzanne O'Hara
'A Practical Guide to the Law of Farming Partnerships' by Philip Whitcomb
'A Practical Guide to the Law of Unlawful Eviction and Harassment – Second Edition' by Stephanie Lovegrove
'A Practical Guide to Costs in Personal Injury Claims – Second Edition' by Matthew Hoe
'A Practical Guide to the General Data Protection Regulation (GDPR) – Second Edition' by Keith Markham
'A Practical Guide to Working with Litigants in Person and McKenzie Friends in Family Cases' by Stuart Barlow
'Protecting Unregistered Brands: A Practical Guide to the Law of Passing Off' by Lorna Brazell
'A Practical Guide to Secondary Liability and Joint Enterprise Post-Jogee' by Joanne Cecil & James Mehigan

‘A Practical Guide to the Pre-Action RTA Claims Protocol for Personal Injury Lawyers’ by Antonia Ford
‘A Practical Guide to Neighbour Disputes and the Law’ by Alexander Walsh
‘A Practical Guide to Coercive Control for Legal Practitioners and Victims’ by Rachel Horman
‘A Practical Guide to the Law of Driverless Cars – Second Edition’
by Alex Glassbrook, Emma Northey & Scarlett Milligan
‘A Practical Guide to TOLATA Claims’ by Greg Williams
‘A Practical Guide to Elderly Law – Second Edition’ by Justin Patten
‘A Practical Guide to Responding to Housing Disrepair and Unfitness Claims’ by Iain Wightwick
‘A Practical Guide to the Law of Bullying and Harassment in the Workplace’ by Philip Hyland
‘How to Be a Freelance Solicitor: A Practical Guide to the SRA-Regulated Freelance Solicitor Model’ by Paul Bennett
‘A Practical Guide to Prison Injury Claims’ by Malcolm Johnson
‘A Practical Guide to Advising Clients at the Police Station’ by Colin Stephen McKeown-Beaumont
‘A Practical Guide to Antisocial Behaviour Injunctions – Second Edition’ by Iain Wightwick
‘Practical Mediation: A Guide for Mediators, Advocates, Advisers, Lawyers, and Students in Civil, Commercial, Business, Property, Workplace, and Employment Cases’ by Jonathan Dingle with John Sephton
‘The Mini-Pupillage Workbook’ by David Boyle
‘A Practical Guide to Crofting Law’ by Brian Inkster
‘A Practical Guide to the Law of Domain Names and Cybersquatting’ by Andrew Clemson
‘A Practical Guide to the Law of Gender Pay Gap Reporting’ by Harini Iyengar
‘NHS Whistleblowing and the Law’ by Joseph England
‘Employment Law and the Gig Economy’ by Nigel Mackay & Annie Powell
‘A Practical Guide to Noise Induced Hearing Loss (NIHL) Claims’ by Andrew Mckie, Ian Skeate, Gareth McAloon
‘An Introduction to Beauty Negligence Claims – A Practical Guide for the Personal Injury Practitioner’ by Greg Almond
‘Intercompany Agreements for Transfer Pricing Compliance’ by Paul Sutton
‘Zen and the Art of Mediation’ by Martin Plowman
‘A Practical Guide to Adoption for Family Lawyers’ by Graham Pegg

'A Practical Guide to Industrial Disease Claims' by Andrew Mckie & Ian Skeate
'A Practical Guide to Conducting a Sheriff Court Proof' by Andrew Stevenson
'A Practical Guide to Vicarious Liability' by Mariel Irvine
'A Practical Guide to Applications for Landlord's Consent and Variation of Leases' by Mark Shelton
'A Practical Guide to Relief from Sanctions Post-Mitchell and Denton' by Peter Causton
'A Practical Guide to Equity Release for Advisors' by Paul Sams
'A Practical Guide to Financial Services Claims' by Chris Hegarty
'A Practical Guide to Financial Ombudsman Service Claims' by Adam Temple & Robert Scrivenor
'A Practical Guide to Running Housing Disrepair and Cavity Wall Claims – Second Edition' by Andrew Mckie & Ian Skeate
'A Practical Guide to Holiday Sickness Claims – Second Edition' by Andrew Mckie & Ian Skeate
'Arguments and Tactics for Personal Injury and Clinical Negligence Claims' by Dorian Williams
'A Practical Guide to Drone Law' by Rufus Ballaster, Andrew Firman, Eleanor Clot
'On Experts: CPR35 for Lawyers and Experts' by David Boyle
'An Introduction to Personal Injury Law' by David Boyle

These books and more are available to order online direct from the publisher at www.lawbriefpublishing.com, where you can also read free sample chapters. For any queries, call us on 0844 587 2383 or email us at mail@lawbriefpublishing.com.

Our books are all generally in stock at www.amazon.co.uk with free next day delivery for Prime members, and at good legal bookshops such as Wildy & Sons.

We are regularly launching new books in our series of practical day-to-day practitioners' guides. Visit our website and join our free newsletter to be kept informed and to receive special offers, free chapters, etc.

You can also follow us on Twitter at www.twitter.com/lawbriefpub.

www.ingramcontent.com/pod-product-compliance
Lightning Source LLC
LaVergne TN
LVHW052242200926
848481LV00002B/241